MW01602392

CASTE, RELIGION AND COUNTRY

A View of Ancient and Medieval India

Caste, Religion and Country

A VIEW OF ANCIENT AND MEDIEVAL INDIA

S.V. Desika Char

Orient Longman

CASTE, RELIGION AND COUNTRY

Orient Longman Limited

Registered Office
3-6-272 Himayatnagar
Hyderabad 500 029 (A.P.)

Other Offices
Kamani Marg, Ballard Estate, Bombay 400 038
17 Chittaranjan Avenue, Calcutta 700 072
160 Anna Salai, Madras 600 002
1/24 Asaf Ali Road, New Delhi 110 002
80/1 Mahatma Gandhi Road, Bangalore 560 001
3-6-272 Himayatnagar, Hyderabad 500 029
Birla Mandir Road, Subzi Bagh, Patna 800 004
S.C. Goswami Road, Panbazar, Guwahati 781 001
"Patiala House", 16-A Ashok Marg, Lucknow 226 001

© Orient Longman Limited 1993
First Published 1993

ISBN 0 86311 255 2

Published by
Orient Longman Limited
1/24 Asaf Ali Road
New Delhi 110 002

Typeset by
Scribe Consultants
B4/30 Safdarjung Enclave
New Delhi 110 029

Printed in India at
Rekha Printers Private Limited
A-102/1 Okhla Industrial Area Phase II
New Delhi 110 020

To the memory of

my esteemed friend K. Venkataraman
and
my beloved daughter Sudha Chakravarthy

Contents

Preface

Early in life, as a post-graduate student and research fellow at the Universities of Mysore and Madras, I made an intensive study of the constitutional reforms of 1919 and 1935, and also ventured to find solutions to some of the vexing problems connected with caste and communal issues. Later, as a research officer attached to the Constituent Assembly of India, I had a closer feel of the intricacies and nuances. I realised then that we were not writing on a clean slate—our attitudes and actions were mostly governed by inherited traditions, customs and values. The intractability of human nature and the role of vested interests to which we attach great importance was limited. My interest in knowing the origins and fundamentals, the prime historical foundations, was roused. The opportunity to work on the subject came late. When Dr. Nihar Ranjan Ray was the Director of the Indian Institute of Advanced Study, Simla, I presented with considerable hesitation, only as an alternative subject, a scheme for probing into the caste and communal problem and the allied issues with reference to the period prior to British rule. I was both surprised and happy when Dr. Ray brushed aside my first choice and enthusiastically opted for the second. He impressed upon me that despite the wide interest evinced in the caste and communal problem as a live issue of our day, few had bestowed enough thought on the origins and foundations, and what I contemplated would be a worthwhile venture. Owing to service conditions and personal problems, I could not initially accept the offer of a fellowship at the Institute made by Dr. Ray. However, soon after, I joined the Institute when Prof. V.K. Gokak was the Director, and was attached to it for eighteen months during 1971-72. After I left the Institute, I found that the basic work I had done there had large gaps. For several years thereafter, amidst other studies and preoccupations, I sought to complete the work to my satisfaction. Surprisingly enough, this field of investigation has remained as unexplored as it was when I first broached the subject with Dr. Ray. My indebtedness to scholars who have thought and expressed their views on several aspects of the subject in the past is immense, and it is writ large in the study. If I have succeeded in bringing into sharper focus several matters discussed by others earlier, and also added a few insights of my own, I would feel amply rewarded. I am convinced that this is primarily a pathfinding study—there are yet several dark corners all along the line that require to be illumined.

My first debt of gratitude goes to the late Dr. Nihar Ranjan Ray. Save for the preliminary discussions I had with him and the rekindling of interest, I may not have ventured on this study. Because of my long interest in the subject, my indebtedness is no less to my old-time research guides who are no more—Prof. K.A. Nilakanta Sastri and Dr. Eddy Asirvatham while I was at the University of Madras, and Dr. Bisheshwar Prasad under whom I worked for my doctorate at the Delhi University. Sir B.N. Rau, Constitutional Adviser when the Constitution of India was framed, was my officer, but I have always regarded him as a teacher of mine. I have discussed several aspects of the subject with my friends at different times. In particular, I owe my understnding of the great significance of some of the theological literature of the Sri Vaisnavas, the followers of Ramanuja, to Dr. S. Prasannam of Madras, a doctor of medicine but deeply versed in the field. I am also indebted to Prof. G.N. Chakravarthy, retired Professor of Sanskrit at Mysore, Dr. B.V. Subbarayappa, noted for his studies in the history of science in India, and Dr. Suryanath Kamath, Chief Editor, Karnataka Gazetteer and a well-known historian. My esteemed friend Sri. K. Venkataraman of the Publications Division of the Council of Scientific and Industrial Research who is no more with us, and Sri. Manu Chakravarthy of the N.M.K.R.V. College, Bangalore, have very kindly gone through the manuscript, and helped me with their valuable suggestions. In the course of my work, I have, in particular, availed of the facilities for research provided by the National Archives of India, New Delhi, the National Library, Calcutta, the State Archives of Tamil Nadu and that of West Bengal, and also the Mythic Society and the Gokhale Institute of Public Affairs in Bangalore. Above all, I am deeply indebted to the Indian Institute of Advanced Study, Simla, for initially sponsoring the study.

March 1992   S.V. DESIKA CHAR
Bangalore

Introduction

The caste and the communal problems of today are commonly regarded as being modern and mostly a creation of the British. Though no scholar of worth would accept such a facile view, not many are aware of their deep roots going back to ancient times, or of their wide spread touching every aspect of life. "The present *is* history", as Arnold Toynbee succinctly put it. The factors governing every social phenomenon of this type are of two kinds. There are the particular circumstances and the short-term factors; there are also the broad general considerations and long-term ones — the nature of society, its perspectives and ideals, and also the traditions, customs and outlook developed through the ages. The former always looms large, but it is the latter that counts far more in reality. Ernest Barker, in his study *National Character* (1948), made a generalization of great significance when he said:

> Just as it has been calculated that only one-tenth of an iceberg appears above the surface, so it may also be agreed that the great mass of national character rides as it were under seas, with a steady permanence. ... The British of the year A.D. 1900 are not likely to be signally different from the British of the year A.D. 1900.

In dealing with the caste and communal problem and allied issues, attention is riveted only on palliatives and instant remedies to get over immediate troubles and little effort is made to understand the deep underlying causes. The present study is a macro one — to view the problem with reference to the pre-modern age, prior to British rule, laying stress upon macro facts and taking a macro view of micro facts. This should help us to understand better specific events and developments, both ancient and modern, viewing them in their larger and long range historical setting. In this endeavour, our present-day concepts of right and wrong, our ideas and

aspirations for a better society, constitute a major hurdle.
Unhappy over our heritage not being better, we are apt to
be over-critical of our past. National pride and communal bias
also colour our judgement. Overcoming these and other
constraints, we are to understand and judge past events in
terms of the then contemporary values and of what was
practicable and best under the conditions and circumstances
of the day. The study reveals many myths and half-truths
concerning earlier times currently held about which we should
be on our guard.

There is a running thread in Hindu* history governing life
in all sectors. It is the acceptance of diversity as a fact of
life and recognition of the right of everyone to his way of
thinking and his way of life. The need for homogeneity and
unity was no doubt felt, but their pursuit found only a second
place. Tolerance, a readiness to compromise, a spirit of live
and let live, seeking homogeneity and synthesis without giving
rise to tensions and conflicts — these were the main
characteristics of the Hindu approach. And they found
manifestation in different fields in diverse ways — eclecticism
and an absence of proselytizing zeal in the realm of religion,
the decentralized social order with its many castes and sects,
village communities occupying the apex of the political
pyramid and not the bottom when viewed from the point of
vitality and strength, and the seminal role played by self-
constituted guilds in the economic sphere. As a necessary
consequence, institutional growth and loyalties at higher levels
were on a low key.

The Hindu approach proved beneficial in several ways and
was the bedrock of great achievements. In the total and the
long-range view, it ensured a peaceful and settled life all
round. There were no sharp differences in the distribution
of wealth and absolute poverty was avoided. Religio-social
inequalities constituted the dominant characteristic of the

---

*   In this study, unless the context indicates otherwise, the term Hindu
      includes Buddhists, Jains and others who are heirs to the indigenous
      religious and socio-cultural heritage of the land. And, the term Aryan
      culture would refer to the indigenous composite culture developed without
      any of the implications arising out of the race factor. See pp. 11-14.

system of caste, but, whatever be the modern perceptions, the constraints and privileges arising solely out of caste or class were not vexatious enough to generate social revolutions. There was wide scope for intellectual freedom and development, but little interest was evinced towards scientific and humanistic studies. The rigidity of caste was a source of strength in day-to-day life, and contributed to stability. But, no less noteworthy was its flexibility when viewed in the long run, and this ensured progress without friction. Caste proliferation was not a sign of decadance as is often made out — it was mostly the product of settlement of acute social conflicts or a sign of spatial mobility and economic development. The caste-profession equation was there, and it helped to conserve knowledge. The linkage was not, however, mandatory or universal. Vocational secularization in the different sectors was of a high order from early times. Even vocational differentiation on which the varna system was based faded very early and ceased to be important. The high and low of caste was no doubt there, but the horizontal spread of caste was more pronounced than the vertical —a point often overlooked. The fight against the high and low of caste itself was ancient and also vigorous at all times. The concessions made from time to time averted crises, and the success registered by reformers was substantial though not spectacular. The rigid restrictions governing connubium and commensality basic to the system of caste could survive, only because they constituted no serious hardship. Even here, there were relaxations in the face of paramount necessity. The doors of Hindu religion and society were not firmly closed on outsiders; but entry was not easy and it took time. The common culture evolved in the country as a whole was in every sense a composite one, though it went by the name Aryan or Hindu. The general success of the system was reflected in the religion and culture of the land, both Brahminical and Buddhist, spreading over the whole of the subcontinent and far beyond, and also in the high level of intellectual attainment and material prosperity maintained down to the modern period. What was most remarkable was the pacific way in which all this was accomplished.

While the Hindu outlook and approach to problems proved beneficial and the system evolved stood the test of time, there were serious shortcomings too. The Hindu society with its numerous sects and countless castes and subcastes lacked homogeneity and solidarity. Eclecticism, absence of proselytizing zeal, and lack of a strong urge to form an integrated religious community led to there being a higher Hindu religion, that of the elite and the upper classes and castes, and a lower Hindu religion, that of the masses at the bottom layers. It was not easy to attain a high degree of unity in public life and political matters in such a society. The weakness showed up specially when there were foreign invasions or confrontations with fundamentalist faiths and cultures. Further, there was too much of tolerance of social evils recognized as such, e.g., the high and low of caste, especially the practice of untouchability, enforced widowhood and sati. Except for the mild protests of saints and religious reformers, the urge for social reform was conspicuously absent. It has also been said that the highly protective role of the well-coordinated village-caste-guild system took away the element of strife and competition necessary for progress. It is a moot point if these and other serious shortcomings could have been wholly overcome without sacrificing a good bit of the benefits derived.

The emergence of the Muslims as a parallel society, governed by a different set of values, created a new situation. In their case, there was unswerving faith in the message of the Prophet; the Shariah was taken to be a complete guide to life. Absolute conformity, unity and solidarity among the faithful, intolerance of dissidence of any type, characterized their basic stand, though the Sufis succeeded in making a dent. Besides, there was the unprecedented proselytizing zeal and the keen desire to convert the whole world into a close-knit Islamic community. Basically, the classical Islamic world view was just the opposite of the Hindu.

From the point of achieving the goals set forth, this approach did not go well with what was practicable in the Indian situation. The invaders were small in number. No doubt there were large scale conversions and a large Muslim community had emerged. But a yawning gulf separated the immigrants from the local converts, because of the racial and class divide. Further, the converts retained most of their Hindu ways and sentiments; it was not easy to wean them from their Hindu background and integrate them with the new comers. The politico-cultural confrontation of the Hindu in the medieval times was primarily with the immigrant Ashraf. The invaders had been able to bring down the Hindu rulers at the top, but failed to pierce the inner ring; their political success was far from complete. Further, land and money power remained with the Hindu. As such, the two sides were more evenly balanced than commonly supposed. In this background, the Muslim approach, so far India was concerned, was more pragmatic than fundamentalist. A contrary impression is created by the destruction of temples on a large scale, and the sweeping mass conversions that took place in the early years. It needs to be stressed that the element of naked force in effecting conversions was much less than generally believed; what really counted was the Muslim political predominance for over six long centuries with material benefits of one type or the other available to converts. Of greater importance were the many weak spots in the Hindu social armour. As is well known, the stresses and strains of the confrontation were great. There were, however, two prime forces operating to bridge the gulf — the Hindu heritage of eclecticism and tolerance, and Muslim pragmatism that sought continuously to overcome its heritage of Islamic fundamentalism.

In the administration of the plural society that had emerged, the Hindu rulers had the advantage of their secular heritage. The Muslims rulers of the day, on the other hand, suffered from many handicaps — their own alienness, the danger from the unreconciled Hindu, the constant pressure from zealous fundamentalists, and the power-hungry nobles within their own camp. The Mughul success lay in establishing a strong centralized government and in reconciling the Hindus to Muslim rule with their liberal policies. The wide popular support gained by the regime could be gauged from the Mughul charisma even in the years of decline. The process of reconciliation that had been initiated in a big way had not, however, gained sufficient momentum and strength when the Mughul power declined, and as such the country fell an easy prey to the British.

It is often held that territorial consciousness among the Hindus was very weak until recent times, and there was little patriotism. This extreme view stems from modern prejudices and high expectations not really warranted. The village and local communities were close-knit. At this level, territorial consciousness was of a very high order, and village Hampdens would not have been wanting. Otherwise, the Muslim invaders would have pierced the inner ring and made a clean sweep. At the higher levels, territorial consciousness was bound to be weak because of the pre-modern means of communication and conditions of life. There was a further weakening because of the heritage that favoured a decentralized pluralistic political system. There was, however, one strong favourable factor. The Hindu religion and culture, as it spread over the land, carried with it a strong sense of homogeneity and oneness. Conceptually, One India was a reality from the earliest times, and the efforts to attain the goal were by no means insignificant. Side by side, there was the operation of subnational forces too. In the ancient period and in the Hindu world in later years as well, the forces of centralization and decentralization complemented each other and helped in evolving a common culture and a relatively homogeneous society in which every part of the country had a sense of belonging. The emergence of clear-cut subnational communities centering round modern vernaculars was a late development, except in the South, and this coincided with the beginnings of Muslim rule. In the centuries that followed, there was not much scope for subnational rivalries and conflicts on linguistic or regional lines, because of Muslim political predominance over the whole land, and later because of British imperial rule. The political and religious issues of the day and the responses to them cut across linguistic and regional boundaries. The rise of the Marathas, the Rajputs and the Sikhs no doubt acquired great strength from the prevalence of subnational sentiment, but their fight was primarily against Muslim hegemony and for the preservation of religious freedom. The emergence of pronounced subnationalism as a counterforce to Indian nationalism in public and political life is a post-Independence phenomenon.

Territorial consciousness among Muslims stood on a different footing. In the medieval period, it was only the attitude of the immigrant Ashraf among them that really mattered. The members of this class had two homes — their spiritual home located outside in the Islamic world, and then the country to which they had migrated and where all their material interests lay. As the years rolled by, external loyalties became weaker and weaker, and the attachment to the land of domicile came to be primary. The Ashraf too entertained the dream of One India. In their case, the governing motive was political ambition, the desire to bring the whole country under Muslim rule. Besides, the need for pan-Indian Muslim unity was great, both at the height of Muslim power and in the years of decline. The contribution of Muslims to the political unification of India and the growth of an all-India outlook in political and public affairs was great. The British only took the country a step further than the Mughuls did.

In the manifestation of patriotism, which is closely linked to territorial consciousness, there was no room for generation of heat or strident expressions in the ancient period, because neither cherished institutions were in jeopardy nor were the material interests of any class seriously affected. The issue assumed importance only with the coming of the Muslims to India. Why did the Hindus fall such an easy prey to a handful of foreigners and live as a subject people for centuries? This is an intriguing fact. The military debacle at the first onslaught may be explained in military terms and in terms of contemporary political conditions. But the absence of adequate resistance after the initial defeats, at the national or the regional level, except in deserts and mountains and other inaccessible regions, can only be explained in terms of a lack of unity among the rulers and the ruling classes arising from the nature of the political heritage. However, the vitality of social and political life at the local levels saved the Hindus from total collapse. More than the political factor, it is the cultural *milieu* and the mental outlook that mattered. There is no substance in the charge that there was a general political and cultural breakdown in the Hindu world. It was the will to resist that had been unconsiously undermined. The inherited spirit of tolerance and readiness to compromise came in the way of putting up a resistance that was sustained and lasting. It would surprise many to know that no loud-enough war cry was raised by any of the religious leaders. Further, it was not the rigidity and the high and low of caste, its restrictions and taboos, that came in the way of offering effective resistance, as is often alleged. On the contrary, it was the very flexibility of the caste system that enabled converts to Islam to form their own caste groups and settle down in peace easily. Even the immigrant Ashraf came to be just another caste. The rapidity with which the Hindu spirit of accommodation and the synthesizing forces came to operate is a point of great significance, the rise of the Bhakti movement being only a pointer. The Sufi response and the pragmatic liberalism of the Muslim rulers also helped to restore peace and normalcy.

Then there is the issue of patriotism with reference to the onset of British rule. Indian resistance was feeble, and the British gathered their plums with little effort. For them, it was more of a diplomatic achievement than a military one; also, it was victory for an organized bureaucracy as opposed to native governments depending for survival on the personality of the ruler of the day. Despite the colossal failure, the eighteenth century was an age of iron, when strong men flourished and the common solider exhibited unflinching loyalty towards his employer, whoever he was, under trying circumstances. The Indian collapse was due entirely to a spiritual vacuum, both in the Hindu and in the Muslim world. The thing most wanting was a worthy cause for the people to fight for. The elite and the ruling classes failed to provide one. What the masses would have felt at the time and the resentment of the common man found spontaneous expression in the Revolt of 1857.

The challenge of modernism and the post-medieval developments form no part of the present study. A few general observations may, however, be made in the light of the past. From the earliest times down to the modern period, there was a set economic mould conditioning the whole of life, and there was limited scope for variations in fundamentals. The phenomenal progress in scientific knowledge, the sea changes brought about by applied science, and the transformations in the structure of society and its functioning, all characteristic of modernism, have left their deep mark on values and attitudes the world over. India cannot be immune to their influence, and life cannot qualitatively be the same as before. But such changes would take a long time to have their full impact. In the interim, it should be remembered, the submerged part of the iceberg in the form of inherited institutions, traditions and outlook continues to have a dominant place in fashioning our lives, whether it be for good or evil. The old-time values do not seem to have suffered serious damage from the impact of modernism. Acceptance of the spirit of science and of the modern way of life has in fact rejuvinated Hindu religious and cultural life more than undermined it. However, the system of caste has no future, whatever be its merits that made for its survival in the past. In particular, the high and low of caste, and the many restrictions and taboos, are clearly on their way out; the best minds even in the past had never approved of them. Still, it is not unlikely that the outer framework of caste groups would survive much longer, hopefully posing no serious social problems. As regards the communal divide, secularism enshrined in the Constitution of India is a part of our precious heritage from Vedic times. With their history behind them, the Hindus could not have opted for anything different. Indian Muslims, most of whom are local converts, are heirs to the same heritage. Despite the role of fundamentalism and separatism arising from the Islamic past, the wounds inflicted by Partition may be expected to heal before long, and the outlook for Hindu-Muslim integration considered bright enough. Indeed, the Hindu, now Indian, spirit of eclecticism, tolerance and readiness to compromise is being put to test in a wider field, the international scene, and it is serving as a beacon light to bring peace to the strife-worn world, and contribute towards emergence of a unified world order. As regards the growth of subnationalism and sharply-parochial attitudes in Independent India, these primarily constitute a struggle to effect improvements in local life as well as to have a larger share in the common pool of benefits available. Despite the present-day travails and disappointments, the struggle may lead to a more uniform development of the different regions. We may view the present trends as constituting the latest phase of the twin forces of localism and national unification battling throughout history, the forces of localism gaining the upper hand at the moment. However, the spiritual roots of One India go so deep that one need not be unduly perturbed over the future. Besides, the economic and material compulsions making for One India are much greater today than they were ever before.

In conclusion, it needs to be stressed again that this is a macro study — it is based upon macro facts and macro views of micro facts. Specially in respect of the latter, judgements and evaluations are bound to be subjective, and there is good room for differences of opinion. I only hope that the picture presented here is fair, clear and true enough.

CHAPTER 1

The Hindu Religion and the System of Caste

Hinduism, its Eclecticism and Tolerance

The problems arising out of the Hindu religion and the system of caste, either as contemporary issues or of historical significance, cannot be understood unless there is a clear appreciation of the seminal factors which conditioned their origin and development through the ages. The Hindu religion, viewed historically and not as generally taken to be today, is best understood if it is not equated with Zoroastrianism, Christianity or Islam, each of which has a founder and a sacred book held to be authoritative. Hinduism represents a cluster of religio-theological traditions native to the soil of India. It is comparable to a river system with many tributaries forming a gigantic stream and then dividing into innumerable branches, making it difficult to tell the main stream from the tributary or branch. The Vedas are often equated with the Bible and the Quran, and considered to be the pillar on which Hinduism rests. Unlike the latter the Vedas are a vast collection of hymns composed by several seers in praise of many gods. The metaphysical views advanced cover most known schools of speculation, including the agnostic; the religious beliefs and theological practices rooted in them are also diverse. Besides the Vedas, the Hindus have a large body of sacred books, venerated and considered to be authoritative in varying degrees — the Itihasas, the Puranas and the

Smritis. There are also the teachings of saints and saint-scholars who flourished in different parts of the country at different times, and these are considered sacred by their respective followers. All these collectively constitute the base on which the religion stands.

Of this vast sacred literature, which of them is central or primary or constitute the last word? It is true the vast majority have regarded the four Vedas to be *apaurusheya* or divinely inspired and authoritative. Though they are songs sung by many seers and not one, eminent saint-scholars like Sankara, Ramanuja and Madhva have viewed the whole of Vedic thought and tradition as one work, and sought to establish that there is complete harmony and consistency in them and the message conveyed is one. But, their own understanding of the Vedic truth has not been the same, and their followers have formed divergent sects. While the learned have debated over the text of the scriptures, the masses have venerated the Vedas only from a distance. For them the spiritual guide-book has always been the general teachings of saint-scholars and the inspired sayings of saints who acquired the essence of the Vedic truth intutively by divine grace and not through a study of the scriptures. Of the latter class, there have been very many — the Saivite and Vaisnavite saints of Tamilnadu of the sixth-ninth centuries A.D., Jnanesvar, Namdev and Tukaram of Maharashtra, Chaitanya, Nanak, Mira Bai and Kabir from the North, and a host of others. They have played a bigger part than saint-scholars in the religious life of the Hindus.

While the Vedas are considered to be the last word by the majority of the Hindus, there have been large sections which have rejected the stand or have qualified their acceptance in different ways. The Buddhists and the Jains were the first to see differently in a big way. Departing from the Vedic tradition, they developed religio-theological systems based solely upon the teachings of their own founders, the Buddha and Mahavira. While these have been marked out as dissenters from early times, the stand taken by many others have been uncertain and equivocal. First, there are those who are free thinkers; they believe it is the right and duty of every individual to judge for himself. However, while making this claim on principle, they find precious gems in

Vedic thought providing full insight, this specially in the Vedanta or the Upanishads, and these have formed the core of their faith. To this class belong the Brahma Samajists and the disciples of Sri Ramakrishna. Then there are those who accept the Vedas unquestioningly, but hold the teachings of the founders of their respective sects as more than adequate for their spiritual education. The attitude of this class to which most Hindus belong is very well brought out by a teacher of the Srivaisnavite school in the South. In his view the Vedas are comparable to the vast ocean. But, they are accessible only to the select and the elect, just as only a few types of animals can live and grow in the salty waters. In contrast, the Dravida Vedam of the Tamil saints is like the clouds high above. The saints have sucked the seas, and filled wells, ponds and lakes with sweet water for all to drink.[1] Here, there is no attempt to snap the Vedic links; on the contrary, the full backing of the prestige of the Vedas is ensured for the teachings of the saints, with which the devotees could rest content. Some sects have, however, consciously sought to snap the Vedic linkage, and assert that they have nothing to do with traditional Hinduism and are outside its fold —to them the teachings of their founding-fathers are the first and the last word. The Sikhs would belong to this class, and they seem to be going the way of the Jains and the Buddhists. It is to be seen if the trend is permanent or trasitory.

It is thus clear that Hinduism has no one teacher or no single belief, view or principle central to it. What stands out is the multiplicity in saints and sects, in their teachings and sacred books. If any one thing can be considered to be its sheet-anchor, it is the belief that truth has many facets and the roads to salvation are multiple. As R.C. Majumdar has observed, "Hinduism is at its best, more a view of life and an attitude of mind than a specific belief or faith."[2] Fearless pursuit of truth is the only goal of the Hindus, and they are a community of truth-seekers. Concretely, Hinduism is a collective name for the cluster of religio-theological traditions native to the soil, and the Hindus comprise all the votaries of these traditions.

Apart from the common outlook being a binding force, the cultural bonds arising out of common living have helped in holding the Hindus together. This community could be equated with the People of the Book, the Islamic concept covering Muslims, Christians, Jews, Zoroastrians and Sabaeans. Its Hindu version would include all the sects accepting the Vedic heritage and also the dissenters, whatever be the degree of dissent, all native to the soil. This community has been one corporate whole for exchanging ideas as well as for learned disputations, and this all through history down to the present day. It has been a world of its own, the votaries of alien religions and theological systems having no place in it. We have a picture of this world, a feeling of its oneness, in a prayer recorded in an old Hoysala inscription and widely current:

> He whom the Saivites worship as Siva, the Vedantins (devoted to the study of metaphysics) as Brahma, the Buddhists as the Buddha, those of the Nyaya school, good at logical reasoning, as Creator, those attached to the Jaina doctrines as Arhat, the Mimamsakas (proficient in Vedic rituals) as Karma or Sacrifice — let Hari (Vishnu), the Lord of the Three Worlds, who stands for all these, bestow on us all that we desire.

This community, this Hindu version of the People of the Book, had no name to identify it at the beginning, for none was needed. When the Muslims first came to the country they gave it a name — the Hindus, the locals who were different from themselves in religion and culture. It covered the whole of the local community and was apt. However, the term Hindus has now acquired a narrower connotation —it refers only to those who hold the Vedic heritage as sacred, the Brahminical Hindus as they are often called to distinguish them from the Buddhists and Jains, the dissenters. This change has come over because of the imposition of the Western concept that a religion must have a founder and a sacred book as in the case of Christians and Muslims. Unless we revert to the earlier concept of Hinduism and of Hindu society, the history of the land would be incomprehensible.[3]

What is relevant and important to this study is the fact that eclecticism is the central and characteristic feature of Hinduism. The spirit of tolerance and the readiness to compromise which have come to be a part of the Hindu psyche have stemmed from this. This open and permissive attitude has given birth to a social system and a way of life that revel in variety and in entertaining even opposites. 'Functioning anarchy', a term used by Prof. Gailberth in a not uncomplimentary sense, would best express the view of Hindu society held by foreigners as well as modern West-oriented Indians. But, the overall unity that made for the successful functioning of the society through the ages is as important as the near-anarchic conditions and conflicting trends one often comes across. Whatever the merits and demerits, it is the psychological attitude, this approach to life, that has exercised the profoundest influence over all aspects of Hindu life, politico-economic as much as socio-cultural. In the course of this study, it will be seen to provide an important key to solve many a historical riddle.

Varna and Caste: Growth, Structure and Vitality

As regards the structure of the Hindu soiety, it comprised four varnas or orders, functionally differentiated -- the Brahmana, acting as the custodian of the sacred lore and performing priestly functions; the Kshatriya responsible for governance and maintenance of peace; the Vaisya, engaged in agriculture, industry and trade; and the Sudra rendering general services to the whole community. These four alone were recognized by the Vedic tradition as basic divisions, and it is in respect of them that rights, duties and privileges were enunciated, both in regard to rituals and mundane matters. Manu had categorically stated that there was no fifth varna, but one did emerge and came to be termed the *Panchama* or the Fifth. The functional position of this varna was the same as that of the Sudra; but, ritualistically and socially, it was ranked lower, and subjected to additional disabilities. As P.V. Kane has stressed, the Panchamas or the Harijans of today, were given a place in Hindu society and not wholly excluded from religious participation.[4]

As regards caste, in the orthodox view, it was not a separate category; it was a by-product of inter-varna marriages, which were not considered normal. However, it was considered proper for a woman to marry a person of a higher varna (*anuloma*), but the reverse (*pratiloma*) was strictly prohibited. Unlike in the case of varna, caste differentiation was based primarily on marriage and birth. The Smritis indicated the varna status of each of the caste groups, however it originated. According to P.V. Kane, there are references to 172 of them.[5] Caste proliferation and differentiation took place in a big way based on other considerations and circumstances too, and it was custom that finally determined the status of each in the varna hierarchy. There was no caste that didn't have a varna label attached to it.

It would not be easy to give a comprehensive definition of caste as it emerged. However, for our purpose, it is enough to note that it was based on several factors: "primarily on endogamy and connubium, and secondarily on race, tribe, sect, tradition, locality, occupation, etc.;" also, "it was a vital, comprehensive social association implanting in man strong prejudices, attitudes and class consciousness."[6] A caste had its divisions and subdivisions governed by the very same factors. Indeed, the ultimate primary unit of Hindu society was the close-knit kinship group with its own head and caste panchayat; it was affiliated closely with others of the same caste or subcaste. According to the Census, there were 800 main castes and 5,000 smaller groups in the whole of India, and 200 castes and 2,000 subcastes in each of the linguistic regions.[7]

For the present study, it is important to note how, from small hazy beginnings, the system of caste grew to be a gigantic phenomenon posing socio-economic problems. It is the functionally-based varna turning into caste that gave the start. The Santi Parva of the *Mahabharata* speaks of pre-varna times. When we first encounter them the Aryans were divided into the first three varnas only, functionally divided and tending to be closed groups, but holding an equal position in religious matters. They were all *Dvijas* or twice-born, entitled to study the Vedas, a right stubbornly withheld from all others during the whole course of development down to the modern period. The fourth varna, the Sudra, emerged out of the racial confrontation between the Aryans and the Dasas or Dasyus, equated with the Dravidians.[8] In the process of mutual accommodation, the Dasas were taken into the Aryan fold to constitute the fourth varna as a distinct and separate group, but given a lower place: they were to have no access to the Vedas, held dear by the Aryans, and the duty assigned to them was to serve the Aryan community. How the admission was viewed at the time is clear from what Panini said: the Sudras were those not kept out (*aniravasita, abahishkrita*) in contrast to others kept out of the Aryan fold (*niravasita, bahishkrita*).[9] In this atmosphere of racial antipathy, there was not much room for social interaction or social intimacy between the two. *Inter alia*, the ban on connubium and the restraints on commensality turned the Aryan *Dvijas* and the Dasas into rigid castes as we know them. Seminal for future development, they provided the first elitist standard to mark off social groups rigidly, and also to demarcate the high from the low, ritualistically and socially. It is this embryonic development that set off forces that gave birth to the caste system. With the various groups within their fold having, or acquiring, caste characteristics, the functionally-based varnas themselves got a caste orientation. Also the orthodox found a ready explanation for caste proliferation, which they could not otherwise explain, in *varna-sankara* or "contaminated" inter-varna marriages. This linking of caste with varna proved very useful, for each caste could be fitted smoothly and easily into the varna hierarchy, which had come down from Vedic times and was sacrosanct. From a practical standpoint too, it would not have been possible to prescribe separately the rights, duties and privileges of each of the caste groups that emerged from time to time.

While the caste system had its origin in the racial divide of the mystic past, its growth and proliferation were conditioned by several other factors. Broadly, they were similar to those which gave rise to closed groups in regard to social relations, specially marriage, in other countries. Only, in India, the groups came to be more compact and rigid than elsewhere. Vocation, economic status, mother-tongue, ancestral home as well as place of current residence, religious belief and sectarian affiliation, ancestry and family bond, dissidence and expulsion from caste — the bonds arising from these and other factors, severally and collectively, contributed towards the emergence of castes. They operated equally in regard to breaking up of castes as well as their fusion and proliferation.

Political turmoils, shifts and changes in socio-economic
conditions, religious movements, etc., all had their impact.
While the process of caste formation was a continuous one,
it acquired accelerated speed in times of turmoil and flux.

We have only a hazy picture of caste proliferation over the
centuries. P.V. Kane discounts the view that the reference
to the four varnas in the Purusha-sukta hymn of the Rigveda
was only conceptual. In his view, in the Vedic period, the
varnas represented the real divisions of society at least to
a very great extent, if not cent per cent, and the references
had a ring of contemporary reality.[10] We have a clear
glimpse of several caste groups in the Buddhist Jatakas. In
the South too, in Sangam literature, we have references to
many endogamous groups that are now in existence.[11] From
these it is clear that the caste system was well entrenched
by the dawn of the historical period. Evidence as to later
developments is scanty. The general view of scholars has been
that caste rigidity and proliferation were much less prior to
the 10th century A.D. than later. In the subsequent period,
the political turmoils following Muslim incursions, the socio-
religious upheavals, including the Bhakti and Sufi movements,
the shifts and changes in trade and the economic set-up with
the coming of the Arabs and European merchants, these
created an atmosphere favourable for caste proliferation on
a large scale. According to Raghuvamshi, travellers of the
early medieval period were silent on the complex subcaste
structure of society, but by the time of the later Mughals,
the institution of caste had grown to maturity, and its
ramifications into sub-castes were numerous.[12]

Endogamy held a caste together. As B.R. Ambedkar
carefully noted, prohibition of rather than observance of,
inter-marriage or endogamy is the only one that can be
called the essence of caste, when rightly understood.[13]
However, the vitality of caste and in fact its very survival
depended upon other ties like common occupation, common
religious beliefs and sectarian allegiance, commensality,
common inheritance rules and familial obligations, etc. What
mattered ultimately was the sense of belonging and
attachment generated within the caste group. Imposing strict
conformity to its way of life in all matters was not only
natural but necessary for the survival of any caste. Among

the lower castes, there were invariably heads of castes and also of panchayats, both holding their positions on the mixed principles of heredity, tradition and custom. These had no scriptural or religious sanction; their existence and power rested solely on custom.[14] Though subject to intervention at times by religious heads and the state, their power was normally unquestioned. They generally had no penal powers; but to be thrown out of caste was tantamount to social death, occupational and residential mobility being virtually absent. Except in rare cases, the upper castes lacked the vigorous organizational machinery to administer their affairs. This was due to their low numerical strength, their wide dispersal, lower vocational homogeneity and greater individualistic spirit. However, religious heads and *ad hoc* bodies of elders and learned men of the community exercised adequate control. The power of castes over their members was undoubted until the modern conditions of life started making deep dents.[15] While Abbé Dubois considered "the institution of caste among the Hindu nations as the happiest effort of their legislation", there were detractors of the eminence of Sir Henry Maine.[16] None, however, disputed the power exercised by caste and its deep impact on society from the earliest times. It is universally recognized that caste and the self-sufficient village system were the two pillars on which the strength and integrity of the whole society depended in the pre-modern age.

Challenges Encountered and the Flexibility of Caste

Varna and caste appeared to be permanent and immutable to contemporaries at all times — stinking cesspools which would never dry up in the eyes of critics who cried for change. It was not Warren Hastings alone who thought Manu ruled and still held the key to the Hindu socio-religious system; it was a view that prevailed down to our own times, and still holds many in its grip. Caste, in its origins, was irrational and based on prejudice; and persistence of this factor gave the system its rigidity. As against this, practical and utilitarian considerations also gave it remarkable flexibility. The importance of this has come to be appreciated increasingly in recent years, thanks to micro-studies by historians and the insight of sociologists. It is now clear that flexibility was as much a part of the system as rigidity and sea changes occurred in it over time.

How flexible the caste system was would be clear from the way tensions and problems were encountered as they arose and were resolved. There were four major sensitive areas of conflict: restrictions on endogamy and commensality; dissidence within and attacks from outside in the field of religion; the functional basis of castes and changing economic needs; and the sentiments and animosities roused by the high and low of caste.

CONSTRAINTS OF ENDOGAMY AND COMMENSALITY

As regards the first issue, endogamy and commensality constituted the prime cementing factors which held a caste together. The restrictions imposed received the severest hammering at the hands of reformers, both on principle and on sentimental grounds, but they could not overcome the silent resistence of the orthodox and conservative forces. Many have wondered how the system could have survived. It has often been overlooked that endogamy and commensality gave rise to no great practical hardships, as Wilson pointed out long ago.[17] When the restrictions regarding commensality could not be adhered to in times of drought, famine and war, there was automatic relaxation. Again, when a caste group experienced continual hardship in a big way in regard to endogamy, the difficulties were overcome by making suitable adjustments with analogous and likeminded castes. Such changes taking place at micro levels did not affect the system as a whole; endogamy and commensality remained the essential divisive factors of the caste system. If it had been otherwise, the system would have disintegrated totally.

VOCATIONAL BASIS OF CASTE AND ECONOMIC DEVELOPMENT

The position was very different with regard to the caste— profession equation. Next to endogamy, a common vocation was the most important binding factor. Economic considerations brought men together and held them together, and the caste-forming propensity in the land turned them into castes. The functionally-based varnas were the first to turn into castes or super-castes. The same process worked through the ages inexorably all along the line, and vocation-based castes came to be the norm down to the modern period. P.V. Kane notes that professional castes like wood-workers, betel-sellers, weavers, etc. were existing and well organized from the earliest times.[18] We have a relatively recent example in the Laukiks and the Vaidiks forming separate subcastes among the Brahmanas in Maharashtra and elsewhere: the Laukiks, grown rich and prosperous, were averse to having marital relations with the Vaidiks; the latter restricted themselves to priestly vocations and orthodox ways and were not over keen on having an alliance with those who had debased themselves by dedicating their labour to worldly affairs.[19] Caste proliferation has often been criticized as it led to multiplication of castes and an increase in social fissures. It is forgotten that, in the pre-modern age, it was mostly a direct consequence of economic changes —diversifications in trade and industry, the spatial mobility of people going out in search of cultivable land the desire to avail of other vocational opportunities, etc. Fewer castes in a region really meant a lower order of economic development. For instance, as Martin noted, even in the early nineteenth century, in less-developed regions like Assam, a number of vocational groups like coppersmiths, blacksmiths, weavers and cultivators did not form separate castes as in advanced Bengal.[20] As already noted, greater caste proliferation after the tenth century was partly the result of greater economic development. Vocational caste groups played a big role in economic development. Their part in preserving, transmitting and developing the knowledge of arts and crafts from generation to generation, and in ensuring economic stability and steady progress, has been widely commended.

VOCATIONAL SECULARIZATION OF VARNA AND CASTE

A vocational caste group naturally expected its members to

stick to the hereditary calling as a matter of course. But, often enough, the vocation of the caste failed to provide full employment to its members, and besides other attractive avenues also showed up. Diversification in calling was the natural result. When this happened in a big way, subcastes that were based on new vocational alignments emerged. Sometimes, the other factors making for the integrity of castes prevailed. In such a situation, the caste did not break up, but the vocation considered to be central to its homogeneity ceased to be so; the profession of the caste group came to be not one, but multiple. While great stress is laid upon the vocational base of caste, the fact that there was a good element of diversification too is often ignored. The extent to which the functional base got disintegrated cannot be individually assessed with reference to the several castes and subcastes. But, what happened to the varnas, which were indeed super-castes, show that sweeping changes were taking place over long periods.

To take the case of the Brahmana varna viewed as a caste first, it would appear that the priestly vocation or devotion to learning could not ensure livelihood for all even in early times. The Buddhist Jatakas refer to the following callings of the Brahmanas: tillage, tending cattle, trade, hunting, carpentry, weaving, policing of caravans, archery, driving of carriages, and even snake-charming. [21] Smriti literature is full of references to Brahmanas unable to pursue the vocation enjoined on them by the scriptures, and the alternative occupations they could take up. Parasara-Madhava, for instance, justified the Brahmanas taking to agriculture, trade, crafts, etc.; only, living on gifts, praised by earlier writers, was held to be unsuitable for the times or the Kali Age.[22] Interestingly, there are very many references to Brahmanas entering the army in every period.[23] They were to be found in trade and business: Manu refers to wealthy and powerful Brahmanas and prescribes their duties;[24] in the eighteenth century, Konkani, Saraswat and Maharashtra Brahmanas figure large in the field.[25] There were ruling families and administrators too from the Kanvas of ancient times to the Peshwas. As regards the position reached in the eighteenth century, Raghuvamshi writes that the Brahmanas had taken to all kinds of secular occupations, including low callings, and "their secularization was well-nigh complete."[26] Buchanan's information regarding the Brahmanas of Mithila is a general indicator of the position of the community all over the country; 10 per cent in literary pursuits, 68 per cent occupying rent-free or assessed lands and attending to cultivation, and 10 per cent serving under zamindars or carrying on business. There were also cultivating Brahmana castes as such in different regions who did not hesitate to put their hands to the plough — the Sanketis of Mysore, the Haigas of Kanara, the Mahastan or Masthans of Orissa, and analogous castes in Tirhut and Bihar.[27] Despite these glaring facts, the illusion that the Brahmanas were mostly a priestly and scholarly class prevailed through the ages. This was due to the fact that Brahmanas alone were entitled to serve as priests, and they were the sole custodians of Vedic knowledge. The position was similar to that among the Jews, as pointed out by W. Tennant: "The priests of Jews were indeed of the tribe of Levi, but all the Leviites were not priests."[28]

Unlike in the case of Brahmanas, the duties prescribed by Vedic tradition for the other varnas were associated with the acquisition of political power and wealth and mundane matters. Religious prescriptions and moral dictums could not prevent people from striving for personal benefit or help them to withstand economic pressures. Prior to the admission of Sudras into the Aryan fold, the Vaisyas were the primary producers and constituted the people (*vis*). With their massive induction and the spread of Aryan culture to new lands wherein the immigrant Aryan element was weak, the Sudras came to be the principal land-owning and tilling community, the primary producers. In this process, the vocation of the Vaisyas came to be confined to banking, trade and commerce. This transformation was so complete that even the memory of the earlier position was lost; it survived only in the Smriti passages and the rituals based on them. The late entrants to the Hindu fold, the Panchamas, were also agriculturists and provided the general labour force. These changes were slow, gradual, unobtrusive, and gave rise to no major socio-economic upheavals.

In the case of the Kshatriya, the claim was for exclusive political power. Even in the Vedic days, neither the Brahmana nor the Kshatriya was content with the duties assigned to him. The power struggle was prolonged, reminiscent of the church-state struggle in the medieval Christian world. In the final count, the Brahmana had to remain content with spiritual authority and vocation of learning. Though he acquired the pride of place in the socio-religious hierarchy, he did not count for much where money and power were involved. The success of the Kshatriya was, however, shortlived, unlike in the case of the Brahmana. The struggle for power knew no bounds of varna, caste or subcaste. Traditionally, with the rise of Mahapadma Nanda, the founder of the Nanda Dynasty, at the beginning of the fourth century B.C. the Kshatriya complexion of the ruling class was lost. The Nandas and the Mauryas were Sudras; the Sungas, the Kanvas, the Kadambas and the Gurjara-Pratiharas were Brahmanas; and the great Guptas were Vaisyas. In several cases, the rulers came from aboriginal tribes, and there were also intruding aliens like the Hunas. Hindu jurists like Kumarila, Medhatithi and Parasara Madhava took note of the fact that rulers came from all the varnas, and were exercised over its theological implications.[29] There was a partial return to the Kshatriya varna as a living concept with the rise of the Rajputs. Considered by the ultra-orthodox as *vratyas* (not of pure breed), they acquired that status in popular esteem for their heroic resistance to the Muslim invaders. There were non-Kshatriya rulers also at the time: the Peshwas were Brahmanas; the rulers of Keladi were Lingayats; and so were many other ruling classes. On the whole, the functional basis of the Kshatriya varna, lost in the early historical period, was never regained.

While the complexion of the ruling class, originally Kshatriya, underwent a sea change, that of the fighting forces did not remain static. It is reasonable to presume that in the Vedic days, it was predominantly Kshatriya; in any case, that was the theoretical stand. Right from early times, soldiers came from all varnas and castes. According to the Sukra Smriti, Sudras, Kshatriyas, Vaisyas, or Mlechchas of mixed castes could be recruited, provided they were brave, restrained, well-built, devoted to their master and their Dharma, and hated the enemy. Tribals and frontier-men were, in particular, considered to be brave and martial.[30] There were at all times some castes and subcastes which were specially drawn to army service, and these, at times, put forward claims to Kshatriya status, e.g., the Jats and the Gujjars. On the whole, the Kshatriya complexion of the ruling class as well as of the army that was lost in the mystic past was never regained. Still, the illusion that the Kshatriyas constituted the warrior class of the Hindus has persisted down to the modern period, and this is reflected in the writings of great scholars like Tarachand, M. Mujeeb, Satishchandra and Nazmul Karim.[31]

Apart from losing its functional rationale early, it would appear that the varna system acquired no deep roots in many parts, particularly those which were Aryanised late. As regards the Tamils, K.K. Pillai writes that there are hardly any references to Kshatriyas in Sangam literature, while a number of the present-day caste groups are referred to. According to U.N. Ghoshal, in the Sultanate period, the pattern of social structure in the South differed from what it was elsewhere: in the kingdom of Vijayanagara, the castes ranked next to Brahmanas were Chettis (merchants), Vir Panchalas (artisans), Kaikkolas (weavers) and barbers. According to the *Ras Mala*, in Gujarat, in the eighteenth century, the Rajputs were not recognized as Kshatriyas; they ranked lower than Waneas, a branch of Vaisyas. In Maharashtra, the refusal of the Brahmanas there to recognize Shivaji and his descendants to be Kshatriyas is a clear indicator of the weak position of the varna in the region. Also, D.R. Gadgil has observed that the predominant position occupied by certain Brahmana subcastes in trade and banking in the region was "indicative of the lack of the Baniya (Vaisya) element in the individual caste structure." Buchanan noted with reference to the Dinajpur District,

> Except familes which have lately migrated into Bengal, there are none in the country who pretend to be Khyetriyos (Kshatriyas) or Vaisyas, and the people may be divided into Brahmins and Sudros.[32]

VOCATIONAL SECULARIZATION: REORDERING OF VARNA AND CASTE AFFAIRS

The disintegration of the vocational bond, partially or totally, did not create unsurmountable problems: either the members got freedom to pursue vocations of their choice without prejudice to the solidarity of the caste or there was a restructuring of the caste itself to suit the new vocational alignment. Further, where a common vocation ceased to be of importance, there were other props to keep a caste group intact, viable and strong. Since the changes introduced, if any, were based on consensus and gradual, the tension and hardship experienced were minimal. But, it was not the same when it came to the varnas. Functional differentiation constituted the very essence of the varna system, the bedrock on which Hindu society stood. As P.V. Kane stated, "Smriti writers try to place all their dicta in the framework of the varnas because the four varnas and their duties and privileges had been more or less clearly defined in the times of the Vedas and Brahmanas, which according to the authors of the Smritis were *sruti*, eternal and infallible."[33] Castes and subcastes as they emerged were fitted into the varna frame by Smriti writers; where they failed, custom took care of the matter.

When the functional base disintegrated, it posed a serious challenge to the whole Vedic concept of varna. Taking a cynical view, the Puranas at times held that the varna system had vanished and only Brahmanas and Sudras subsisted during the Kali Age.[34] Echoing the same view, Raghunandana of Navadvipa (Nadia), a renowned scholar of the sixteenth century, observed that "the Kshatriyas had ceased to exist ever since the time of Mahapadma Nanda, and like the Kshatriyas, the Vaisyas and Ambasthas too had become Sudras on account of non-performance of appropriate duties."[35] A more constructive view was taken by Visvarupa, Medhatithi and Vijnanesvara with reference to kingship. They held it to be independent of Kshatriya birth — a king regardless of the varna to which he belonged was to abide by the maxims prescribed for Kshatriya rulers, and the subjects were to reciprocate as if he were a Kshatriya.[36] It does not, however, appear that any Smriti writer was bold enough to uphold the granting of ritual Kshatriya status to a non-Kshatriya. The Brahmanas of Maharashtra objected when Shivaji chose to wear the sacred thread, because they considered him to be of Sudra varna, and as such not entitled to it.[37]

While Smriti writers found it difficult to overcome the scriptural impediment, a shortcut was found in practice —tradition and genealogical tables were fabricated to establish the "fact" of birth in a higher varna. Money and power could buy anything, and social acceptance was all that mattered. The legitimization of the social position acquired by men of lower castes was taking place often all the time. Referring to this aspect, Burton Stein observes, "The capacity of both ancient and medieval Indian society to ascribe to its actual rulers, frequently men of low social origins, a 'clean' or 'Kshatriya' (high caste warrior) rank may afford one of the explanations for the durability and longevity of the unique civilization of India."[38]

VOCATIONAL SECULARIZATION: THE EIGHTEENTH CENTURY

The changes which took place in the vocational field denoted secularization of economic life as a whole. The freedom given to individuals to choose the vocation they wanted was not the only indicator. It was not even the prime one, as it is often considered; it was to be seen much more in the proliferation of castes to meet economic challenges. While the outer framework of Hindu society remained religious and non-secular, there were radical changes in pith and substance. If we keep in view the conditions of life in the medieval period, the level of secularization reached by the dawn of the modern age was indeed remarkable. Colebrooke observed in 1793, "Every profession, with few exceptions, is open to every description of persons; and the discouragement arising from religious prejudices is not greater than what exists in Great Britain from the effects of municipal and corporation laws."[39] B.A. Irving went to the extent of saying, "If we except the priesthood, caste has not necessarily any effect on the line of life in which a man embarks", an extreme statement according to G.H. Ghurye.[40] However, at the lower levels of economic activity, the caste profession met the needs of most, and many craft-centred castes continued to flourish in villages. It was at the higher levels of trade and general business that greater mobility was seen, both among the Hindus and the Muslims. The caste factor was, however, still of great importance in the business world. One or the other caste group held a predominant position in particular regions — the Bohras in Gujarat, the Lohanas in Sind, the Khatris in the Punjab, the Vaisnava and Jaina Baniyas of Rajasthan in Uttar Pradesh, Bihar and Central India, the Komatis in Andhra Pradesh, the Chettis in Tamil Nadu, and the Konkani and Saraswat Brahmanas on the West Coast, etc. Also, members of different business communities operating in the same region did not "show a similarity of behaviour patterns or a degree of social cohesion which would justify their being called members of one business class." Despite these limitations, D.R. Gadgil observes, "The more I looked into the historical materials, the more I was struck by the element of continuity in the evolution of modern business and the extent of integration which appeared through the ebb and flow of individual communities."[41] It needs to be stressed that the level of secularization reached was the product of forces at work from the earliest times as described above and not merely the result of Western trade contacts as some are inclined to believe.

Challenges to Religion and Culture

SPREAD OF HINDUISM AND BUDDHISM — ECLECTICISM AN ASSET

Next to the bond of vocation, religious beliefs and common culture were major binding factors in respect of the several caste groups and of the Hindus as a whole. How did Hindu society react to the challenge of sectarian developments within and that posed by other religions?

Since the Vedic days there was no period when saints and religious teachers did not flourish, or new ideas and beliefs did not crop up. It did not begin with the Buddha or end with Sri Ramakrishna. While in the case of other civilizations, the rise of a successful teacher with a new message often proved to be cataclysmic, he only joined the long line of revered ones in India. The impact on the community was profound and lasting, but the tempo and manner of transformation were neither sanguinary nor revolutionary. This was wholly due to the nature of the Hindu religion and culture — its eclecticism and tolerance, its *laissez-faire* spirit.

The working of this spirit was first and best seen in the spread of Hindu religion and culture. Originating in the land of the Sapta Sindhus in the Punjab, the whole of the Indian subcontinent and several parts of South-East Asia were covered before Islam appeared on the scene. Buddhism, now classed as a separate religion, was a major branch of the same wide-spread religio-cultural stream of the land, and its spread over China, Japan and South-East Asia was a part of the same process. Hinduism and Buddhism were not proselitizing by nature or intent upon making converts in the manner of Christianity or Islam in later days. Usually, religion and culture went together. The process of change was a backdoor affair affecting groups as a whole rather than individuals. The nature of Hindu expansion could be likened to a meandering river with its still waters broadening its course to vast dimensions by slowly eroding its banks. While it is usual to refer to it as the spread of Vedic religion and Aryan culture, it must be noted that the displaced faiths and cultures did not lack in vitality. The fact that both sides were eclectic made for peaceful meetings and exchanges; the victors and the vanquished lost their identities in the new synthesis that was forged. What emerged was something composite, not wholly Vedic or Aryan. With reference to the developments in pre-historic times, Suniti Kumar Chatterjee observes, "in certain matters the Dravidian and the Austric contributions are deeper and more extensive than that of the Aryans." As regards the confrontation with the Dravidians, K.K. Pillai writes, "The impact of the Aryans on Tamilaham (the land of the Tamils) is not comparable to the Romanization of Gaul", and "it would be more appropriate to compare it with the Greek contact with the Aegean civilization as a result of which the later Hellenic culture developed." It was the same in respect of the confrontation with later-day immigrants such as the Sakas and the Hunas. In summing up the emerging position, K.M. Panikkar goes to the extent of saying that the so-called Aryan culture "was predominantly of the conquered people".[42]

The spread of Hinduism and Buddhism in Ceylon, Burma

and South-East Asia was on the same lines as on the mainland, the general conditions being very similar. In China and Japan, the situation was very different. Here, virile, highly-developed civilizations flourished, in no way inferior to the Hindu or Aryan. As such, it was only as a "religious" faith that Buddhism came to be adopted. The tradition of Confucianism and Laoism in China and of Shintoism in Japan, and the social systems of both countries remained intact. The point to be noted is that wherever Hindu religion and culture faced equally eclectic and tolerant systems, the meetings and exchanges were marked by amity.

THE CHALLENGE FROM FUNDAMENTALIST RELIGIONS — THE GENERAL HINDU ATTITUDE UNALTERED

An entirely different situation arose when the challenge came from Islam and Christianity, both associated with highly-developed and organized cultural systems. They were exclusive, and held that they alone provided pathways to salvation. The Jewish and Parsee communities also had a similar outlook, but they did not clash with others as they were closed groups that did not take in converts. For the Muslims and Christians, however, proselytism was an article of faith; the divine message was to be carried to the ends of the world, and they sought to discharge this duty zealously. Compromise in matters of faith with idolators or heathens was unthinkable; to toy with Hindu eclecticism was to play with the devil. Rev. C.T.E. Rhenius, a missionary of the early nineteenth century, wrote that Hindu toleration was "so comprehensive that it amounted to indifference to truth". Rev. William Cockburn (1805) referred to "the religious harm of the ancient world, and the facility with which most nations embraced, or at least respected, each other's superstitions", and held that Christianity could not have spread over the world but for "the exclusive and intolerant zeal of the Christians".[43] This was an attitude both necessary and inescapable if missionary activity was to be successful, whether Muslim or Christian or any other faith.

Surprising as it may seem, the Hindu attitude underwent no change in the face of this challenge. It is true that Hindu theologians and scholars did not take to any serious study of Islam, because of the deep divide between intellectuals of the two religions; but many of the Bhakti saints added Islam to the list of the many paths to salvation in their teachings. Increased Christian missionary activity during the eighteenth and nineteenth centuries also effected no change in the basic Hindu attitude. In the Preface to the Code of Hindu Laws prepared at the instance of Warren Hastings, the Brahmana pandits, in the words of Rev. C.T.E. Rhenius, said:

> Contraries of belief and diversities of religion... are in fact part of the scheme of Providence; for as a painter gives beauty to a picture by a variety of colours, or as a gardener embellishes his garden with flowers of every hue, so God appointed to every tribe its own faith, and every sect its own religion that man might glorify Him in diverse modes, all having the same end and being equally acceptable in his sight.[44]

The persistence of Hindu eclecticism and tolerance in the face of grave provocation, and the sharp diversity in the attitudes of the opposing camps, were to be seen in the acrimonious controversy between Rev. R. Tylor and Ram Mohan Roy in 1823, the latter placing Hinduism and Christianity on par in his esteem, and the former considering this view to be blasphemous.[45]

Several contemporary writers refer to this eclectic and tolerant attitude prevailing among the Hindu masses as well. Friar Jordanus (early fourteenth century) wrote, "And let me tell you that among the idolators a man may with safety expound the Word of the Lord... nor is any one from among the idolators hindered from being baptized throughout all the East, whether they be Tartars or Indians, or what not." ShaykhZaynud-Din,a Malabari Muslim, wrote in the fifteenth century, "The unbelievers never punish such of their countrymen who embrace Islam, but treat them with the same respect shown to the rest of the Muslims, though the converts belong to the lowest grades of society." Rev. William Tennant, writing at the close of the eighteenth century, said, "Numbers listen with silent respect to the Christians and Mahomedans, when worshipping a Deity to them unknown; their conduct he deems pious and commendable; and their system, however good, the Hindu is satisfied must be inferior to that perfect wisdom which breathes in his own." John Henry Grose (mid-eighteenth century) wrote, "Nothing appeared more paradoxical to me than the violent tenaciousness of the Gentoos in their religion and customs; and at the same time their perfect acquiescence, humanity and toleration of others who differ from them in those points that are so sacred to them." Also, while not proselytizing themselves, "when any of their religion renounces it, even in the countries where they are masters, they charitably suppose it was through a conscientious persuasion, unless by cutting off all communion with them, and expelling them irrevocably out of the cast or tribe in which they were born."[46] In Hindu eyes, it may be noted, such outcasting was not inconsistent with the spirit of tolerance. After disowning the faith central to his caste, one could have no claim on the caste or continue to be its member; it was only proper that he should join the caste or communal group whose faith he had adopted.

The above analysis should be taken to be a macro view of the total situation. Human nature being what it is, we have to make ample allowance for dissatisfactions and bickerings and minor-scale conflicts.

SECTARIAN DEVELOPMENTS: TENSIONS CONTAINED

Hindu catholicity and eclecticism did not make it bereft of new religious ideas and movements. On the contrary, freedom made for multiplicity. Apart from general movements, there was a good crop of sects professing sharply divergent views and evolving new rites and practices. Some died; others took their place. While Jainism survived, Buddhism almost vanished. While the Kapalikas, Kalamukhas and other Tantric sects had their heyday and disappeared, several Sakta, Saiva and Vaisnava sects emerged and continued to flourish. A new sect could not escape being fundamentalist and bigoted or avoid adopting aggressive postures. Active proselytism, gaining converts, forming closed communities of followers, were all part of the life of a sect until it lost its dynamism and settled down to a static condition in peace with others.

There were perennial tensions and conflicts arising out of

sectatian rivalries, and a long list of them can easily be compiled. Even in the case of Asoka, P.V. Kane has noted, "In the latter part of his life, he seems to gloat over the fact that the gods worshipped as divinities in Jambudvipa had been rendered false", and also Harsha's restrictions on meat eating should have caused inconvenience.[47] Lalmani Joshi attaches greater importance than others to allegations of persecution of the Buddhists, as "the tradition is too weighty".[48] Many other later instances can be cited — the well-known *Dhurtakhyana* of the Jains disparaging the Hindu Puranas and epics, the impalement of 8,000 Jains referred to in the Tamil Puranas, Ramanuja and Basavesvara leaving their homes to escape persecution, the self-immolation of the Saivas in protest against the installation of a *dhvaja-sthamba* (flagpole) opposite the Govindaraja temple at Chidambaram, and the many fights between the Jains and orthodox Hindus, the Brahmanas and Lingayats, and the Saivites and Vaisnavites throughout the medieval period.[49] Also, "Archaeological evidence is not wanting to show that the hostility of the creeds was not often quite mild and that the appropriation of the sanctuary of one religion by another and effacing the religious symbols of the former by the latter were sometimes practised."[50]

To contemporaries, the sectarian conflicts would have been matters of great moment, and their importance and significance should not be underestimated in any study of local history. What stood out was the general spirit of amity and tolerance that prevailed within the Hindu fold. The credit for this should go largely to the flexibility of the caste system. As noted in the matter of vocation, individual members of a caste enjoyed a certain degree of freedom in religious matters. When it passed the limit of tolerance, the dissenters had to form a community of their own. However, differences in faith or religious beliefs did not always give rise to new sects or break the solidarity of caste. In the present-day caste structure too, there are castes whose members profess different sectarian faiths.

HINDU SYNCRETISM AND THE FEARS ROUSED

Besides generating a spirit of tolerance which helped to

maintain peace and harmony, Hindu catholicity and eclecticism also provided a good ground for the operation of syncretic forces and growth of homogeneity. Cultural exchanges between opposed groups were relatively easy in an atmosphere free from rancour and there were many significant developments all through. For instance, the composition of the *Brahma Sutra* and the commentaries on it by Sankara, Ramanuja, Madhvacharya and others were valiant efforts to view Vedic thought as one whole, holding that the Vedas spoke with one voice. Sankara's Advaita absorbed Buddhistic Nihilism, and Madhusudana Sarasvati sought to reconcile Dvaita and Advaita views in his Prasthana Bheda. D.D. Koshambi characterized the *Bhagavad-Gita* as a cap that would fit all heads.[51] This may be viewed not as a shortcoming but as a merit, a notable instance of syncretism in the realm of thought. The absorption of Buddhistic ideas and of Buddhists was itself a major achievement, but it is important to note that Hinduism did not remain the same as earlier. Jainism and Jains succeeded in maintaining their identity and importance, but were seen as just another Hindu sect or caste, one step removed. While these were major developments, syncretism in matters of detail in religious practices and relationships was continuous and bountiful.

Though the hurdles were great and seemed unsurmountable, there was a visible trend towards Hindu approach in regard to Islam taking the same course, if the response was favourable. This is seen in the teachings of the Bhakti saints and the rise of many syncretic sects among the Hindus. The lengths to which the Hindu could sometimes go is indeed surprising. A Hindu courtier of Akbar went so far as to produce an apocryphal chapter of the *Atharva Veda* entitled *Allah Upanishad*, beginning with a salutation to Ganesha and an invocation of the mystic *Om*.[52] We may dismiss this as just a courtier's writing. There is another baffling instance. According to the conservative, orthodox tradition of the Srivaisnava sect, a sacred Vishnu idol, now enshrined in the Tirunarayanaswami temple at Melukote in Karnataka, was earlier among the looted treasures in the possession of the Sultan of Delhi. The story goes that God appeared to the great saint Ramanuja in his dream, and bade him to get back the idol for worship. The Sultan was struck by the personality of Ramanuja and the miracle he performed, and parted with the idol. But the idol happened to be the favourite of the Sultan's daughter, who could not reconcile herself to the loss. She followed Ramanuja in haste, reached Melukote, and as a crowning event, became one with the Lord — the Muslim princess was an incarnation of the Mother Goddess, Lakshmi. There is a shrine dedicated to the princess (*Tulukka Nachchiar Sannidhi*) in the temple complex of Sri Ranganatha Swami at Srirangam, where Ramanuja spent most of his life. Both Melukote and Srirangam are famous Vaisnavite pilgrim centres of all-India importance.[53] Perhaps, no other example brings out better the basic Hindu temperament. A systematic survey would reveal other similar instances.

Hindu syncretism could match well with Hindu religious tradition, temperament and outlook. But, for the fundamentalists of the opposite faiths, this was a fatal bear-hug to be avoided at all cost. The fears roused in the heart of the Mulsim orthodox could have been of no small measure. At the beginning, with the total collapse of Hindu power and the phenomenal success in proselytization, there was no room for any fear of the Hindu. But the position soon changed. On the political front, Hindu resistance at lower levels acted as a brake on the exercise of Muslim power. On the religious side, the Bhakti saints checkmated Islam's advance, and even started recovering lost ground. By the time of the Great Mughuls, the age of conversions was over; under them and in later times, Islam was not expanding and was more on the defensive. The syncretic teachings of the Bhakti saints could have no impact on the Muslim orthodox. As Tylor said with reference to Christianity, as mentioned earlier, to equate Islam with Hinduism was blasphemous. Hindu syncretism was a treacherous bog one was to avoid. It was of the utmost importance to wean Mulsims from Hindu ways, acquired or surviving, and integrate Muslim society. This was the goal of Muslim Revivalism, a powerful force from the time of Shaikh Ahmad of Sirhind (1563-1624) until recently. When Aziz Ahmed and others refer to "the Muslim feeling of insecurity" under the Great Mughuls, one is inclined to scoff, but it was more of a reality than otherwise.[54] It was more unconscious than conscious and was masked by aggressive postures. It came to the surface and became overt with the fall of the Mughuls, and could be seen in the lamentations of Waliullah on the lot of Muslims in the eighteenth century. The crux of the communal problem in the modern period also lies in this feeling of insecurity and fear of loss of identity.

This phenomenon could be observed in the case of the Sikhs too, though this study would take us well into the modern period. So long as the Sikh community was expanding and power too came its way, all went well. There was a change of fortune in the nineteenth century. With the collapse of Muslim power, the political *raison d'etre* for the rise of the Sikhs vanished; with the Punjab falling into the hands of the British, the advantages which power brought were lost. Though well organized and in large numbers, the Sikhs were now no more than one of the reformist sects which had emerged among Hindus. As a reformist sect too, the Sikhs found a rival in the Arya Samaj, which was as much anti-caste and opposed to idol worship as themselves, and was becoming very popular among Punjabi Hindus. The rise of the Nirankaris, Radhasvamis of Beas and Namdharis, who occupied a mid-position between Sikhism and orthodox Hinduism, was a pointer. In this situation, it was not surprising that many like Lord Dalhousie and Sir Denzil Ibbetson felt that before long the Sikhs would be absorbed into the Hindu fold.[55] It is here that the British came to the rescue. By recognizing the Sikhs as a religious community separate from the Hindus, they gave an official stamp to a line of demarcation that was not there in the minds of either the Sikhs or the Hindus at the time. Further, with the development of the Canal Colony, the Sikhs became rich and prosperous; also with Sikhs being preferred for army service, one gained by being a Kesadhari Sikh. These may not have been enough if the Sikhs themselves were not firm in their determination to retain their identity and integrity. This could only be achieved in the classical way — by insisting upon strict adherence to the Sikh view and way of life every bit by every member. As Khushwant Singh observes, "The sense of belonging to the Sikh community requires both the belief in the teachings of Adi Granth and the observance of the Khalsa tradition initiated by Guru Govind Singh; and ... there is no such thing as a clean-shaven Sikh — he is simply a

Hindu believing in Sikhism." Along with the efforts to maintain their identity as a religious community unimpaired, they also fought for political rights and privileges that could be got — separate electorates and a share in ministerial posts and public services during the British days, and later on the struggle for a Punjabi Subah in which Sikhs would be predominant. Religion and politics were closely intertwined in Sikh history. To quote Khushwant Singh again, "Sikh resistance to being absorbed by Hinduism and the movement for a Sikh state — the two are more intimately related to each other than is generally realised or admitted."[56] To all this, the Hindu had only one answer, to insist on Sikhs and Hindus being basically one, and hoping that the fissures would heal soon—the typical traditional attitude.

In this connection, a pertinent question has to be answered: whether Muslims would have been absorbed like the Hunas and the Sakas earlier if they did not have the backing of political power.[57] We are told that the Turks left behind by Muhammad of Ghazni were "absorbed into Rajput clans and castes like that of Kolis, Khantas, etc.(*Tarikh-i-Sorath*) "[58] Whenever the local situation permitted, it may be presumed that this would have happened in other cases too. As against this, we have several instances where Muslims held their own. The Arabs who had settled down in Kerala for purposes of trade from very early times maintained their separate religio-cultural identity without any political backing to speak of. In this they were not alone: the Syrian Christian community of Kerala and the Parsis were not absorbed and no great headway made towards this end. This leads up to one conclusion. What mattered was the vitality and will of the community concerned to survive, not the attitude of the Hindus as such — the doors of the Hindu religion and society were always open, to enter or to leave, or to reach any compromise that was thought best.

Fight Against the High and Low of Caste

THE STRUGGLE AND THE PROGRESS

We have so far seen how the Hindu social system

proved flexible enough in tackling problems posed by
occupational and general economic changes and the different
challenges in the realm of faith. Another dominant issue was
the hierarchy based on ritualistic standing and the high and
low of caste. The voice of protest was ever there since Vedic
days, no less loud and strident than now. The Buddha, the
Saiva and Vaisnava saints of Tamilnadu, Ramanuja with
whom a new Bhakti era began, and the Bhakti saints of the
medieval age — they sought to cut at the root of the system
by laying stress on the spiritual equality of man. Even at
the close of the medieval period, several radical reformist sects
emerged and kept the torch burning: the Satnami sect of
Dulandas in Uttar Pradesh, the Sivanarayana sect founded
by a Rajput from Gorakpur, the Apapanthis of Oudh, Ghasidas
of Chattisgarh, Charan Dasis of Delhi, and others.[59] The
well-known protestant movements of the nineteenth century,
the Brahma Samaj and the Arya Samaj, were only parts of
an unbroken reformist tradition.

In this struggle, the issues raised concerned metaphysical
and theological concepts of spiritual equality as well as social
conduct in day-to-day life. The traditionalist held fast to the
conservative spirit and the concepts of the system of caste.
The spiritual and ritualistic pre-eminence of the Brahmana-
born was an article of faith; salvation lay only through being
born a Brahmana in the cycle of births as a result of good
deeds. Further, in regard to inter-caste relations, the code
of conduct prescribed by the sacred books was sacrosanct, and
tradition and customs were to be honoured. The accent was
on maintenance of *status quo*. The reformer rejected the very
principle of pre-eminence based on birth or caste. He held
that spiritual life was open to all in equal measure, and
salvation lay within everyone's grasp. In his view, no sanctity
was to be attached to the prevailing restrictions and taboos
regarding connubium and commensality, and other matters.
They could be dropped whenever they were in the way of
good life, spiritual or mundane.

In this struggle between the two groups, we get the
impression that the reformists were knocking vainly against
the granite rocks of orthodoxy. This is largely due to the *outer
framework* of varna and caste surviving unimpaired and
remaining intact through the ages. There has been very

inadequate appreciation of the substantial changes effected *within the framework*, because the process was always very slow and extended over long periods. Indeed, one is reminded of the Chinese proverb, "There is nothing harder than stone, nothing softer than water; but water dissolves stones." An in-depth examination would reveal that the very success of the reformers, both radical and moderate, lay in their role in defusing social crises as they were building up and in preventing the emergence of revolutionary situations.

Total rejection of caste and all that it implied came to be an article of faith with two major communities, the Lingayats in the South and the Sikhs in the North, besides other small sects. The Brahma Samaj, the Prarthana Samaj and the Arya Samaj of later days belonged to the same group. Together, they constituted a sizeable minority of the Hindus. However, as the dissenters were regarded as only 'castes' of the Hindu world, their contribution towards the creation of a casteless society failed to impress. Besides, in their internal structure and working, they were unable to overcome the problems of caste, just as converts to Islam and Christianity.

Of much greater significance than the success of the attempts to establish a casteless Hindu society was the tranformation effected in the outlook and life of those who remained attached to orthodoxy, and constituted the substantial majority of the Hindus. The process had several facets. First, there was the accent placed on the 'ideal' of the varna system, decrying the degeneration that had set in. Character and merit, not birth, marked one's 'true' varna. A 'true' Brahmana was to be honoured in whatever caste he was born; but this did not imply or constitute an attack on the system of caste as it prevailed, for it had other utilitarian aspects too. Honouring and canonizing reformers coming from lower varnas and castes existed from the earliest times. Hailing the Buddha as an incarnation of Vishnu in India and as of Siva in Greater India was the first classic instance in the historical period. Indulging in obvious sophistry, the orthodox held that God had incarnated as the Buddha to mislead people for a divine purpose, and what he preached could not override the Vedas.[60] In later times, we have the formal canonization of the sixty-three Nainmars (Saivite saints) and twelve Alvars (Vaisnavite saints), most of whom were non-Brahmanas, and many hailed from the lowest castes. Among Srivaisnavas, it may be noted, Nammalvar, a Sudra, who is assigned fifth century A.D., was recognized as the father-founder of the sect (*Kutastha*); Ramanuja's greatness lay in his giving the faith its Vedic linkage through his commentary on the Brahma Sutra and being its first great propagator. Azahiya Manavala Perumal Nayanar, a direct Brahmana disciple of Ramanuja, in his *Acharya Hridayam*, said that Nammalvar had incarnated in the fourth varna as though to point out the dangers arising from pride by birth in a higher varna. Holding that spiritual standing was all that mattered, he further said, if a *mlechha* (lowest of the low by birth) was a 'true' *bhakta* (devotee), he was to be honoured as one's *guru* (teacher), his feet washed and the water thus made holy drunk, and the food prepared by him eaten as *prasad* (food regarded holy).[61] This practice of honouring and canonizing low-born saint-reformers was a universal phenomenon among the Hindus at all times, both at the level of the masses and of the elite. The basic principle underlying the whole process had found acceptance quite early in a general way — the Smritis held that there was no distinction of varna among those who renounced the world, the *Sanyasins*.

Another major trend concerned access to the Vedas and other sacred books, the treasure house of spiritual knowledge. As stated earlier, only the first three varnas were entitled to study them, and of them, only the Brahmana was permitted both to study and teach. The Sudras and Panchamas, who constituted most of the population, were totally excluded. P.V. Kane cites the only instance known of a sage named Badari advocating the right of a Sudra to study the Vedas and perform Vedic sacrifices.[62] Further, as the sacred books increased vastly in number and Sanskrit ceased to be spoken, the knowledge came to be in fewer and fewer hands even among Brahmanas. One way to reform was to permit members of all the varnas to study the Vedas. This would have meant victory for a principle, but benefited only a few. Presumably, respect for tradition and the Brahmana, and the difficulty in mastering the Vedas in old-time Sanskrit, both came in the way. Instead, conveying the spiritual knowledge in the language of the people was much easier, more beneficial

and popular. The growth of the vernacular languages itself
came to be closely linked with the spread of Vedic knowledge
and Aryan culture throughout the land. These covered both
high metaphysics as well as simple religious concepts and
practices understood by the common people. The all-round
success achieved may perhaps be best seen in Tamilnadu,
the heartland of the old Dravidians. Here, it could safely be
asserted that the Vedic orange was squeezed into Tamil until
the last drop of juice was extracted.

Side by side, there was another associated development.
The teachings of the saint-reformers, mostly in the language
of the people, came to be venerated and even accorded the
ritualistic status of the Vedas. While this was the general
trend all through and everywhere, the path pursued may be
illustrated with reference, to Srivaisnavism in Tamilnadu.
Here, the hymns of the twelve Alvars in Tamil constituting
the Prabandham gained the appellation Dravida Vedam or
the Tamil Veda. Scholars of the sect were bestowed the
honorific *Ubhaya Vedanta Pravartaka*, meaning proficient in
both the systems of Vedanta, viz., the Prabandham and the
Vedas. Both the sacred books were given an honoured place
in day-to-day rituals. Only there was a sharp difference of
opinion over the precedence to be accorded — the Tengalai
subsect favoured the Tamil Prabandham and the Vedagalai
subsect the Vedas. There was a similar development among
the Lingayats. The teachings of their saints, known as
Vachanas, came to be hailed as Vachana Veda or Vachana-
agama. The process may be said to have reached its
culmination among the Sikhs —their sacred book, the *Granth
Sahiba*, in the Punjabi language and Gurumukhi script, came
to be the sole object of worship. This was not due to any
hostility towards or lack of respect for the Vedas; it was due
to weaker linkage with Vedic scholarship and strong
opposition to idol worship.

In line with these developments, there was the strong trend
towards simplifying religion and religious practices, a counter
to inaccessibility, theological sophistication and elitism, which
had come to be the bane. P.V. Kane has described in detail
the far-reaching changes which helped in the rehabilitation
of Hinduism at the close of the Ancient period — *Pauranica
mantras* used along with Vedic ones even at funeral

ceremonies, emphasis on "*ahimsa*, charity (*dana*), pilgrimages and *vratas*" as being more "efficacious than even Vedic sacrifices", etc.[63] U.N. Ghoshal observes that the growth of the Puranas and the Tantras opened to the Sudras full participation in religious knowledge and practices. Image worship and the abundant pantheon, "so far from heralding the decadance of the Indian people, turned out to be one of the pillars of their strength in the life and death struggle with the foreign invader."[64] Indeed, Srivaisnavas in particular developed the doctrine of *Archavatara* (affirmation of the special presence of God in the idols worshipped); also, Ramanuja was noted for popularizing the Pancharatra form of worship in preference to the Vaikhanasa, and making worship in temples simpler and subject to fewer constraints. More important, all the teachers and saints laid stress upon the supreme efficacy of devotion as the pathway to salvation. Simple faith and chanting of the divine name (*nama sankirtana*) were held to be as rewarding as a life of scholarship or meticulous observance of the rituals prescribed in the sacred books. Many of the saints canonized by the orthodox came from among the lowest castes and the unlettered — Tiruppana Alvar among the Vaisnavite saints, Nandanar among the Saivite saints, and Haraliah among the Lingayats belonged to the untouchable caste. There was also the system of formal initiation into the new sects with appropriate rites; all members of the sect without distinction had to get initiated in the prescribed way. This was analogous to the Vedic ceremony of *Upanayanam* for initiating novices to the study of the Vedas. On the whole, the deep urge to make religion simple, comprehensible and accessible to one and all found powerful expression.

Further, proselytism and making converts, foreign to Hinduism as a whole, became characteristic of every one of the new faiths and sects, and there was feverish activity. Converts came mostly from the middle ranks, specially traders and artisans — this was as much true of the Bhakti cults as of Jainism and Buddhism earlier. Although many of the saints were from the lowest castes and the reformers cried themselves hoarse against the high and low of caste, the message did not percolate to the bottom in adequate measure. This is borne out by several macro facts — persistence of caste distinctions and the high-and-low beliefs and practices even within the new reformist sects though low-ranking subcastes among them were fewer in number; and most important, the very high proportion of Hindus who crossed over to Islam and Christianity or remained as Untouchables within the Hindu fold without improving their status.

As regards connubium and commensality which marked the height of intimacy in social relationship, even moderate reformers at times went to lengths one could hardly conceive. The Sahajiya sect, which was of importance in the seventeenth-eighteenth centuries, was noted for its total opposition to caste and rejection of the Brahmana claim to superiority. G.S. Ghurye writes, "If the Sahajiya sect was rather a revolt, Vaisnavism could not be looked upon as such. Yet its attitude to caste was not far different. Srinivasa, a Brahmin, Ramachandra, a Vaisya, Narottam, Kayastha, were all Vaisnavas and as such were not afraid to take their meals from the same plate."[65] Again, Periyavachchan Pillai, a noted scholar of the Srivaisnava sect who lived in Tamilnadu in the thirteenth century, commenting upon Hymn 42 of *Tirumalai* of Tondaradipodi Alvar, said that the spiritual relationship among devotees was what mattered most, and caste restrictions regarding marriage, inter-dining and such other mundane matters were based on custom only and had no sanctity.[66]

REASONS FOR THE PERSISTENCE OF THE
HIGH AND LOW OF CASTE

Despite these developments, the high and low of caste was very much in evidence down to the modern period; it continues to be a vexed problem to this day. What stood in the way of greater progress? Many have laid stress upon the failure of the Brahmanas to rise up to their responsibility as the spiritual and intellectual elite of the community. It is also stated that the leadership for reform came mostly from those adversely affected — the non-Brahmanas. Presenting this point of view, Tarachand observes, "a majority of these devoted messengers of tolerance belonged to castes other than Brahmana", and gives a long list of them.[67] To view the developments in terms of Brahmana — non-Brahmana would be an inadequate appreciation of the total situation. The issue at stake was the high and low of the entire hierarchical order of caste, sustained by claims to superiority at every stage except the lowest. The lack of greater progress in the path of reform cannot be wholly attributed to the obduracy or opposition of any one particular caste, including the Brahmana; it was due to the inherent nature and limitations of the whole system. The Brahmana being the special target of attack is to be accounted for by his occupying the apex of the caste pyramid, and as such symbolizing the persisting inequality.

While it is not correct to look at the issue in terms of Brahmana — non-Brahmana, it must be made clear that the Brahmana, individually and not as a caste group, played a prominent part in the work of reform at all times. In the time of Mahavira and the Buddha, if the religious upheaval was a Brahmana-Kshatriya confrontation, as often characterized, it would be useful to remember that the fight was between the two higher varnas or elitist groups, still closely linked with one another. Even so, the Buddha had a good Brahmana following, and we are specifically told that the principal disciples of Mahavira, eleven in number, were Brahmanas.[68] The Vaisnavite and Saivite saints of the sixth-ninth centuries in Tamilnadu no doubt came mostly from non-Brahmana castes. But it is the Brahmana *Acharyas* (scholars) who linked their teachings with the Vedic tradition, canonized them, and made them acceptable to the whole community. Here, the role of Ramanuja and his Brahmana disciples is of particular importance. Also, it is the Northern School of Srivaisnavism beginning with Ramananda that spearheaded the Bhakti movement, with moderates like Tulsi Das and Chaitanya, and radicals like Nanak and Kabir. Basavesvara with whom the Lingayat movement came to its own was a Brahmana though Allama Prabhu, a non-Brahmana, held the pride of place on the spiritual side. Among the leading followers of Chaitanya, in the sixteenth and seventeenth centuries, out of total of 490 listed, 239 were Brahmanas, 37 Vaidyas, and 29 Kayasthas; most of the disciples came from other castes.[69] At the close of the eighteenth century, a large number of leading religious men

among the Sikhs were Brahmanas. In modern times, Sri
Ramakrishna was a Brahmana, but Vivekananda was a
Kayastha. Though small in numbers as a community, the role
of the Brahmana was throughout important and seminal. This
is not surprising since it is generally accepted that all reform
and revolutionary movements originate as schisms within the
ranks of the elite. Indeed, the charge of failure on the part
of the Brahmana itself arises from the fact that more was
expected of him, not without justification.

The main inhibiting factor in the way of greater progress
really lay in the nature of the movements. All the saint
reformers showed deep concern for the poor and proclaimed
the brotherhood and equality of man. The vigour and
forthrightness with which many of them spoke, and set an
example by their own conduct, can hardly be paralleled by
modern social reformers of the radical type. With all this,
they did not seek to lead a social or economic revolution; their
sole concern was spiritual upliftment. This was true from the
Buddha to Sri Ramakrishna. Referring to the "erroneous
opinion" that Buddha attacked the caste system, Anand K.
Coomaraswamy writes, "What he actually did was to
distinguish the Brahman by mere birth from the true
Brahman by gnosis, and to point out that the religious
vocation is open to a man of any birth." Berth in *Religions
of India* dubbed the theory that Hinayana Buddhism was a
reaction against the regime of caste and the spiritual yoke
of the Brahmanas "a fiction of romance".[70] The position was
no different with the Bhakti saints of later periods also. While
holding that their influence was wide and far-reaching, U.N.
Ghoshal writes, "It must, however, be admitted that such a
fundamental Hindu institution as caste remained for the most
part unaffected by their teachings. Still less influence was
exercised by them on the contemporary political life."[71] R.C.
Majumdar observes that even Chaitanya who admitted all,
including Muslims, to his faith followed "a middle path" in
regard to caste.[72] This was true even of Sikhism in the early
stages. Hari Ram Gupta observes, "His (Nanak's) opposition
to caste system was so mild that no Brahman or any other
high caste Hindu organized any opposition to him. On the
contrary, he was loved by one and all." It is only in the days
of the later-day Gurus that the movement leaned distinctly

towards social reform. Guru Amar Das, pontiff from 1552 to
1574, introduced the practice "of obliging all visitors to partake
of food in his free kitchen before seeing them, thus regularizing
the system of inter-dining (*pahle pangat pichhe sangat*)."[73]
Though others had made incipient moves in this direction,
Sikhism should get full credit for demolishing one of the two
bastions of the high and low of caste, the other one being
inter-caste marriage. Despite the socio-political turn taken
by the Sikh movement, Sikhism was essentially a religious
movement. The same old traditional attitude was exhibited
even by Sri Ramakrishna, though he was a contemporary of
the noted social reformers Keshab Chandra Sen and Iswara
Chandra Vidyasagar , and in close touch with them. In the
massive work *The Gospel of Sri Ramakrishna*, there are
hardly more than two or three references to caste. In one
of them, he says, "You asked about caste distinctions. There
is only one way to remove them, and that is by love of God.
Lovers of God have no caste. Through this divine love the
Untouchable becomes pure, the paraiah no longer remains
paraiah. Chaitanya embraced all including the paraiahs."[74]

Inadequate motivation arising out of mundane matters
seems to offer the best explanation for the fact that the
opposition to the high and low of caste did not gather
sufficient strength to demolish it. On the economic front, the
self-sufficient village, the joint family and caste provided an
insurance against absolute poverty. Despite apparent rigidity,
the caste structure did not impose an absolute bar on
vocational changes or hinder economic advancement, whether
of individuals or of groups. Group rivalries and conflicting
interests of castes or sects did not lead to emergence of high-
and-low blocks pitted against each other. This was perhaps
because there was a continuous trend towards improvement
in caste status whenever there was a marked improvement
in socio-economic standing. Judging by the outcome, economic
motivation for a social revolution was very poor.

On the social front, restrictions in regard to connubium and
commensality constituted the prime bases of the high and
low of caste. As already stated, they posed no great hardship,
and as such could provide no foundation for the rise of
tensions. Therefore, the fight was primarily on sentimental
grounds and on principle. That this was the position is obvious

from another fact. It is customary to view the hierarchical structure of caste as being vertical with the several rungs of the ladder rising sharply one above the other. But the fact was that the horizontal spread was very much more pronounced, a point often overlooked. Several subcastes within a caste group, even several of the principal castes, stood on par in regard to social status, with no sense of high and low operating; but there was no relaxation in the restrictions on connubium and even commensality, and this caused no resentment. The vertical incline was pronounced at the varna level. It was at this level that the spirit of high and low operated in a big way, reinforced by caste restrictions governing social relations and ritualistic practices. The pride arising out of it was condemned with different emphasis by all saint-reformers, whether radical or conservative, and people applauded. But this did not come in the way of their accepting the system of caste as it stood.

VARNA AND CASTE AT THE DAWN OF THE MODERN AGE

Vocational secularization and the constant attacks on the high and low of caste affected the varna system more than caste. Castes could proliferate or undergo other changes, but the varnas could not. Their number and what they were to be were unalterably set in Vedic days and described in the Smritis and other sacred books. This had also left a permanent impress on the Hindu psyche, life and attitudes. As explained earlier, the theologians struggled manfully to find a way out in the face of the challenges posed, but they could not do much without disowning the Vedic tradition. They had reached an impasse, and matters drifted. While varna remained in Hindu consciousness, it ceased to have any great relevance in their life. G.S. Ghurye has characterized varna as "the junk of Indian tradition", and M.N. Srinivas has observed that the exaggerated importance attached to it is a modern phenomenon and due to a variety of circumstances.[75] The observations are well warranted, but it is important to note that varna had not become moribund. Not much importance need be given to varna distinctions in rituals and religious observances, for even those officiating hardly understood their

significance. The continued relevance of varna lay primarily
in its providing a cognizable framework for the high and low
of caste permeating Hindu society, with sub-claims to
superiority based on tradition and custom in regard to castes
falling within a varna group. Castes were not merely close-
knit endogamous groups spread over the land; they were
attached, however loosely, to the hierarchical varna frame
recognized by society.

In this general process of waning, two of the varnas, the
Brahmana and the Panchama, which had turned into
supercaste-groups, survived, viable and important, and as all-
India categories. Not only did the Brahmana retain his
individuality and ritualistic pre-eminence everywhere, but also
constituted for the most part the intellectual elite of the land.
Several factors contributed towards this. First even though
most Brahmanas took to other occupations, the sacred lore
and the priestly functions remained with them. Indeed, when
new sects cropped up within the Hindu fold, there was always
a Brahmana element among the converts, and they came to
constitute their priestly class, forming a subcaste. This
phenomenon could be noticed among the Jains, Lingayats and
others. There was always a Brahmana-like caste, by whatever
name known, to attend to priestly duties. Another important
reason for the survival of the varna was the fascination that
the ideal of *the true Brahmana* exercised over men's minds
through the ages. The attack was never against the ideal,
but on its being grounded on mere birth. P.V. Kane has
observed that the restrictions on a Brahmana taking up other
vocations was only to insist that he should live a high spiritual
life and not yield to worldly temptations. "As a class they
(the Brahmanas) performed three of their appointed tasks
— of study, teaching and comparative renunciation", and the
community benefited from the performance of its best men.[76]
U.N. Ghoshal observes that there was hardly any evidence
of stubborn opposition to the Brahmanas in the pre-modern
age, and the only conspicuous and organized anti-Brahmana
movement was that of the Lingayats.[77] Another factor, no
less important, was economic. The vocation of the Brahmana
was not such as to evoke envy or serious competition. Though
many a Brahmana acquired power and wealth and became
a part of the competitive world, as a caste group, the

Brahmana remained low in economic status. 'The poor Brahmana' was a saying current at all times. Everyone valued his services as a priest and astrologer, as a literate person, and as a scholar; no one was keen on supplanting him. The challenge to him in his secular role came primarily from the literate classes, Kayasthas in the North, Prabhus in Maharashtra, etc. It is also said that the humbling of the Kshatriya element, the Rajputs, consequent to Muslim invasion, improved the standing of the Brahmana.[78] Finally, there was the Brahmana's own desire and instinct to hold on to his caste status, for he occupied the top in social ranking and any change meant going down.

The stability of the Panchama at the other end of the caste hierarchy was also significant. Unlike the Brahmana, he sought change; he wanted to climb up the social ladder. Many like the Hadis and Doms in Bengal succeeded when circumstances favoured. But the hard core remained stationary. This stability of the two ends of the caste hierarchy was only an instance of a general sociological principle. It is the size of the core that is significant — the Panchama or the Untouchable would have constituted more than a third of the Hindus prior to the inroads by Islam and Christianity. This was clearly due to the non-proselytizing spirit of Hinduism as a whole and the slow pace of Sanskritization. Also, the sectarian religious movements lacked social purpose; where they exhibited something of it, the spirit did not last long.

On the whole, the varna system had undergone great metamorphosis, and survived only in an attenuated form. However, castes and subcastes retained their vigour ad vitality; only the props on which they rested changed from time to time. Life centred round caste and village; both were primary and important. As there was a general acceptance of the system by the ruling class and the community at large, inter-caste relations were smooth and cordial, except for minor irritants.

The Hindu State and the Caste-based Society

WHAT THE DHARMA PRESCRIBED

The nature of the Hindu state and the policies adopted by

it to tackle problems arising from caste were conditioned by
the social system and the socio-religious tradition. Divinity
was attached to the position of the king and his rule was
personal. But, it could not be termed absolutist or despotic,
for there were two important checks. Socio-economic life was
highly decentralized, and the state had only a limited role
to play. Life centred round villages, castes and guilds, which
were autonomous; their freedom was encroached upon only
rarely. The other check concerned the basis of political
obligation — the nature of the tie between the rulers and
the ruled. As T.G.P. Spear pointed out, it was democracy with
the Greeks; the Romans spoke of democracy, but believed in
law; medieval Europe saw no salvation outside the church;
revolutionary France believed in nationalism and Rousseau's
model of democracy but, was more concerned with equality
than liberty; old Germany had a mystic faith in ' State'; for
the Hindus, it was Dharma — "It was the religious duty of
the subject to obey, the religious duty of the king to rule
well."[79] Tradition and custom and right conduct as
understood by the virtuous and the best minds, constituted
Dharma. There was no permanent machinery to ascertain and
lay down the Dharma in terms of legislative norms; the
decisions taken were *ad hoc*. The political process was at no
stage inspired by individualism or democracy. The individual
was lost in the group — village, caste and guild. In arriving
at decisions, the stress was not on counting heads and
ascertaining the wishes of the majority; it was on arriving
at a consensus acceptable to all sections. Panchayats were
representative of caste groups and vocational interests, the
elders acting as spokesmen or members. At higher levels too,
whether for purposes of representation at state functions, or
for formal or informal consultations on state matters, the
rulers took cognizance primarily of the groups. The strength
and vitality of this form of democratic process were reflected
in the Smritis and other evidence available. During early
British rule, the Paternalists like Metcalfe, Thomas Munroe,
John Malcolm and Elphinstone understood the functioning
of the system, and they set high store by it for ascertaining
the wishes of the people. Non-development of an individualistic
spirit and of democratic institutions of the Western type were
as much due to the hold the Hindu view of political obligation

had over men's mind and the strength of the grass-root socio-political institutions as to the pre-industrial conditions of life.

Administration on the basis of Dharma had another significant aspect. Hindu society was highly complex and pluralistic; it was nurtured in an eclectic socio-religious tradition. To allow the different castes and sects to live their own lives unhindered came to it naturally enough; it was a part of Dharma. That was not all — the state was to cherish and further in equal measure the faiths, customs and usages of every community. Precepts to this effect were contained in every Smriti work. P.V. Kane writes, "Smritikaras like Yajnyavalkya laid down that when an Indian king reduced a kingdom to subjection, it was the conqueror's duty to honour the usages, the transactions and family traditions of the conquered country ,and to protect them." Even the usages of the heretical sects were to be respected and enforced.[80]

In a Hindu state, the king could not act contrary to tradition and custom, and as such could not enact laws in the modern sense. The Dharma as interpreted by the wise was to be enforced. The diversity in law books and the opinions expressed gave great elasticity to the system. This apart, the Smriti writers themselves recognized the futility of laying down the Dharma as applicable to all situations and all times. The Smriti maxims and precepts were to be suitably modified according to circumstances. Giving a free hand in the matter, Medhatithi, the doyen of commentators, observed, in the determination of Dharma, "the satisfaction of the learned and the virtuous is a vital test; it may find what appears to be *dharma* as *adharma*, and what appears as *adharma* as *dharma*. When those learned in the Vedas feel that a thing is pure, it is to be deemed as pure."[81] P.V. Kane states that Manu, Yajnyavalkya, Vishnu-dharma-sutra, Vishnu and other Puranas expressly required one to give up what was once Dharma, "if it has come to be hateful to the people and if it would end in unhappiness."[82] Going a step further, Medhatithi said that the Smritis coming down from the ancients were not the last word; new Smritis had to be there to meet the needs of the future.[83] Thus, it would be wrong to hold that the Smriti approach was rigid.

The weakness lay not in the basic approach, but in there not being a recognized machinery to expound the Dharma from time to time; stray commentaries on the ancient texts could hardly meet the need. In this situation, with a conservative, pedantic, legal tradition gaining the upper hand, the discordance between Smriti interpretations and the life as lived was bound to be great. The following glaring instances would show how the Smritis, expected to serve as guides, were getting distanced from life as time passed: the persistence of the *varna-sankara* theory to explain the proliferation of castes and turning a blind eye to the emergence of castes and subcastes under a variety of circumstances; the divergence between the juristic theory on slavery as expounded in *Vyavahara Mayukha* of Nilakantha Bhatta (seventeenth century), recognized as authoritative in Maratha courts, specially in Gujarat, and the usage as gleaned from contemporary records; and *Smriti Chandrika* reiterating the ban on sea voyage as found in the earlier Smritis — that too at a time when Indian colonies in South-East Asia had sprung up, and there was considerable maritime activity.[84] In this situation, the Smritis, as a part of the sacred literature, continued to command great sentimental attachment, specially among the elite; but their relevance to life was limited, save in ritualistic matters. What held the ground everywhere through the ages was tradition, custom and usage. 'Justice, equity and good conscience', formally enthroned by the British in India, had a free play in the land from the earliest times. This taken along with the tolerance of diversity referred to earlier, ensured socio-religious freedom to all castes and communities, Hindu and non-Hindu.

INEQUITIES AND PRIVILEGES

The overfree and non-regulatory approach towards social life and the policy of drift account for the many inequities and claims to privileges, major and minor, perhaps more than in any other cultural system. There was first the taint of untouchability attached to the Panchamas, who had not been absorbed fully into Hindu society; this gave rise to many inequities and oppressions in day-to-day life. Again, there was the high and low of caste throughout the hierarchical system. This found expression in many points of etiquette, claims to precedence and privilege, etc. which affected every aspect of life — having an umbrella carried over one's head as a mark of distinction, and even the right to carry an umbrella; travelling on a horse or seated in a palanquin; the honour of being borne seated in a palanquin carried crosswise (*adda-pallakki*); the bridegroom riding a horse in a marriage procession; claims to precedence and a share in offerings to gods in temples and at religious functions; wearing a turban or having an upper cloth over one's body before one's social superiors, etc. A long list of them could be drawn up. Fights to conserve one's rights were frequent, and called for intervention by local functionaries or the state. Besides, there was the privileged position accorded to the upper castes in the administration of justice. The Smritis went by varna status in laying down the composition of judicial panels, priorities to be accorded in taking up cases, weight to be attached to evidence received, penalties to be imposed, etc. There were also the many privileges conferred specially on Brahmanas by the state or the community: tax concessions, land grants, free services or service at concessional rates rendered by barbers, ferrymen and others, gifts by way of charity or on religious occasions, etc.

While evidence regarding the existence of apparent inequities and privileges is to be found in plenty, it is most difficult to determine the actual extent to which they prevailed and were burdensome, since many issues were involved. It could be said, on the whole, where sentiment and pride were involved, they caused constant friction and tended to survive; where material interests were involved in a big way, they were sharply scaled down to meet the realities of the situation. If this had not happened, the system would not have had that measure of general acceptance that it enjoyed, since there was no one to enforce it with an iron hand. The position may be examined with reference to certain major sectors.

First there were the land grants and tax concessions by the state. In most cases, they were for services rendered to the state or the community, and these were made to persons of all castes. Here, there was no question of privilege or inequity. This apart, there were the grants and concessions to Brahmanas and religious men, and also those made to temples and religious institutions. These were at the time the principal means of extending state support to education and higher learning, and to Hindu religious and spiritual life. The Smritis invariably stressed that the beneficiaries should be merited. For instance, Manu said, "A gift to one who is not a Brahmana (yields) the ordinary (reward; a gift) to one who calls himself a Brahmana, a double (reward); a gift to a well-read Brahmana, a hundred-thousand-fold (reward); (a gift) to one who knows the Veda and the Anga (Vedaparaga, a reward) without end."[85] There is no reason to believe that the grants and concessions were made to persons other than the merited, though the beneficiaries were usually Brahmanas under the system; it is the king or the state that suffered from indiscriminate benefactions.[86] P.V. Kane has pointed out that Brahmanas as a class had to pay the usual taxes like others, and "the (Smriti) claims to exemptions were probably exaggerated, and not respected in practice."[87] As in the working of any system, there would have been lapses. In M.G. Ranade's opinion, for instance, the revenue concessions to Brahmanas imposed "an unnecessary burden upon the finances of the land and contributed not a little to the breakdown of the Peshwa's power."[88]

In day-to-day life, the Brahmanas and religious men were accorded small concessions based on custom in a religious spirit or as an act of charity. Such matters of minor moment apart, on the basis of a special study of the agricultural wages in Madras as prevalent in the nineteenth century, Dharma Kumar has expressed the view that the wages paid depended upon the caste of the labourer as well as that of the employer; generally, the lowest castes were paid the lowest wages; and all over India the Brahmanas paid different and lower fees for various village services than those paid by others.[89] The existence of certain disparties is not unlikely, but, as a generalization, the view runs counter to the practical and pragmatic spirit of the people where material interests were involved. It is probable that Dharma Kumar has placed excesive reliance on mere wage structure without taking adequate account of perquisites and other material considerations. This is more than likely, because we get a different picture of the condition of the lowest classes from the report of the First Indian Law Commission on slavery (1841). The Commission noted that the slaves were well-fed and clothed, and humanely treated, and their condition was as good or better than that of free labourers "in respect of the supply of physical wants, and particularly of the certainty of that supply", and as such there was no general desire for freedom among them. Indeed, the Act of 1843, a welcome measure in itself, was promulgated more to placate the missionaries and the anti-slavery lobby in England than to put an end to a crying evil requiring urgent redressal.[90]

That there was not much discrimination on grounds of caste to pose a major challenge is also seen from another macro fact — caste considerations did not count for much in the distribution of harvest. Writing on the agrarian structure in Uttar Pradesh in the late eighteenth and the early nineteenth centuries, Sulekh Chandra Gupta observes:

> The rights and privileges of various groups within the village community were not always governed by the considerations of caste, at least during the period preceding the British conquest. Caste was important only for regulating the broad division of labour within the village community between such groups as artisans, agricultural labourers (who were few in number), and cultivators. But the rights and privileges of the different groups were determined by their functional relationship to the village economy and the nature of the work done by them.

Again, regarding the distribution of harvest in the Delhi region, Percival Spear writes, "Thus, the lowly chamar, cobbler and dresser of unclean leather received the highest allowance of all, while the priest or Brahmin was given by the hard-headed people the least." The Brahmana had to supplement his income with astrology and other means. The position was the same in South India as testified by Buchanan and others.[91]

As regards inequities in the administration of justice, no doubt the general attitude of the Smritis was to project and uphold the privileges of the Brahmanas and the upper varnas in this as in other matters. In fairness, it should also be noted that there was a running stress placed upon responsibility to go with privilege. This is reflected in Manu who said where a common man was liable to be fined one *karshapana* (an old-time coin), the king should be fined a thousand. In cases of theft, the guilt of a Sudra was to be deemed eightfold, of a Vaisya sixteenfold, of a Kshatriya two-and-thirtyfold, "of a Brahmana sixty-fourfold, or quite a hundredfold, or (even) twice four-and-sixtyfold, each of them knowing the nature of the offence."[92] As explained earlier, as in other matters, it would be hazardous to take Smriti texts laying down discriminatory punishments or granting special privileges to the upper castes as conclusive and authoritative. The considered opinion of P.V. Kane with reference to the Brahmana at the close of the ancient period would be applicable to all the upper castes in regard to later periods as well. He writes, "The only special privilege claimed for the Brahmana in the law courts of the land was freedom from death sentence or corporal punishment like whipping, though rarely he was liable to be sentenced to death also. He was subject to the indignities of branding and being paraded on the back of an ass, to fines and banishment, etc. These claims were very moderate when compared with the absurd length to which the doctrine of the 'benefit of clergy' was carried in England and other Western countries."[93] Though the sentiment in favour of the Brahmana was generally there, H.H. Dodwell writes that, in the eighteenth century, Brahmanas were executed under special circumstances, and the Peshwa would not have hesitated to have a Brahmana hanged if he was guilty of a crime against the state.[94]

While the Hindu society was an unequal one at the dawn of the modern age, and inequities based on caste and class were in plenty, the situation was not critical or explosive. The measure of social acceptance of the system as it stood was very high. This is reflected in a statement of Ananda Rangam Pillai, the Dubash of Dupleix, himself not a member of a higher varna: "No good can come ... of treating the low born with unaccustomed respect, or of employing anyone in occupations for which he is by descent unqualified. The foundation of prosperity and good government is the due subordination of the castes."[95] Pillai would render his superiors their due; he expected those below him to know their position and do the same. In the prevailing atmosphere, everyone was after gaining a small advantage, and fought hard for it; only a few, the saint-reformers, were for ending the inequitous system, and that in their own way.

In this background, the policy of the Hindu state in matters of caste and religion was highly pragmatic; it was to uphold the system as it stood and was generally accepted. To allow the different castes and social groups to live their own lives according to their individual customs, tradition and usage without undue intervention was the rule. However, it was the duty of the king to hear complaints and redress grievances; he was also to resolve intergroup differences and conflicts over rights and privileges. It was his duty to sustain the social order that had come down and gained acceptance. It was not his duty, nor the right thing to do, to innovate, reform or strike a new path. What was important was to hold the balance even and be fair to all. The Hindu state was not non-interventionist in the strict sense; its policy could best be described as constructive secularism, without being reformist, or being unfair to any religious group, sect or caste in dispensing favours or in any other matter. Holding the balance even and maintaining the *status quo* without giving room for friction were the wise norms to be adhered to.

Maratha administration exemplified the way the Hindu state functioned and we have good evidence about its working. There are many references in the records to state intervention in caste matters: infringement of caste rules; expulsions from and readmissions to caste; prohibition of marriages in the Hindu month of Kartik; punishment of a Brahmana for giving lessons in *Rudra* to a Lingayat priest contrary to usage; adoption by a Brahmana widow without obtaining government permission, etc.[96] With regard to inter-caste relations, the policy was to maintain existing rights and privileges, equitable or otherwise, or to help in working out a new consensus. By way of illustration, we may refer to a conflict between the Mahar and the Kumbhi castes of Nagaur in 1776–77. The former complained that, contrary to custom, they were prevented by the latter from taking hides of dead cattle, other than those of plough bullocks. They also had complaints against members of the Mang caste who were not allowing them to receive "the five dishes and rice offered to gods on the Dasara day"; they unlawfully claimed "half a share in the buffaloes led in procession round the town on the Dasara

day and the jar of sweets carried behind it"; their bridegrooms
rode on horses instead of bullocks, "a privilege which belonged
to the Mahars"; etc. After due enquiry, the government issued
orders for the redressal of the grievances of the Mahars in
all the provinces.[97] To cite a few other instances, carpenters
were restored their right to precedence over eleven other
castes practising different crafts; the priorities to be observed
in reciting the Vedic hymns by Brahmanas of different sects
were laid down on the lines recommended by a *parishat*
(conference); Prabhus were barred from learning or reciting
the Vedas consequent to objections raised by Brahmanas;
certain Brahmanas were restrained from giving their
daughters in marriage to their nephews on complaints being
received; the right of the Kasar caste to take out marriage
processions accompanied by a *kalasha* (an ornamented pot
of water considered to be an auspicious symbol) was
recognized; etc.[98] The policy pursued by other Hindu kings
was similar. E.A. Gait notes that the relative ranks of castes
were adjudged by rulers, often in consultation with
Brahmanas; no caste was allowed to make spurious
claims.[99].

The Peshwa government considered it its duty to play a
similar role in regard to its non-Hindu subjects, and the latter
sought its intervention at times. It settled a dispute over
priesthood among the Parsis, confirmed a claim to priesthood
by a Portuguese clergyman, and arbitrated in the matter of
taking out *tazias* in Poona.[100] It may be noted that both
Muslim rulers and the British in India also did not disclaim
the right to intervene in caste affairs. As regards the British,
the Parliamentary Committee of Secrecy (1773) advised that
a measure of control should be maintained over caste councils
"as a direct assertion of the subordination of the Hindoos,
who are a very considerable majority of the subjects."[101]
While this was the policy during the early years of British
rule, the function of settling caste and inter-caste disputes
was transferred to the civil courts later, since there was great
opposition to a Christian Government associating itself with
the functioning of the heathen religion and its social
system.

PUBLIC SERVICES AND THE CASTE FACTOR

As regards the manning of public posts, there was no positive ban on any suitable person being selected, except for posts requiring knowledge of sacred books, which was the preserve of the Brahmana. But the caste factor had its impact in a big enough way: .the vocational base of caste and its preferences and antipathies, the socio-economic standing of the caste, lineage and family status of the individuals concerned, all these mattered. At the village level, the all-powerful Patel was a member of the dominant land-owning caste; the Kulakarni (Accountant) was of the upper literate caste; and the village servants, Talwar, Thoti and others came from the lower castes. In the bureaucratic setup of the state in general, it is held that white-collar posts, specially financial and judicial, were the preserve of the Brahmana, though the Kayastha displaced him in a number of regions in the North. Taking the total situation into consideration, there is a case for presuming wider employment of other literate classes in this sector. Until recently, it was taken for granted that Brahmanas were mostly engaged in priestly and scholarly occupations, and this is found to be incorrect. A closer look may reveal that the extent of Brahmana monopoly in this sector may also not have been as much as assumed. As regards police and watch and ward, these were in the hands of lower castes. There were often close-knit caste groups such as Bhils, Kolis and Bedas who pursued this as their major occupation.[102] As regards the army, it has been stated earlier that recruitment was broad-based, and several castes, upper and lower, were represented. Even so, a closer look may reveal the existence of small caste or subcaste groups that could be classified as 'martial' as, for instance, the Military Brahmanas referred to above. Broadly, while there was sufficient diversification of the bureaucracy and the army, certain caste groups were predominant in particular sectors. There was no conscious effort on the part of the state to give equal opportunities for all to enter its services as in modern times.

Caste politics was bound to be present in a caste-based society at all times. Rivalries and fights over spoils of office and patronage in different fields, particularly among those caste groups which had reasonable claims, were inescapable. Great stress has been laid by some scholars on the Maratha-Brahmana divide under the Peshwas. As mentioned earlier, M.G. Ranade holds that the undue favouring of Brahmanas was a major cause for the Maratha collapse. Appeasement of influential caste groups and balancing acts were very much a part of statecraft. We can get a good view of it from S.N. Sen's account of the administration of forts under Shivaji whose arrangements continued to the very end of Maratha rule. Forts were under the charge of three officers having the same rank and exercising conjoint authority — the Havaldar or the head of the garrison, a Maratha of good family; the Sabnis in charge of accounts, a Brahmana; and a Kharkhani in charge of commissariat work, a Prabhu. "Their duties were so adroitly apportioned and so cleverly adjusted that nothing could be accomplished without the knowledge of all the three." S.N. Sen further observes that this caste-wise apportionment was not conditioned by caste-vocation: Brahmana generals were not wanting; a Prabhu could be an efficient Sabnis. This was resorted "to minimise the chances of their joint action against the king and placate the three principal castes of Maharashtra by an equitable distribution of state patronage in a manner best suited to the peculiar genius and traditions of each. The Brahmin was not well disposed towards the Prabhu, the Prabhu had no kindly feeling towards the Brahmins, who had bitterly opposed his claims to Vedic rites, and a Maratha could be ordinarily expected to be more loyal to the king of his own caste than to his own colleagues of a superior caste".[103]

CASTE CONFLICTS AND MAINTENANCE OF PEACE

It would appear from contemporary records that on the whole, caste and sectarian conflicts were of minor moment, no more than ripples providing excitement to an otherwise placid life. In his study on the panchayats under the Peshwas, H.G. Franks writes, "In all the records that have been examined in the Poona Daftar, the present investigator has not found a single instance of that caste hatred and quarrellings that are common in these days." Further, with reference to the depressed classes, he says, "Not one of the many dozens of reports of British officials makes any reference to the problems which today confront the social reform of the people of India."[104] There are also hardly any references to any serious law and order problems arising out of caste conflicts in the travelogues and other records of the seventeenth-eighteenth centuries.

There is one exception to what has been said above — the strained relations and frequency of conflicts between the Left Hand and the Right Hand castes of South India. These were caste blocs rather than castes in the accepted sense. Buchanan observes that they were not united "by any common tie of religion, occupation or kindred;" theirs was "merely a struggle for certain honorary distinctions." However, this does not explain how the blocs came into being or their antiquity. There are references to these groups in the inscriptions of the eleventh century. Opinion is divided about their origin. One view is that it was socio-religious, "an anti-Brahminic movement directed towards reclaiming the lower strata to a higher position" in the process of checking conversions from Buddhism to Hinduism. However, the caste groups concerned now belong to the orthodox Hindu wing. Another view is that advanced by B.E.F. Beck. In his view, it originated from the conflict of interests between the village-based landowning castes and the town-based artisan castes; the line of demarcation arising out of this factor grew thin over time. In whatever way they originated, in the eighteenth century, the fights were over customary socio-religious practices involving sentiment and prestige, as noted by Buchanan. Beck states that the conflicts "reached a peak of intensity" in the late eighteenth and the early nineteenth centuries because the Right Hand castes resented being placed on par with their rivals by the East India Company. Later on, the relations were less strained.[105]

Impact of Religion and Caste on Economic Progress and Intellectual Development

It is often stated that economic progress and intellectual development were greatly impeded by the nature of the Hindu religion and its social system. As regards economic progress, judged by pre-Industrial Revolution standards, the view is untenable — India did not lag behind others in the eighteenth century or the earlier periods. Land was plentiful. If taxes were heavy and there was oppression, people migrated freely, and this was the best check against arbitrary government. The agricultural know-how was sufficiently advanced, and there was not much scope for any major improvements before the introduction of modern techniques.[106] As regards industries, citing Moreland, who was not likely to exaggerate Indian achievements, Tarachand observes, "Although Indian industry remained in the pre-capitalist stage and India did not evolve the industrial middle class, yet, both in variety of output and techniques of production, she was, at the time, more advanced industrially than contemporary Europe." In the matter of foreign trade, India was the largest exporter of industrial goods, and in the absence of corresponding imports, a noted 'sink of precious metals', as those trading with India complained. She retained her creditor position even during the first half of the nineteenth century.[107] The great maritime tradition which led to the colonization of South-East Asia lasted till the thirteenth century. Later, the Indians were gradually ousted first by the Arabs and then by the Western traders. Even so, Indian trade and shipping had no negligible place even in the eighteenth century. India failed to retain her high position only because the rulers, both Hindu and Muslim, did not ensure protection against piracy and unfair competition, not because of the weakness of the Hindu social system.[108] As regards indigenous banking, it was linked with both trade and the collection of revenue, and was strong and viable. Though industries were village-based, D.R. Gadgil has noted that the degree of urbanization about 1750 was comparable to that of England, France and Italy.[109] The general prosperity of the land received high encomiums from discerning foreigners — Lt. Col. Moore regarding Tipu's Mysore, Elphinstone regarding Maharashtra and Alexander Dow regarding Bengal.[110] Despite castewise imbalances, the state of general education was very good in Madras, Bengal and elsewhere, as seen from the well-known Adam's reports on education. In the opinion of Sir Thomas Munro, it was much better than that which existed "till very lately in most countries in Europe."[111] There was also uniform praise for the administrative system and performance of the Mughuls. The gulf separating the Muslim rulers from their Hindu subjects did not prevent India from maintaining a high standard all round, and this can be explained only in terms of the strength of the village and the caste at the grass-roots level. This should lay to rest the criticism that economic progress was impeded by the nature of the Hindu religion and its social system, specially caste.

The weaknesses of the system which were an obstacle to greater progress being achieved should, however, be noted. These came from the very factors which gave it strength. First was the protective role of caste and village, which C. Rajagopalachari termed 'decentralized socialism'.[112] When it was overplayed, the spirit of individualism and scope for personal enterprise suffered, and this is a point rightly stressed often by scholars. However, holding a contrary view, Sulekh Chandra Gupta has maintained that the right balance was struck. "Not to let the inequality of wealth grow beyond a point, and yet to introduce a certain degree of inequality for providing economic incentives was the main strategy of pre-British Indian rulers. It succeeded in so far as it sustained the internal solidarity and vigour of the village communities."[113] Again, vocation-centred castes made for conservation of craft knowledge and tradition, but it would have also acted as a damper when one wanted to strike a new line. There were also taboos and restrictions governing commensality, sea travel, etc. The castes most affected generally ignored them, and often enough, the Smritis condoned infractions taking refuge under the law of necessity. This is clearly seen in the Smriti provisions governing sea-travel.[114] Though, often enough, safety valves were provided and the restrictions were not rigidly enforced, the whole exercise would have cost something. The impact of such adverse factors should not, however, be exaggerated.

We will also need to consider if Hindu religion and caste stood in the way of intellectual development and scientific progress. There is first the criticism that the scholarship base was too narrow — Brahmanas were the sole possessors of Vedic knowledge and they constituted the intellectual elite. This view requires to be qualified in many ways. The

Brahmanas were not a small coterie, but a large community, divided into castes and subcastes and evenly spread over the whole land. Also, the ritualistic bar concerned only study of the Vedas, not of other subjects. On the authority of Martin, Adams and Buchanan, Raghuvamshi writes that Baidyas, Kayasthas and a number of artisan classes studied Sanskrit, particularly concerning their profession.[115] This does not appear to have been any new development: in the time of the Chalukyas of Kalyani (973-1200A.D.), there were Sudra *sishyas* (pupils), who were proficient in Sanskrit grammar, etc. and who in turn became teachers.[116] Apart from institutions devoted to Vedic and theological studies into which only Brahmanas were admitted, there were always general schools open to all who sought admission. In these, in the early nineteenth century, the Brahmana proportion was about a quarter, the other castes making up the balance — "vaidyas and kayasths in Bengal, kayasths, banyas and rajputs in U.P., prabhoos in south Konkan, wanees and combees in Gujarat (Ahmedabad collectorate), wanees and sudr in Khandesh, to give a few examples." In these schools, the stress was on imparting literacy and knowledge of numeration "useful for small trade, revenue collection and revenue administration".[117] Brahmana predominance would have been the highest in the field of higher eduation at all times — in the early years of the last century, according to Adams' report, in Murshidabad, none of the 437 students of the higher schools were non-Brahmanas.[118] Broadly, the educational system of the day was need-based and not conceived in the spirit of imparting universal education; this virtually left out most part of the community, the lower castes. Despite this limitation, it could be said that the educational base castewise was more broad-based than often supposed, and it was no more narrow than in most other countries of the day.[119]

Another factor highlighted as coming in the way of progress is the absence of cross-fertilization in regard to ideas and techniques, because of the high and low of caste and its vocational base. There was no free mixing of intellectuals with craftsmen, no meeting of those engaged in one occupation with those of others. According to many students of the history of science in India, this was a major impediment to scientific development. Only for a short period, the Tantric cults cut

asunder caste restrictions and taboos; it was then that the
Siddha Vaidya and the Rasa Vidya, associated with research
for the elixir of life, flourished.[120] This argument is valid up
to a point, but the position does not appear to have been
as gloomy as often made out. As explained earlier, there was
a relatively good measure of flexibility in choice of vocation,
either by a caste group or by individuals, from very early
times. The rigidity of caste in this respect is based upon
assumptions made and taken for granted by scholars a few
decades back, as noted earlier. Again, it is admitted that crafts
in India were entirely village-based. The people in a village
formed a close-knit community. While craftsmen worked,
others watched. Their techniques were not complicated nor
was any secrecy attached to them, save in rare cases. There
were inhibitions not easy to overcome only in cases such as
the profession of the *chamar* or leather worker.

There is then the question of freedom of thought and
expression, basic to intellectual development and growth of
knowledge. In the highly explosive field of religion, boldness
and an uninhibited spirit of enquiry marked the Upanishads
and the agnostic schools founded by Mahavira and the
Buddha. There was no break in the tradition set up: the
diverse schools of Mahayana Buddhism, the growth of Nyaya
(Logic) in the clash between orthodox Hinduism and heterodox
Buddhism, the philosophical schools founded by the great
savants like Sankara, Ramanuja and Madhvacharya, the
many religious sects, moderate and radical, which flourished,
these showed that the springs of individualism and freedom
of thought were never choked. Among the Hindus, there was
no Vatican issuing infallible decrees or an Inquisition. True,
there was the rigidity of caste to contend with; to be put
out of caste was tantamount to death. But a certain degree
of conservatism was basic to stability. It cannot be said that,
on the whole and in the long run, the Hindu social system
was not flexible enough to accommodate new ideas and new
forces.

The real trouble lay not in want of freedom of thought or
expression, but in the value attached to things, in the focus
of interest. At the beginning, the Vedic Aryans had a balanced
view of life. The concept of *Rta* or natural order was central
to Vedic thought; it showed that "the Vedic People had an

instinctive conviction in the natural order — a conviction which is of prime importance for sustenance of scientific attitude." That the two sets of values, spiritual and humanistic, were given the same place is seen in the Vedic hymn, "Give sight to our eyes, sight to our bodies, so that they can see. May we see the world as a whole, may we see it in detail."[121] This was what Max Lerner termed "the metaphysic of secular promise with the desire for ultimate spiritual liberation."[122] This balance which the Vedic Aryans held high was not easy to maintain. Perhaps, in the whole of recorded history, only the Greeks strove truly towards this goal, as vividly brought out by Edith Hamilton in *The Greek Way to Western Civilization* (1952). With the Hindus, it was all different from the time of the Buddha: there was a clear lack of interest in the material side of life — it was the same with agnostic Buddhism as with the later theistic Bhakti cults. Dhirendra Narain has urged that there was nothing weak or inferior about this attitude; on the contrary, it was stronger and more sublime than that of the West.[123] This aspect of the question apart, it was a fact that the best minds among the Hindus were always drawn to the realm of the spirit —metaphysics, mysticism and religion. The entire stress was on seeing "the world as a whole", not on seeing it "in detail". Even so, the strong pull of the materialistic world could not be escaped. The high order of material culture sustained down to the modern period clearly indicated that the pull was by no means weak. Also, recent studies in the history of science have shown that, judged from medieval standards, India did not, in fact, lag behind other countries in scientific studies or technological development; her contributions in the field of mathematics, astronomy and medicine were noteworthy. It is in the field of humanistic studies that the progress was particularly weak. Not much attention was paid to social and political problems, except in a practical way as and when they cropped up, and no social and political philosophy of value was developed as a discipline. While Hindu intellectual development in scientific and humanistic studies was not on the whole poor as judged by contemporary standards, India was left far behind by the post-Renaissance developments in Europe. It is this that made India backward *vis-a-vis* the West. If the balanced view of life projected by the Vedic

Aryans had not been largely abandoned, if the inquiring mind so active in the realm of the spirit had evinced equal interest in the material world and human affairs, the Hindus might have ushered in the Renaissance much earlier.

Further to the factors internal to the Hindu standing in the way of progress, there was the impact of the Muslim invasions disrupting life over the whole land, and the fact of Muslim rule for over six centuries. Though opinion may differ as to the extent of damage caused, there is no doubt that loss of power and political subjection greatly hampered the intellectual development and cultural progress of the Hindus. Long periods of political unsettlement intervened before peace returned. This apart, it was the attack on focal points nourishing intellectual and cultural life that mattered. In war time, temples were the special targets of attack; with the Hindus, temples and holy places were the main centres of learning. The burning of libraries, big and small, the flight of scholars leaving their treasures behind, mattered more than destruction of stone edifices. Of the disastrous consequence of the invasions of Muhammad of Ghazni, al-Biruni wrote, "Hindu sciences have retired far away from those parts of the country that have been conquered by us, and have fled to places which our hand cannot yet reach, to Kashmir, Banaras and other places."[124] In Central Asia, Al-Biruni noted that the scribes, priests and libraries of Khoreznians were destroyed. As a consequence, it was found later that they had lost their written language and had to depend upon memory.[125] Nothing of that magnitude may have happened in India. How much of their rich heritage the Hindus lost, there can be no estimate; one can only guess. The location of a copy of the famous Kautilya's *Arthasastra* only in the early years of the present century is a rough indicator of the possible losses suffered, both in the matter of heritage and in continuity.

Return to peace did not mean restoration of normalcy for the Hindus. Under Muslim rule, the beneficiaries of the state patronage were mostly scholars who flocked from different parts of the world of Islam. No doubt some Hindu scholars too benefited, but such patronage was very limited and fitful, dependent upon the spirit of tolerance and political wisdom of individual rulers. Since Muslim rulers were generally

pragmatic in their administrative policies, there was no
positive animus towards Hindu learning or any active
persecution; it was a case of indifference, even under
the Mughuls as M.L. Roy Choudhury has observed.[126] As a
result, Hindu learning flourished mostly in areas under Hindu
rulers. M.A. Mehendale and A.D. Pusalkar have noted,
"Regional survey indicates that the bulk of (Sanskritic)
production came from the South, followed by Bengal, Mithila
and Western India. Kashmir recedes into the background."[127]

The plight of the Hindus also worsened because of other
factors. The conquest and conversion to Islam of the whole
of the North-Western belt and the loss of control over the
seas with the entry of the Arabs deprived the Hindus of their
external cultural contacts; even the links with their colonies
in South-East Asia were snapped. Tibet remained the only
outlet. There was a drift of scholars to that land, and Tibetan
Buddhism came to flourish in a big way. At the same time,
regional insularity also increased. Earlier, Sanskritic learning
had an all-India base and purview. The absence of patronage
discouraged the movement of scholars, and development of
Sanskritic learning came to be increasingly regional. There
was another development which heightened this insularity.
After Asoka, the unity provided by the Brahmi script was
mostly eroded with the regional changes in the style of
writing. Even so, the post-Brahmi Siddhamatrika or Kutila
script provided a good measure of unity between the sixth
and ninth centuries A.D.[128] Thereafter, there was the rapid
growth of the vernacular languages, each of them coming to
have its own individualised script, though all the scripts came
from the same stock. Sanskrit and other classical languages,
which made for the religio-cultural unity of the Hindus, came
to be written in the local scripts. For instance, even in the
early decades of the present century, Sanskrit books used by
traditional scholars in Karnataka and Andhra Pradesh were
printed mostly in the Telugu script, and in Tamilnadu, they
were printed in Grantha, a variant of the Tamil script. The
trend to adopt the Devanagari as the common script for
Sanskrit throughout the country is a recent development. The
loss of script unity was an impediment of no small measure
for the progress of Sanskritic scholarship throughout the
medieval period.

There was one positive aspect to Muslim rule and contacts with outside Islamic cultures. The invaders brought with them not only a new faith, but a new intellectual and cultural tradition, an amalgam of Arabic and Persian. With this was associated the Graeco-Roman heritage in the realm of scholarship. If the cultural contact had given Hindu thought a decidedly humanistic turn, as it did in the case of Christian Europe, India may have been the forerunner of the Renaissance, and possibly of the Industrial Revolution as well. Unfortunately, the confrontation between the two was limited to the realm of religion and faith, not the field of intellect. Akbar's Ibadat Khana, the Conference Hall of All-Religions, and his common schools bringing Hindu and Muslim scholars under the same roof, held out hopes of change, but the experiment proved to be stillborn.[129] Soldiers crossed swords in the field of battle and hugged each other when peace came; the ruling classes compromised; saints on both the sides preached harmony; but the intellectuals kept aloof. As Tarachand observed, "The Hindu and Muslim learned circles moved largely within their own orbits, and so, with a few exceptions, they did not exchange their knowledge and thus failed to fertilise one other's mind."[130]

However much we may regret, under the prevailing circumstances, this was unavoidable. With political power in their hands, with their fundamentalist and proselytizing tradition, the Muslim Ashraf were aggressive and uncompromising; they saw little merit in the learning and culture of the Kafir. For the Hindu, the challenge posed by Islam was a new experience. If Muslims had entered India in the way others did earlier, he would have been patient and understanding, exhibiting his traditional tolerance and poise. The loss of political power and constant attacks on his cherished institutions made him sullen and retire into a shell. Proud and aloof, he was sure Islamic culture had nothing to give him, and he would have none of it in any case. Neither Hindu religion nor the system of caste as such could be faulted for this alienation and aloofness. This is amply proved by the dawn of the Bengal Renaissance within a few decades after Plassey, and the readiness with which the Hindu elite took to Western education and scientific culture, without compromising their faith and traditional culture and values.

It would be clear from the above that, despite limitations and shortcomings, India did not lag behind others, judged by medieval standards. Most of those who level the charge of backwardness have at the back of their mind the phenomenal progress made by the West following the Renaissance and the Industrial Revolution. These were unique events, comparable to the flowering of Greek culture, the historic role of Roman Law and the system of governance, and the emergence of the Upanishadic thought and the Hindu way of life. The unique occurs only once, when there is synchronization of specially favourable factors. Politically divided and internecine warfare rampant, but economically prosperous because of the trade with the East, morally debased with the old values of the Mother Church crumbling and the Papacy itself in disrepute, Italy was, for all appearances, hardly fit for the great role it played. What really mattered was the emergence of an intellectual elite holding old values in scorn and ready to question everything. It was, indeed, fortuitous that, just at this juncture, the Arabs brought the West into contact with its own lost heritage with its pronounced humanistic and secular values and scientific spirit. Hope quenched disillusionment, intellectual curiosity opened up a vista, and these augured a new era. India could have formed the base for the great leap forward if there had been healthy cross-fertilization between the Hindu and Islamic intellectual traditions, but this did not come to pass. It would be good to remember that it was not given to China either, though rooted in Confucianism, with its highly secular and pragmatic outlook on life, and with a casteless society. Even the Arabs came to be only the purveyors of the Graeco-Roman heritage, their own fundamentalist tradition coming in the way of their benefiting from it.

Notes

1. *Acharya Hrdayam*, 86-7, 90.
2. R.C. Majumdar in Nanavati and Vakil, 73. The Vedas are not considered authoritative in the same sense or spirit the Bible and the Quran are. "The ultimate authority in Indian religion is experience (*anubhava*) as Sankara says." — S.S. Rama Rao in Pranabanand Joshi, 317.
3. See p. 240, Note 17.
4. P.V. Kane, Vol. II. Part I, 176-7.

5. Tarachand, Vol. I, 90.
6. Raghuvamshi, 53.
7. Tarachand, Vol. I, 90
8. No doubt the racial explanation is often not accepted by scholars. However, what seems certain is that there were two antithetical cultural groups in the beginning — one exclusive, assertive, upcoming and dominant, the other continuously on the defensive. It is the interaction between the two, with a good element of the racial divide not ruled out, that gave rise to the system of caste.
9. R.C. Majumdar, *The Age of Imperial Unity*, 549.
10. P.V. Kane, Vol. II, Part I, 47. Also, G.S. Ghurye, *Vedic India*, 298.
11. K.K. Pillay — The Caste System in the Sangam Age, *Journal of Indian History*, Vol. XL, Sl. No. 120, 513-20.
12. Raghuvamshi, 17-8. Also, P.V. Kane, Vol. V, Part II, 1266.
13. B.R. Ambedkar, 7.
14. P.V. Kane, Vol. II, Part I, 23.
15. Caste Panchayats under the Marathas — H.G. Franks, 70 *et seqq.* Adverse impact of British policy —Raghuvamshi, 84, 278-307.
16. P.V. Kane, Vol. II, Part I, 19-22.
17. Raghuvamshi, 76.
18. P.V. Kane, Vol. II, Part I, 66-8.
19. Buchanan, *Mysore, Canara and Malabar*, 21. Mithila Brahmanas were in the same position as the Vaidiks — Buchanan, *Purnea*, 275.
20. Raghuvamshi, 59-63.
21. R.C. Majumdar, *The Age of Imperial Unity*, 548.
22. P.V. Kane, Vol. II, Part I, 118-20. Also, U.N. Ghoshal in R.C. Majumdar, *The Delhi Sultanate*, 576, 603.
23. P.V. Kane, Vol. II, Part I, 122-3, regarding Kautilya's reference to Brahmanaka wherein Brahmanas followed the profession of arms and other similar instances in the Smriti literature. B.R. Gopal, pp. 407 & 422, refers to Brahmana colonies (*agraharas*) of those trained in arms. Also, U.N. Ghoshal, in R.C. Majumdar, *Imperial Kanauj*, 235; *The Struggle for Empire*, 476.
24. G. Buhler, Chap. VIII, 411-2.
25. D.R. Gadgil, 19.
26. Raghuvamshi, 61-3. Also, Tarachand, Vol. I, 146.
27. Buchanan, *Northern Parts of Kanara*, 107. Sterling, 37.
28. W. Tennant, Vol. I, 89.
29. P.V. Kane, Vol. III, 39. U.N. Ghoshal in R.C. Majumdar, *Imperial Kanauj*, 232-3, and *The Struggle for Empire*, 269-70.
30. P.V. Kane, Vol. III, 202. Of the character of the Bengal army prior to British conquest, T.C. Das Gupta writes, "There was no caste distinction among soldiers who were recruited from all sections of the community. Even foreigners were employed, of whom the Telugus (the Madrasis) were prominent." — xxxi.
31. Tarachand writes that in Hindu India, villages took no direct part in war, "which was the business of kings and of the caste whose vocation was fighting." — Vol. I, 108. A.K. Nazrul Karim observes that Brahmanas and Kshatriyas were functionally divorced from

production and a parasitic class. — pp. 68 and 84. According to M. Mujeeb, because of the caste system and the position of the Kshatriyas, the total resources of the state could not be used in wars. — p. 29. Also, Satishchandra in *Spirit of India*, Vol. II, 80.

32. K.K. Pillay, The Caste System in the Sangam Age —*Journal of Indian History,*Vol. XLI, Sl. 120 (1962), 517. U.N. Ghoshal in R.C. Majumdar, *The Delhi Sultanate*, 582. H.G. Rawlinson (Ed.), *Rasa Mala*, Vol. II, 236. Buchanan, *Dinajpur*, 99. D.R. Gadgil, 19.

33. P.V. Kane, Vol. II, Part I, 47.

34. *Ibid*, Vol. III, 873.

35. B.B. Majumdar in R.C. Majumdar, *The Mughul Empire*, 637.

36. U.N. Ghoshal in R.C. Majumdar, *Imperial Kanauj*, 231-2, and *The Struggle for Empire*, 269-70.

37. For an account of the festering controversy from the time of Shivaji to our own times, see A.C. Paranjpe, section on historical background. Also, *Selections from the Peshwa Daftar*, Vol. 42, Introduction, p. 2.

38. Burton Stein, in J. Silverberg, 79.

39. Raghuvamshi, 61, 63.

40. G. S. Ghurye, *Caste and Class in India*, 17-18.

41. D. R. Gadgil, ii-iii *et seqq.*

42. K.K. Pillay in *Journal of Indian History*, Vol. XL, Sl. No. 120 p. 517. S.K. Chatterjee in R.C. Majumdar, *Vedic Age*, 160. K.M. Panikkar, *Survey of Indian History*, 6. Krishna Chaitanya, 294, also, Chaps. 7-9 *et seqq.*

43. C.T.E. Rhenius, 114. W. Cockburn, 31.

44. C.T.E. Rhenius, 114.

45. Sisir Kumar Das in Bisheshwar Prasad, 75-6.

46. Friar Jordanus, 24. *Tuhafat-ul-Mujahidin*, 52. W. Tennant, 179-80. J.H. Grose, 182, 184.

47. P.V. Kane, Vol. V, Part II, 1015-17.

48. Lalmani Joshi, 396. R.C. Mitra (*p. 128 et seqq.*) cites several instances of persecution of Buddhists, but holds that toleration was the general rule. Also, Phra Khantipolo for a similar view, 29, 130.

49. Dhurtakhyana — R.C. Majumdar, *Imperial Kanauj*, 207; impalement of Jains — *The Struggle for Empire*, 404; self-immolation of Saivas — *The Mughul Empire*, 641.

50. H.D. Bhattacharya in R.C. Majumdar, *Imperial Kanauj*, 327.

51. D.D. Kosambi, *Myth and Reality*, 15.

52. B.B. Majumdar in R.C. Majumdar, *The Mughul Empire*, 654.

53. B.R. Gopal, *Ramanuja in Karnataka*, 11.

54. See pp. 106-7 and p. 113, Note 70.

55. N. Macnicol, 286-8, Khushwant Singh, Vol. II, 119.

56. Khushwant Singh, Vol. II, 302-3.

57. Satishchandra raises the issue, but gives no answer. —*The Spirit of India*, Vol. II, 76.

58. K. Satchidananda Murty, 70.

59. Raghuvamshi, 24, 143-6.

60. *Sankara Digvijaya*, p. 4, states, "In the days of yore, it was to favour us that Lord Vishnu incarnated Himself as the Buddha and diverted

unrighteousmen from contaminating the Vedic path, by preaching a new religion for them." Another renowned Srivaisnava saint-scholar Manavala Mamunihal wrote that the Sankhya of Kapila Muni and the teachings of the Buddha, though God's own words, could not be, accepted as they were contrary to the Vedas. — *Acharya Hrdayam*, Part III, Sutra 194, page 149.

61. *Acharya Hrdayam*, Part I, Sutras 84-5. Also, 103, 108-12.

62. P.V. Kane, Vol. V, Part II, 1642. Kane also points out that in the Vedic days, Rathakaras and Nishadas were allowed to participate in *Yajnas* and repeat *mantras. Ibid.*

63. *Ibid., 1024-5*. The predominance of the popular non-Vedic Smriti tradition over the elitist *srauta* rites — Richard Salmon in Pranabanand Joshi, 329.

64. U.N. Ghoshal, 523.

65. G.S. Ghurye, *Caste and Class in India*, 108.

66. *Tirumalai*, 472-3. P.V. Kane observes, "The caste system, the joint family system, and the laws of succession and inheritance that are peculiar to Hindus are really social matters and not religious matters." Also, his account of the far-reaching, radical views regarding *dharma* advanced by Dharma Nirnaya Mandal, a society formed to arrive at definitive conclusions on matters of *dharma*, which hold its deliberations during 1934-59. — Vol. V, Part II, 1703-7

67. Tarachand, Vol. I, 97, 147-8.

68. A.K. Narain writes, "One has only to go through the Pali canonical literature to see how strong in number were the Brahmana followers of the Buddha who had rejected the claim of their Brahmanahood by birth. It has been shown that 40 per cent. of the leading monks and nuns taken together belonged to the Brahmana caste. Many of the key personalities through its history in India came from this social group,"— p. xxvii. Also, B.G. Gokhale in A.K. Narain, 74-5. Regarding Jains, see *Bharatiya Samskriti Kosh*, Vol. II, 703.

69. B.B. Majumdar in R.C. Majumdar, *The Mughul Empire*, 645.

70. Anand K. Coomaraswamy, 25-6. P.V. Kane, Vol. V, Part II, 1007. Lalmani Joshi, 407. De Barry, 131-6. B.C. Law, 95-6. Mahavira's approach was the same as that of the Buddha. —*Bharatiya Samskriti Kosh*, Vol. VII, 247.

71. U.N. Ghoshal, 264.

72. R.C. Majumdar, *The Delhi Sultanate*, 568.

73. Hari Ram Gupta in R.C. Majumdar, *The Mughul Empire*, 660-4.

74. *The Gospel of Sri Ramakrishna*, 159-60. Indeed, Sri Ramakrishna favoured adherance to accepted caste rules and practices until these got dropped through one's spiritual attainments. — *Teachings of Sri Ramakrishna*, Advaita Asrama, Calcutta, 1972, pp. 240-1.

75. G.S. Ghurye, *Anthropo-Sociological Papers*, 238. M.N. Srinivas, 6.

76. P.V. Kane, Vol. II, Part I, 124, 136-7.

77. U.N. Ghoshal, 530.

78. Sir Denzil Ibbetson's view referred to by A.K. Nazrul Karim, 66.

79. T.G.P. Spear, 5-6. Also, P.V. Kane, Vol. III, 25-8 *et seqq.*

80. P.V. Kane, Vol. V, Part II, 1011; Vol. III, 882.

81. R.C. Majumdar, *Imperial Kanauj*, xviii.
82. P.V. Kane, Vol. V, Part II, 1619, 1629-30. Also, U.N. Ghoshal in R.C. Majumdar, *Imperial Kanauj*, 235.
83. A.S. Altekar in Katre and Gode, 25.
84. Sea voyage — U.N. Ghoshal in R.C. Majumdar, *The Struggle for Empire*, 493. Slavery — B.P. Murdeswar in Tikekar, 283-4. Smriti punishments— U.N. Ghoshal in R.C. Majumdar, *The Delhi Sultanate*, 580.
85. Buhler, Chap. VII, 85.
86. P.V. Kane, Vol. III, 195; Vol. II, Part I, 143-6.
87. Ibid.
88. S.N. Sen, *Maratha Administrative System* , 290.
89. Dharam Kumar in Tapan Ray Chaudhuri, Vol. II, 63-73.
90. S.V. Desika Char, *Centralised Legislation*, 190-4.
91. S.C. Gupta in Tapan Ray Chaudhuri, Vol. I, 22. Percival Spear, 121. Buchanan, *Mysore, Canara and Malabar*, Vol.I, 265-7, 299-300, 388-9, 414. N. Guha, 13. Sivarama Krishnan in P.P.S.T. Bulletin, No. 12, Sept. 1987, pp. 36-56.
92. Buhler, Chapter VIII, 336-8.
93. P.V. Kane, Vol. II, Part I, 142.
94. H.H. Dodwell in *Ananda Rangam Pillai Diary*, Vol. XII, 290-1.
95. H.H. Dodwell in *ibid*, Introduction, xxiii.
96. *Selections from the Peshwa Daftar*, Vol. 7, No. 58; Vol. 32, Nos. 205-6; Vol. 39, No. 137; Vol. 43, Nos. 8, 22, 25, 92, 107, 110.
97. K.B. Marathe, Vol. II, No. 816.
98. *Selections from the Peshwa Daftar*, Vol. 43, Nos. 9, 27, 69, *et seqq.* Also, S.N. Sen, *Maratha Administrative System*, 403-5.
99. E.A. Gait in *Encyclopaedia of Religion and Ethics*, Vol. 3 — "Caste". Also, M.N. Srinivas, 81.
100. S.N. Sen, *Maratha Administrative System*, 400. *Selections from the Peshwa Daftar*, Vol. 43, No. 33, regarding the role of Tahsildars in the settlement of caste disputes.
101. Raghuvamshi, 84. Buchanan, *Mysore, Canara and Malabar*, Vol. II, 294.
102. The Report from the Committee of Police at Tanjore, 4 April, 1813, noted, "The body of *Cavilgars* (police) of Tanjore consists chiefly of tribes, each connected within itself, and in many instances with others, by the ties of blood and clanship, and maintained by constant intermarriages." *The Cavilgars* held their posts hereditarily, and were a difficult class to control. — Paras 38, 65. Mss. Record, Madras Record Office, Vol. 8 A, No. 29, pp. 1683-1838.
103. S.N. Sen, *Maratha Military System*, 81-4.
104. H.G. Franks, 67.
105. Buchanan, *Mysore, Canara and Malabar*, 79. Brenda E.F. Beck —The Right Hand and Left Hand Divisions of South Indian Society, *The Journal of Asian Studies*, Vol. XXIX, No. 4 (August 1970), 779-98. Raghuvamshi, 70. U.N. Ghoshal in R.C. Majumdar, *The Struggle for Empire*, 478.
106. Lallanji Gopal in B.V. Subbarayappa, 237, 242.
107. Tarachand, Vol. I, 176-7, 180. Also, R.K. Mukherjee in R.C. Majumdar, *The Maratha Supremacy*, 782-9.

108. R.K. Mukherjee, *ibid.*
109. D.R. Gadgil, 8.
110. Raghuvamshi, 312-8. S.N. Sen, *The Maratha Administrative System*, 305. Alexander Dow, Vol. I, cxvii.
111. M. Elphinstone, *History of India*, 203.
112. C. Rajagopalachari, 33-6.
113. S.C. Gupta in Tapan Ray Chaudhuri, Vol. I, 41.
114. P.V. Kane, Vol. III, 933-8.
115. Raghuvamshi, 176-82, 187-90.
116. B.R. Gopal, *Chalukyas and Kalachuris*, 408.
117. S. Shukla in Bisheshwar Prasad, 127. Tarachand, Vol. II, 201. Dharampal, 15.
118. Tarachand, Vol. I, 215.
119. Dharampal, 14-23 *et seqq*, an in-depth study.
120. Sen and Subbarayappa, 588. B.V. Subbrayappa, 263.
121. B.V. Subbarayappa, 455. For a detailed exposition of the concept of *Rta*, see G.N. Chakravarthy, *et seqq.*
122. K.M. Panikkar, *The Foundations of New India*, 244.
123. Dhirendra Narain, 42, *et seqq.*
124. R.C. Majumdar, *The Struggle for Empire*, 513.
125. Sen and Subbarayappa, 47.
126. M.L. Roy Chaudhuri, 324.
127. M.A. Mehandale & A.D. Pusalkar in R.C. Majumdar, *The Delhi Sultanate*, 465.
128. K.V. Ramesh, 74.
129. "We see in Akbar, perhaps for the first time in Muhammadan history, a Muslim monarch sincerely eager to further the education of the Hindus and the Muhammadans alike. We also notice for the first time the Hindus and the Muhammadans studying in the same schools and colleges." — N.N. Law, 160-1.
130. Tarachand, Vol. II, 175.

10   *Caste, Religion and Country*

greater today than they were ever before.

In conclusion, it needs to be stressed again that this is a macro study — it is based upon macro facts and macro views of micro facts. Specially in respect of the latter, judgements and evaluations are bound to be subjective, and there is good room for differences of opinion. I only hope that the picture presented here is fair, clear and true enough.

CHAPTER 2

Muslims: A Parallel Society

The Emergence of Muslims as a Parallel Community

Before the Muslim invasion from the north-west, Hindu society was sufficiently homogeneous, despite the heterogeneity arising out of its social setup and the continental character of the country. There had earlier been invaders and immigrants from outside, the Hunas, Scythians, Bactrians and others. Invariably, they brought with them their own faiths and cultures. They were all absorbed and lost their separate identity in course of time. As in the case of the meeting of the Aryans and the Dravidians, the religio-cultural exchanges were a two-way traffic, though the predominance of the older indigenous Hindu culture was maintained. Whatever may have been the socio-political problems encountered, they were transitory. There were only a few minor cases of non-absorption — the Syrian Christians of Kerala who date back to the second century A.D., the Arab settlers in the south from the ninth century onwards, and the Parsi refugees who came to India at the close of the tenth century. They were, however, acculturated and indigenized to a great extent, and fitted neatly into society.

A sea change occurred in the situation with the invasion of Muslims and the rise of the Muslim power in India. The beginnings are associated with the Arab invasion of Sind under Muhammad-bin-Kasim in 712 A.D. After the initial success, the Arabs could only maintain a precarious foothold over the frontier towns of Multan and al-Mansurah. Even the raids of Muhammad of Ghazni three centuries later only gave the Muslims a good base for operations in the Punjab, which came to be a frontier province of the Ghaznavid empire. The real conquest of India began at the close of the twelfth century. By the second quarter of the fourteenth century, the Ghurids, the Mamluks and the Khaljis succeeded in shattering Hindu power everywhere. Although a well-knit empire did not emerge at once, the Delhi Sultanate symbolised Muslim political predominance throughout the land. It is the Mughuls who consolidated the gains of the past, and founded an empire which lasted in good strength for over two centuries. This political predominance, lasting over nearly six centuries, was of seminal importance for the growth of Muslims as a large parallel community.

As regards the formation and composition of the community, only the Arab traders came by sea, and settled down in Kerala and other parts of the west coast. For the rest, whether they came as invaders or migrants, the entry was through the north-western passes. All of them came from the world of Islam, mostly Arabia, Western and Central Asia, Iran and Afghanistan. Of them, the Turanis, Turko-Mongol by race, "were far more numerous than any other foreign Muslim people who settled in India." The Pathans too formed a substantial part of the community everywhere.[1] The immigration reached its peak during the thirteenth –fourteenth centuries in the wake of pressures from the Mongols. The influx was not much after the Mughuls came, because of their hostility towards both the Afghans and the Uzbegs; the Iranians were also generally unwelcome as they were Shias. Whatever be the tribal composition and the timing of their coming, their number was small, and their impact on the ethnic composition of the country was negligible. As Tarachand observes, the immigrants were "ethnically hardly different from the inhabitants of north-western India" and "were not numerous enough to produce any considerable change in the racial, economic or social life of the country."[2] In 1911, Muslims constituted 21.26 per cent of the population of India. Of these, not more than five to ten percent could have been descendants of persons of foreign origin, the others being descendants of local converts.[3] According to M. Mujeeb, the fifteenth-sixteenth centuries were the great age of conversions.[4] Though not large in numbers, the mobility and dynamism of the incoming Muslims were such that, by the close of the thirteenth century, "the Muslim Turks had permanently settled in large parts of northern India, and formed an important community", and "Sufi monasteries were already scattered far and wide throughout the country."[5] With the large-scale conversions effected Muslims came to be a large majority or a substantial part of the population in the north-western and north-eastern regions of the country. In the rest of India, they were a minority, unevenly spread and mostly urban. By the time of the Mughuls, the Hindus and Muslims formed a composite community everywhere, their destinies being linked together at all levels, local, regional and all-India.

HETEROGENEITY, TENSIONS AND PROBLEMS

Though the concept of Muslim brotherhood (*Quam*) was central to Islam, Indian Muslims were as divided as the Hindus in their social structure. The immigrant Muslims came from different lands and tribes, and the differences arising therefrom persisted. Coming in as conquerors or in their train, they maintained their distance from the local converts, and the yawning gulf could not be easily bridged. Among the converts, change of faith did not lead to shedding of caste, and the caste factor persisted. There was also the sectarian factor. The Shia-Sunni divide went back to the early days of Islam, and affected the whole of the Muslim world. Besides, there were the Sufis who did not tread the orthodox path, and also small dissident sects centering round charismatic leaders that emerged from time to time. We are told that there were as many as 72 sects in Akbar's days. Linguistic and regional factors were also of importance. Muhammad Yasin has laid stress upon a vital aspect when he says, "The veneer of unreal homogeneity of the Muslim community of India is more or less an aerial view that joins together patches of humanity here and there on the hard earth of realities below. Such a vision is pleasing to all, and inspiring only to the philosopher or the politician."[6]

THE ASHRAF – AJLAF DIVIDE

There were several aspects to the tensions and problems arising out of the heterogeneity internal to the Muslim community. First there was the wide gulf that separated the immigrants and their descendants (the Ashraf) from the local converts (the Ajlaf). The Ashraf constituted the ruling class monopolising all higher administrative and army posts and other gainful ways of living, and formed the intellectual and ecclesiastical elite of the community. They did not put their hand to the plough or take up any work involving manual labour or any low occupation. In contrast, the Ajlaf came from the lower castes of the Hindus. They continued with their old-time occupations, and there was no significant improvement in their economic and social status. The lucky few who were able to climb up were unwilling to own up to their ancestry and tried to pass off for the Ashraf.[7] Converts from among the Rajputs were an exception. They retained their higher status and tried to improve upon it; they came to be ranked below the Muslim Ashraf, but above the other Hindu converts. Between the Ashraf and the Ajlaf, to the feeling of superiority arising out of higher socio-economic status and the fact of belonging to the ruling class, there were added racial pride and colour consciousness. Ghaus Ansari has compared the gulf that separated the two to the Aryo-Dravidian divide of olden times which gave birth to the system of caste.[8] Also, the position was no different in any respect from what it was between the Europeans and the Indian Christians under British rule.[9] On the racial issue, *Seir Mutaqherin* noted, "All white Mussalmans are called Mughals in India, as well as their descendants, as all white Christians are called Feringhis."[10] As regards the antipathy and antagonism roused in the early years, Aziz Ahmed writes, "The Turkish aristocracy strictly forbade an equal treatment and held the new Muslims in scorn and contempt."[11] The seventeenth century travellers, Roe and Fryer, commented that the Mughuls "prided themselves to be called whites ... in scorn of the Indians who were blacks."[12] And, M. Mujeeb observes, "Maintenance of the purity of the family stock has all through been an important consideration with those who claimed to belong to the 'noble' class, and their attitude was

regarded as a sign of respectability."[13] Moncton Jones'
comment that "the various branches of the conquering
Mahomedans still remained distinct from the people as a
whole" in the eighteenth century is confirmed by
Buchanan.[14] The socio-political importance of this factor in
medieval life is reflected in the scornful rejection of the
proposal for a matrimonial alliance made by Tipu to the
Nizam, and the good prospect of the two great powers joining
hands being dashed to pieces, as Cornwallis gleefully
noted.[15]

THE TRIBAL FACTOR AMONG THE ASHRAF

There were four principal *dhats* or *quams* among the Ashraf,
based on the country of origin: Arabs or Sayyids, Iranians
or Persians, Turks or Mughuls, and Afghans or Pathans. The
Turks and the Afghans constituted the bulk of the immigrant
Muslims. They were noted primarily as warriors, and were
the chief contenders for power all through. The Iranians were
Shias, unlike all the others who were Sunnis. They had a
long cultural heritage, and formed the cultural elite. Finance
and administration were their special preserve. The Arabs
were settled in large numbers on the west coast as traders.
Besides, priesthood and theology were regarded as their
special field and prerogative. Buchanan noted that in Kerala,
the Tangals, the chief priests of the Mapillas, said they were
Arabs and claimed to be superior to the Tartar Muslims. The
same claim to superiority over all other classes was put forward
by the Sayyids, as noted by Mrs. Meer Hussein Ali.[16]

While the four sections of the Ashraf inherited their tribal
and sub-tribal loyalties and prejudices from their forefathers,
and these persisted through generations, their contacts with
the Hindus gave their social structure a distinctive caste turn.
Even prior to their entry into India, during Islam's eastward
expansion through Iran, there arose three social orders similar
to the varna groupings of the Hindus: the priesthood, the
ruling class and the commoners. In India, the Muslims
developed "a graded scheme of society — a modified caste
system", with the Ashraf occupying the same position that
the Brahmanas and Kshatriyas traditionally occupied in

Hindu society. The priesthood was not hereditary in the beginning, but became so gradually — "sons began to succeed their fathers; thereafter, *Astana* and *Takiya* (sects of preaching and special guidance) became a family monopoly." Ibbetson and Blunt noted in the census reports that the Ashraf were "bound by social and tribal customs than any rules of religion." And, Ghaus Ansari observed, "The Ashraf ... do not believe in the system of caste and consider it contrary to the tenets of Islam, but in actual practice their attitude towards social problems are almost identical to the caste-practising Hindus."[17] As more and more of the ethos of the caste system was absorbed, the very idea of its incongruity with Islam was lost, and "the elite accepted the endogamous pattern of community formation, qualified further by allied considerations of wealth and power in the case of influential families."[18]

In regard to social and political life, it was not so much caste or religion that mattered as the tribal divide. Power being wholly in the hands of the Muslim Ashraf, the struggle was primarily within their ranks centering round the tribal factor. On this aspect, S.N. Sen writes, "The brotherhood of Islam was recognized in theory alone; in practice, a Persian was a Persian, a Turk was a Turk, an Afghan was an Afghan when their political interest was affected and racial instincts got the better of their religious precepts."[19] Throughout the medieval period, it was the struggle between the Afghan and the Turk that was primary; the other two tribes the Arabs and the Iranians, played only a secondary role. When the Mughuls came to power, the Afghans were kept down and were always suspect. When the Mughul chips were down and Ahmad Shah Abdali was on the scene, *Seir Mutaqherin* describes the transitory change in the political climate: "This much is certain, that the Peshto language and Abdali dress have gained all the northern parts of Hindostan as far as Lucknow, where the Sovereign wears it in winter, and speaks a few words of Peshto, and where even the women of the seraglio make it a point to mix some words of it in their speech."[20] The Afghan-Mughul rivalry and animosity even found expression in a popular game in the countryside of Bihar and Bengal, known as "Mughul-Pathan".[21] Side by side, administration tended to be broad-based and inter-tribal marriages frequent. There was a definite narrowing of the tribal divide as years rolled by. According to Satishchandra, by the early eighteenth century, secularization in Mughul court life and politics had made great strides — "The general assumption that parties and politics at the court of the later Mughals were based on ethnic or religious groupings among the nobility is not borne out. The groups which were formed at the court towards the end of Aurangzib's reign were based on clan and family relationships or personal affiliations and interests. ... It would appear that slogans of race and religion were raised by individual nobles only to suit their convenience, and that the actual groupings cut across ethnic and religious divisions."[22] This trend was hastened by the rapid decline in Muslim power. With the total eclipse of that power, the operation of the tribal factor got merged with the general caste and communal problem. Its continuing relevance is to be seen in what V.K. Bawa says of mid-nineteenth century Hyderabad, wherein the Mughal tradition had survived: "Turks and Persians, Pathans, Arabs and Siddis were as important as Kayasths and Khatris, Maratha Brahmins, Reddis and Mudaliyars in the social and economic life of the state in the power game, and the tribal affinity, in each case, was more important than Hindu or Muslim, and Shia or Sunni."[23]

THE POSITION OF THE HINDU CONVERTS

As regards Hindu converts to Islam, as stated earlier, they constituted most part of the community. There was little change in the pattern of their vocational life or any improvement in their economic condition. In social status too, the gulf separating them from the Ashraf was no less wide than that which prevailed between them and the upper Hindu castes prior to conversion; indeed, the position was perhaps worse because of the sharper class divide. In this background, their political importance was negligible, much lower than that of the Hindus. However, there was the fact that they had some sense of belonging to the ruling class because of common faith, and their loyalty was promoted by small concessions and by a few of the converts rising to high positions. This was the position till the eighteenth century when the process of integrating the Ashraf with the Muslim commoners gained momentum.

From the socio-religious angle too, the change of faith brought about no significant change in the life of the converts. Caste stuck to them like their skin. It has been said earlier that, within the Hindu fold, whenever new sects cropped up. corresponding new subcastes emerged. The same thing happened when Hindus embraced Islam or Christianity. The new Muslim groups had their own caste organizations (*Jamatbandi*) and the ageold customary life remained unchanged. This was as much true of the upper classes as the lower. S.C. Misra writes of the Rajput Muslims of Gujarat, "when they accepted Islam, they admitted only a superficial tinge of Islamization and continued to observe their traditional practices and therefore were served after conversion by their (own) priests and *barots*."[24] Untouchability of a sort also stuck to the converts from Unclean Castes. In Uttar Pradesh and Bengal, they were inadequately integrated with Muslim society. The doors of mosques were barred to them; when permitted to attend prayers, they were expected not to proceed beyond the entrance steps. When they were allowed to learn the Quran, they were required not to teach it.[25] Everywhere, observance of the rule of the Shariat (Islamic law) "was limited to urban areas and even there only where the disputants reached the Qazi courts." Mostly only the 'foreign' Muslims or the Ashraf were attached to the Shariat.[26] On the whole, Indian Muslim society was a caste-based society just like the Hindu, though in a mitigated form. The mitigation was there because the social inequality ingrained in the system of caste was opposed to the avowed tenets of Islam. Also, since Islamic proselytization did not affect all the layers of the Hindu society in equal measure, caste hierarchy among Muslims was not as comprehensive and graded as among the Hindus. Further, despite the great influence wielded by religious leaders, a charismatic priesthood analogous to Brahmanas did not emerge. The major problem faced by the proselytizers was not one of effecting conversions; it was that of weaning converts from their Hindu ways, and transforming their socio-cultural life to conform to the pattern of orthodox Islamic society as envisaged. This was a stupendous task, slow and tardy in its progress; to the end, the success was limited. As a result, Indian Muslims came to be *sui generis* or a class by themselves in the Muslim world.

Dissidence in Religious Matters

THE SHIA – SUNNI DIVIDE

Apart/from the social divisions and problems arising from foreign origin and tribal and caste factors, there were those connected with sectarian developments and dissidence in religious matters. The most important was the Shia – Sunni divide. Frustrating the hope of creating a single monolithic community of the faithful, Islam was cleft into two even in the early years, because of the religio-political struggle for power and predominance. The animosity roused was so deep, so lasting and permanent, that it bedevilled life, secular as much as religious, throughout the Muslim world. The Shias migrated to India in large numbers because of persecution at home. The Muslim rulers in India were generally tolerant and extended patronage to those who came from the world of Islam outside, and this encouraged Shia immigration. At the same time, the activities of Shia saints gained a large number of converts from among the Hindus. The world over, Shias were a minority, only four per cent of the Muslim community, and mostly concentrated in Iran. India had the largest number of Shias outside Iran, about ten per cent of the Indian Muslims (1921 Census). Apart from pockets of concentration such as Lucknow and Bijapur, they were evenly spread over the whole land. As regards their role in the medieval world, most Shias among the Ashraf were Iranians. Being a small group only, their political role in the power struggle was secondary. Only in the South, Shiite rulers like the Adil Shahis of Bijapur emerged. The major contribution of the Shia Ashraf lay in the field of administration, and Mughul dependence on the group was great. The antipathy evinced towards Shias on the part of the Sunni Ashraf, who held the reins of power all along, was a constant feature, finding expression in court politics, administrative life and political and inter-state relations. In the life of the common folk, it manifested itself in recurring Muharram clashes between the two sects. However, on the whole, the Shia –Sunni divide was much less in India than in the rest of the world. As Aziz Ahmed observes, "In the syncretic atmosphere of India, Sunnism has tried to compromise with Shiaism."27

THE ULLEMAS AND THE SUFIS

Orthodox Islam was fundamentalist in outlook and inimical to freethinking. The Quran and the Sayings of the Prophet (*Sunnah*) were considered to be complete guides in all matters, temporal as much as spiritual; there was to be no deviation from what was laid down. Further, Islam had aimed at setting up an integrated world community of the faithful, headed by the Khalif, supreme in all matters, religious as well as secular. After some initial success in this direction was registered, the Muslim world was cleft into two by the rise of the Shias, and also every Muslim ruler sought to act independently in religious matters, recognizing no superior. Even so, there were constant efforts to maintain a facade of unity, a factor of no small importance: the Khalif received the homage of all the Sunnis the world over, and the Shias recognized the Shah of Iran as their leader. Organizational unity did not amount to much in the field of religion; there were no hierarchically organized established churches as among the Christians. The role of religious men too was unspecific and ill-defined as among the Hindus. Subject to these limitations, those knowledgeable in the Shariah, the Ullemas, were highly respected and influential. They were the interpreters of the sacred law; they also advised how far specific deviations from the letter of the Quranic law conformed to its spirit, and could be permitted. Four schools of jurisprudence emerged which sought to adapt the Shariah to the needs of changing society — the Malaki, Shafaii, Hanbali and Hanafi. Of these, the Hanafi was known for its liberal outlook. It was this that was most popular in India and served as a guide to Muslim rulers. The importance of this factor would be well appreciated if we note their respective views in regard to the Hindus: while the Hanafi accorded them the status of Zimmis and all the rights and privileges attached to it, the others refused to do so — in their view of the Shariah, the Hindu could be allowed "no other alternative but Death or Islam."[28]

Unlike the orthodox view of Islam based on faith, Sufism was a profound expression of the age-old conflict between faith and reason, between authority and freedom. Despite the prevailing fundamentalist atmosphere, the irrpressibility of the human spirit was such that many Sufi saints flourished. Their personal character and contributions were such that they gained ascendancy over the mind of the intelligentsia and the heart of the masses. The development of Sufi thought was almost entirely outside India. In the opinion of M. Habib, it reached its maturity by the early decades of the thirteenth century and entered India as a complete system, and there were at that time twelve different schools of Sufis.[29] India's own contribution to Sufism was in the field of mystic practices, particularly by the Shattari school, not in the realm of thought. Scholars often refer to the impact of Vedanta on Sufism, but there is no solid foundation for saying that it amounted to much. Before Islam's entry into India, contacts with the concerned regions and communities were limited; later, the atmosphere of mutual hostility and repugnance came in the way of intellectuals and religious men of the two communities coming into close contact for exchange of views. However, at different stages, the Chisti, Shattari and Qadiri schools exhibited profound Hindu influence in their local manifestations, and were most tolerant towards the Hindus.

Of great importance was the way the Ullemas and the Sufis reacted to each other. To the Sufis, the Ullemas were irrational, ununderstanding and obscurantist; to the Ullemas, the Sufis were audacious and heretical in as much as they sat in judgement over the words of the Prophet. Neither could carry the intelligentsia and the masses wholly with them. In the long run, there were naturally attempts to syncretize and accommodate the differing viewpoints — Sufi thought, it was held by many of the Sufis, did not run counter to the teachings of the Prophet; on the contrary, it helped people to understand his message better. Aziz Ahmed observes that the teachings of eight out of the seventeen Sufi schools mentioned by Abul Fazl were integrated with the Shariah, and accepted by the orthodox.[30] Shaikh Ahmad of Sirhind (1563–1624), who had been initiated into all the Sufi systems, preferred Naqshbandia "because it regarded meticulous obedience to religious law (Shariat) as superior to mystic discipline and knowledge."[31]

As regards the extent of the hold and significance of Sufism, W.C. Smith has cautioned against overstress; in his opinion, "the classical version of Islam remained official and has always remained socially important."[32] While the observation is true of India too, it has been generally held that the hold of the Sufis has been much greater here than in any other part of the world. Aziz Ahmed observes, "In India, Sufis rather than the Ullemas were the real inspiration of the Muslim intelligentsia and the masses." Further, "Sufis in India regarded themselves as responsible for the spiritual welfare of the people, and considered themselves entrusted with spiritual government, parallel to the political government exercised by the Sultans and their amirs." The Sufi hierarchy divided a state by regions, and each *Wali* (saint) had a *Wilayat* to administer.[33] In the sixteenth-seventeenth centuries, it is said that it was usual for every religious-minded person to get himself attached to one or other Sufi school, and it was a sign of respectability and religious awareness.[34] Most of the mass conversions too were because of their proselytizing zeal, and they retained a continuous hold on the masses. In all probability, the great success of Sufism in India was also due in large measure to the tolerant and eclectic Hindu tradition to which the converts to Islam were heirs.

IRREGULAR SUFISM AND UNORTHODOX SECTS

Besides the recognized Sufi schools, there was also a good bit of irregular Sufism emanating largely from religious fervour and messianic spirit. The wandering Qalandars founded no schools, lived a simple ascetic life, and were popular with the masses. The Wahabis sought to take Islam back to its pristine purity. There were many sects of local importance only. The Pagal Panthis of Mymensingh District in East Bengal emerged in the last quarter of the eighteenth century; they were involved in the agrarian troubles of the early nineteenth century and in the Revolt of 1857 before they vanished.[35] Din Ilahi of Akbar, with only nineteen followers, was an elitist sect of the same group. Besides, there were impositions by successful adventurers: *Seir Mutaqherin* refers to one Mir Muhammad Hussain *alias* Nomad, an Iranian who came from Kabul. He founded a heretical sect, had a large following including many nobles, and was visited by Farruckshyar. The imposture came to be exposed only after his death in the time of his son by a discontented follower.[36]

While dissidence was not uncommon, the hold of classical Islam, with its passionate desire to maintain the integrity of the Muslim community, acted as a high-rise dam preventing the emergence of strong, long-lasting sects. This was in sharp contrast to what was happening within the Hindu fold. Despite the hurdle, some sectarian groups did arise. Of them the Ismaili Bohra of Gujarat, the Khoja or Satpanti founded by Pir Sadr-ud-Din, and the Ahmadiya founded by Ghulam Ahmad of Qadiyam (Punjab) are best known. The Khoja and the Ahmadiya were syncretic sects which compromised with Hinduism and the orthodox could hardly accept them. The Ismaili Bohra was a Shia sect, and the success of the Shia saints of this school was an eyesore to the Sunni rulers. The troubled history of this sect, beginning from the twelfth century, shows what dissidents generally had to face. Satish Misra writes, "The foundation of the Ismaili community in Gujarat is an unique fact in Indian history. Nowhere else in India did these communities come into being in any sizable dimensions; nowhere else was the penetration of Islam as peaceful, or the rise of the new communities so imperceptible. No other Muslim community in India suffered more at the hands of the iconoclastic Sunni rulers." The rigour of persecution, which began in the fifteenth century, was such that the majority became Sunnis. Those who stood steadfast migrated to other regions, took to trading and became urbanised. The several subsects or castes into which the community got divided in the Hindu fashion was also an interesting feature.[37]

The broad picture that emerges is that at the dawn of the modern age, Indian Muslim society was as divided as the Hindu; there was only "the veneer of unreal homogeneity of the Muslim community", as Mohammad Yasin observed. There were, however, stronger forces to bring about integration and consolidate Muslims at all levels than among the Hindus.

The Limits of Muslim Socio-Economic Power

In the divided society that had emerged, the Muslims were strong and well-entrenched from the start. The political predominance they had attained in the country as a whole was there for all to see. The six centuries following the coming of the Ghurids are regarded as the period of Muslim rule. It should be noted that the Muslim rulers never attained the preeminence or universal domain of the British in the sub-continent. Some areas never came under Muslim rule; some were subject to it only for a short period; and even in the vast regions where their rule was firm and lasting, the government's position was weak, because of the grass-roots strength of the Hindu zamindars and chiefs. In general, though the Hindus lived under the government of an alien-spirited, dominant minority, their position was not so abject or helpless as is often made out.

The first source of Hindu strength came from the ownership of land. Land was mostly owned by the Hindus, and superior rights of ownership also remained with them even in areas where the peasantry was primarily Muslim as in East Bengal. The Hindu zamindars and chiefs and the village communities were neatly fitted into the new administrative system, and they acted as buffers between the government and the rural folk. There is little divergence of opinion among scholars about the general position in this respect. In his succinct survey, Tarachand has noted that in Uttar Pradesh, the heartland of Muslim power all through, the predominance of Hindu zamindars could be seen at the end of the sixteenth century as in the mid-nineteenth. The position was the same in Bengal and elsewhere in 1765, at the time of the transfer of the Diwani to the East India Company. "It may be reasonably concluded", he writes, "that in the whole of India, excepting the western Punjab, superior rights in land had come to vest in the hands of the Hindus."[38] Commenting upon the relationship between the Mansabdari and the Zamindari,

Satishchandra ı observes that there was hardly any area in which there was no well-established zamindari class ranging from self-cultivating zamindars to chiefs, and they were to be found even in *Khalsa* or crown lands.[39] Dispossession of lands held by Hindu cultivating peasants or peasant communities was rare. Buchanan writes that while there was no right to property in land, none could be denied his right to cultivate: "Even in the reign of Tippoo, such an act would have been looked upon as an astonishing grievance." Of Dinajpur in Bengal, he writes, "Many of the officers of Government and almost all the lands being in the hands of Hindus, the Muhammadans are rather sufferers, not however to an outrageous degree."[40]

The second source of strength lay in the Hindu monopoly of banking and trade and other sources of non-agricultural wealth. The hereditary Hindu business classes, the Khatri, the Baniya, the Komati and others carried on their vocation without impediment as before. The new ruling classes had no interest in doing business, and as D.R. Gadgil noted, "no important cases were recorded of Muslim traders rising to military or administrative positions."[41] The Muslim trading castes or classes were outside the charmed circle. The Arab traders who settled down in Kerala were under Hindu rulers. The Ismailia Bohras had taken to trading and prospered in the face of Sunni persecution. The others like the Lohanas had no special links with the governing classes. Also, it may be noted that there was no clash of interest between the Muslim rulers and the predominantly Hindu trading and industrial classes of the type which led to the economic exploitation of India by the British.

In the realm of government also, though power was tightly held by Muslim rulers, administration could not be carried on without Hindu help. The zamindars and chiefs and other Hindu elite had to be conciliated and minimum cooperation ensured. This was no insignificant factor under British rule too. In his penetrating study of the administration of the Madras Presidency, D.A. Washbrooke has brought out very well how, even in the early years of the present century, the all-powerful British Collector was often enough helpless before the local zamindar and the merchant chief, and the administration had to acquiesce.[42]

All in all, the position under Muslim rule should not be viewed only in terms of Muslim political predominance as often done. We should note that Muslim political power and Hindu land and money power were more or less evenly matched.

The Hindu Response to Islam's Challenge

FACTORS GOVERNING CONVERSIONS TO ISLAM

From the socio-cultural angle, the survival of the Hindu in strength was as significant as the emergence of Indian Muslims as a parallel community, accounting for more than a fifth of the population. The Hindus did not succumb to the extent others had done elsewhere. While the political challenge was there, of no less importance was the cultural one. A most sensitive and controversial issue has been as to how far the large-scale conversions were due to the employment of force and the offer of material benefits and how far to the charisma of Islam and the proselytizing zeal of its ministers and the inherent weaknesses of the Hindu socio-religious system. As a result of the complexes developed, the popular Hindu view is that it was mostly a case of force and graft, and this absolves their religion and social system of any responsibility for what happened. The Muslims, in turn, would like to believe that nothing improper was done in the spread of their cherished faith. Touching upon the sensitivity of the issue, K.G. Saiyidain writes, "The most harmful are the wounds that have healed, but whose memories remain in the pages of history to condemn or invite reprisal.[43] No doubt there is a point here. Still, it would be wise to correct the *idee fixe* of both, not only in the interest of historical veracity but also to place Hindu-Muslim relationship on a sounder and healthier footing.

There is abundant evidence to show that force figured large in the spread of Islam in India as elsewhere. To spread the good word and save souls even if it were at the point of the sword was a weak spot common to every fundamentalist faith — there was the Jesuit phase in the history of Christianity.

It is to this aspect that Jadunath Sarkar refers when he writes, "The poison lay in the very core of Islamic theocracy. Under it there can be only one faith, one people, one all-overriding authority. The state is a religious trust administered solely by His People (the Faithful) acting in obedience to the Commander of the Faithful. ... There could be no place for non-believers."[44] And, Quranic society was more or less a missionary society; it was the solemn duty of everyone to spread the Prophet's message and help to integrate the world into one Muslim land. It is important to remember that taken in the right spirit the conquest was to be of the mind and the heart. But excessive zeal and fanaticism opened the door wide for the use of force and other questionable means for gaining converts. What happened in the first phase of Islamic expansion in Western and Central Asia and elsewhere is too well known to bear repetition. In the case of India, even by the time of the invasions of Muhammad of Ghazni, there was distinct cooling of fanatical zeal, but a good bit of it continued to be in evidence. In any case, the embers were stirred frequently for political and military ends. Whatever be the extent and effectiveness of forced conversions, there is the mute evidence of fanaticism running riot in the ruins of hundreds of temples destroyed all over the land. The inscription at the entrance of the famous Quwwat-ul-Islam mosque, near Qutb Minar, proudly states that it was built out of the materials of 27 Hindu and Jain temples. Ibn Batutah found at its eastern entrance "two very big idols of copper connected together by stones," and noted, "Everyone who comes in and goes out of the mosque treads over them."[45] This was symbolic of the fanaticism of the first invaders and the travails the country passed through. Making ample allowance for conventional hyperboles and exaggerations, the proud boasts of the Muslim chroniclers reflect the times.

The worst was over with the first flush of invasions and the early years of Muslim rule. Less fanaticism and a moderate policy were necessitated even before the Mughuls appeared on the scene. The gradual emergence of syncretic faiths by the fifteenth century, both among the Hindus and the Muslims, marked the end of the age of fanaticism. The destruction of a number of temples in Mughul times as reported, the anti-Hindu measures of Aurangzib and other manifestations of fanaticism did not amount to much when compared to earlier times. With the change in environment, there was little scope for forced conversions. The only major cases reported were those made for special reasons or under exceptional circumstances, and these were held to be legitimate. Tipu's conversion of Coorgis and Nayars and of Canara Christians and the transportation and forced conversion of the Bedas of Chitradurga by his father were politically motivated. S.N. Sen writes, "The loss of caste was and is regarded by the Hindus as the greatest disgrace, and the letters of Tipu hardly leave any doubt that he regarded conversion as an extreme form of punishment."[46]

As regards the crucial question as to how far forced conversions contributed towards the growth of the Muslim community, there can be no definite answer. All that can be said positively is that it would have been of importance only during the first flush of invasions and the early years of Muslim rule. M. Mujeeb's view is the last word in this regard: "Force was used on occasions, but the existing historical evidence does not enable us to estimate either the scale or the effectiveness of such conversions."[47]

While further accumulation of micro evidence may not be of real help in this regard, there is good enough macro evidence to caution us strongly against giving this factor an exaggerated importance. There is first the way the Muslim population is spread over the land. There is at least one striking instance wherein the element of force would not have figured. Malabar in Kerala has a sizable Muslim community, and its growth under Hindu rulers was linked with peaceful trade. The whole region was outside the bounds of Muslim rulers until Haidar Ali and Tipu Sultan entered the scene.[48] Again, as mentioned earlier, the rise of the Ismailia Bohra sect in Gujarat was entirely peaceful as noted by S.C. Misra.[49] It is also a significant point that the proportion of Muslims has been very much on the low side in the heartland of Muslim power from the earliest times — Delhi, Agra and Lucknow. The editor of *Qanun-i-Islam* noted with surprise that Muslims should have been more numerous in North Bihar, "the seat of Hindu and Brahminical domination than round the old Muhammadan centres in South Bihar, Patna and Monghyr."[50] This was also true of most other regional centres of Muslim power.

Doubts have also been raised regarding employment of force and making converts with reference to areas of Muslim predominance population-wise in the north-western and north-eastern regions of the country. Scholars have noted that these were just the areas where Buddhism had been strongly entrenched. They suggest that Islamic missionary effort met with thumping success in these regions because of Hindu-Buddhist antagonism. S.N. Sen observes, "It cannot be an accident that the Punjab, Kashmir, the district around Behar Sharif, North-East Bengal, where Muslims now predominate, were all strong Buddhist centres in the pre-Muslim days." He goes on to refer to the peaceful large-scale conversion of the people in the old-time Federal Malay States, and the Islamic leanings of the Buddhist rulers of Arakan; the latter added Muslim designations to their names, and even issued medallions bearing the *Kalima* in Arabic script.[51] R.C. Mitra, in his classic study on the decline of Buddhism in India, has observed, "Bad blood between the Hindus and the Buddhists might conceivably have favoured conversion to Islam, and this may partly account for the large percentage of Muslim population in Bengal."[52]

This view rests on shaky foundations. To view Buddhist society as having been something different from the Hindu seems to be incorrect. As R.C. Mitra and others have stressed, the decline of Buddhism was due in large measure to the absence of a well-organized laity with well-formed caste groups unlike in the case of Jains who were able to survive. It was the caste factor that was important. Further, there is little evidence to show that there was any great measure of antagonism between Buddhism and Brahminical Hinduism at the social level, not even to the extent we find in respect of the Jains in the South. There is the further fact that, at the time of the Muslim invasion, "Buddhism was already an exhausted volcano, whose smouldering ashes were incapable of rekindling a new fire," as R.C. Mitra stated.[53] The Muslim invaders only destroyed monasteries and monks with no following.

Looking at the whole question afresh, it would appear that Muslim predominance in population in the whole of the north-western belt was due primarily to proximity to the Muslim countries outside India. The whole region experienced the rigours of every invasion; it was subject to Muslim rule longest; and it was most exposed to ethnic and cultural influences of the Islamic world. It is not improbable that the element of force in effecting conversions figured here more than elsewhere.

This explanation would not hold good in the case of East Bengal, which was far removed from the world of Islam. Here, we have no alternative but to give credit to missionary effort, unless large-scale employment of force can be substantiated. M.T. Titus is clearly on the right track when he observes, "In this part of India, Hinduism was not nearly so well-organized and consolidated as in the northern, western and southern parts of the country. The inhabitants were under the influence of a very crude form of Buddhism; and, despised as they were by their proud Aryan rulers, who held them in disdain, they apparently welcomed the Muslim missionaries gladly."[54] Presumably, these were inadequately integrated with the main stream, whether it be termed Hindu or Buddhist, to a much greater extent than elsewhere and they could be more easily weaned away. R.C. Majumdar has however queried the strength of the argument, and observed, "We have no reliable and positive evidence in support of the view that the missionary efforts, pure and simple, should be counted as a very important, far less dominant factor, not to speak of the major factor in the conversion of Hindus to Islam in India, in general, and in Bengal in particular."[55] Though there is paucity of evidence, intense missionary activity has to be presumed to account for such mass conversions that proved to be stable and lasting. There is no reason to believe that force and graft operated here more than elsewhere. In this connection, it is of interest to note that, according to Buchanan, in the Dinajpur District of East Bengal, the number of reputed saints who had monuments erected to their memory was astonishing.[56]

The classes from which most of the converts came also militate against the force theory. Scholars agree that most of the converts came from the lower strata of Hindu society. There were exceptions as in the case of the Rajput Muslims. If force was the major factor leading to conversions, it is legitimate to ask why the upper castes were in general spared.

The discussion so far about the use and non-use of force in effecting conversions is subject to an important caveat —voluntary conversion is not to be equated with change of faith as a matter of conscience alone. While we would do well to remember the role of charismatic faqirs operating among the poor and the neglected, R.C. Majumdar has a point when he says, "No one outside a lunatic asylum would seriously believe that in such mass scale conversions, sincere faith in Islam or anything like it would count in the least."[57] Several factors besides the charisma and teachings of the faqirs would have gone to make for the voluntary conversions — the socio-political climate of dominance for six centuries, intensive missionary activity aided by the ruling classes in different ways and varying degrees, material inducements of various types offered, and positive disabilities imposed upon those who remained Hindus. While the state was not a direct participant in the missionary activities, it is difficult to accept without qualification Aziz Ahmed's view that it adopted "a general attitude of neutrality to the problem of conversion."[58] This is not true wholly even of the Government of India's attitude during British rule in regard to Christian missionary activities. The dangling of the proverbial Qanungoship for embracing Islam was there, though only a few could have benefited. The Ashraf took care to keep the plum cake to themselves, and the rise of converts to high positions was limited. But, as M.L. Roy Choudhury noted, "In the lower ranks of service, the Hindu efficiency was utilised mostly from the converts as in the case of Qanungos and Karoris."[59] In the case of most of the lower classes who embraced Islam small inducements would have been enough; if one could escape Jizya, whenever and wherever imposed, by reciting the Kalima (the Muslim article of faith) one could as well do it. How the little tiltings could have operated in the long run could be gauged from Khushwant Singh's observations regarding Sikh proselytism and the growth of the Sikh community in the latter half of the nineteenth century: "The prosperity ushered in by the development of the canal colonies and the preference shown towards the Sikhs in recruitment to the Imperial army had an important bearing on the future and the caste complex of the community. The economic advantages of being Sikh checked the disintegration of Sikhism and its lapse into Hinduism. On the contrary, the last decade of the nineteenth century and the first decade of the twentieth, saw a phenomenal rise in the number of Sikhs. This was due largely to the patronage of the government, which required posts reserved for Sikhs in the army (and later in the civilian services) to be filled exclusively by the *Kesadhari* Khalsa. This patronage paved the way for the success of the proselytization movement, the Singh Sabha."[60] Indirect state support and material inducements have figured large in Christian proselytization also. Besides these, in Muslim India, those propagating Islam had full freedom, but a similar right was denied to the Hindu; the conversion of a Muslim to another faith was punishable with death, whatever be the extent to which the law could be enforced in practice. On the whole, considering the long period of Muslim rule and the advantages which power gave, it is reasonable to hold that these went a long way to help in gaining converts and in the growth of the Muslim community.

There is another side to the case which should receive equal attention — the weakness of the Hindus and their socio-religious system which made such mass depletions from their ranks possible. Many of the issues involved are discussed elsewhere, and only the points relevant to the matter under consideration are recapitulated here briefly. Compactness and rigidity and the capacity to hold together were characteristic of caste and subcaste groups; but the Hindu society as a whole was decentralized, lacking an adequate degree of homogeneity. Sanskritization was the process of taking the culture of the upper castes to those at the lower end, and unifying the community as a whole. In the absence of proselytizing zeal or a set object to this effect, it was too slow a process, indirect rather than direct, unconscious rather than conscious. As a result, Hindu society had two layers of castes — the upper one comprised those adequately integrated and having a deep sense of belonging; the lower one included half-assimilated and unassimilated castes and groups, which were nevertheless considered to be Hindu. Great stress has been laid upon the fact that converts to Islam and Christianity came from the second group, economically depressed and socially neglected. It is important to remember that the castes of this group

were not   worse off than the analogous classes in other
countries of the contemporary world. It is not economic
wellbeing or social status as is often made out or hinted at
that really mattered; it is the permissive nature of Hindu
religion and culture which allowed an elitist Hinduism and
a lower class Hinduism, with a yawning gulf separating them,
to exist side by side; it is the absence of a clear-cut objective
and zeal for creating a homogeneous religious community.
All through, the problem was how far a religion and culture
wedded to eclecticism or non-fundamentalism could go the
fundamentalist way, that is, with what vigour the religious
beliefs and culture of the lower castes could be tampered with
through Sanskritization or spread of sectarian faiths. In the
absence of active proselytization with a view to gaining
converts, the several religious movements from the time of
the Buddha failed to reach these classes in adequate measure,
and transform their lives. Their success lay mostly among
the upper and middle castes and classes, for it is at these
levels people were progressive enough to comprehend their
message, felt attracted, and followed on their own. These could
not be weaned away easily by Islam or Christianity. It is
the caste groups of the lower strata that were highly
susceptible. Their strength among the Hindus may be
estimated at one-third or even more, this by taking account
of the Census figures for Muslims, Christians and the
Depressed Classes in pre-Partition India along with other
relevant factors.

The same factors which made Hindu society loose-knit also
incapacitated it from offering effective resistance when
subjected to attack by fundamentalist Islam and Christianity.
Despite the gravity of the challenge, both political and religio-
cultural, the Hindu did not consider Islam or Muslims as
enemies, and react in that spirit. The Hindu saints continued
to speak in terms of amity and tolerance and respect for all
faiths; though hundreds of temples were destroyed, there were
no reprisals; there were no conscious, determined moves to
stem the tide until the Sikhs and the Arya Samaj appeared
on the scene late in the day; the Hindu just stood by watching.
This attitude of non-resistance cost heavily in the political
sector too, a point that will be considered later.

As regards the role of the system of caste as such, it played a double role giving rise to opposite results. The compactness and rigidity of castes taken individually proved to be a great saviour, a point emphasised by many scholars. To be put out of caste was tantamount to death in the medieval world; as such, the scope for conversions of individuals was extremely limited. Where a caste was integrated well enough with the core of the Hindu society, the proselytizing efforts of the alien faiths had little chance of success. It is this factor which ensured the safety of the Hindu society at the upper and middle levels and a good bit of the lower one too. There was also another side to the system of caste — its flexibility when viewed as a whole. When large numbers of a caste group came to be attracted by the new faith, the group adversely affected could do nothing; ostracism, its only weapon, was ineffective. True to tradition, those who strayed away formed their own caste group, and after initial rubs, often pronounced, came to live in harmony with others. Much is made of the unwillingness of caste groups to take back converts, and this is advanced as a reason for the growth of the Muslim community. There is no evidence at all to show that caste groups were obdurate in cases where conversions were effected by force or there were other extenuating factors. Presumption of such an attitude would be contrary to the way the system of caste functioned through the ages. However, a good degree of rigidity was bound to be there, for the caste group would not have survived without it.

In sharp contrast to the Hindus, the Muslims were much better placed and in a position to achieve quick results. They were imbued with the faith that their religion alone provided the way to salvation; they had a sense of mission in their proselytizing activities. It would be resonable to presume that the missionaries had the capacity to awaken the masses and exercised great charisma; otherwise, conversions on such a large scale could not have been effected and endured, whetever may have been the other factors at work. It should be noted that the conversions were at first superficial, more emotional and sentimental than based on full understanding. Of greater importance than gaining converts was the perseverance with which converts were persuaded to give up their Hindu ways and reversions to the ancestral faith prevented. Conversions on large scale had practically stopped by the time of the

Mughuls. The great achievement of the Muslim revivalist movement in full swing from the close of the sixteenth century was Islamization of those already converted and evolving of a homogeneous Muslim society.

It would be futile to try to quantify with exactitude the extent to which the several factors so far considered contributed towards the emergence of Muslims as a strong parallel society. However, in the macro view, it would appear that Muslim political predominance and material inducements proffered mattered most in gaining converts, not so much employment of brute force. Of equal importance was the basic weaknesses of the Hindus which made the task of Islamic missionaries easy — their lack of homogeneity, their eclecticism and spirit of tolerance, and also the attitude of non-resistance to proselytization by others. In this balancing act, the charismatic leadership and zeal of the missionaries in gaining converts, and also the perseverance with which they worked throughout the period to consolidate the community, should not be underestimated. As regards the message of Islam, there was nothing new in the assertion of the brotherhood of man or faith in monotheism so far as the Hindu was concerned. What really mattered was the paramount stress laid upon these aspects, and the zeal with which the message was carried to the unprivileged Hindu masses.

THE RESPONSE OF THE TRADITIONALISTS TO THE CHALLENGE OF ISLAM

The Hindu response to the challenge of Islam and Islamic culture, as has been explained, was not offensive; it was purely defensive. Both consciously and unconsciously, there were great efforts to put the Hindu house in order to stem the tide. The response of the traditionalists and the old guard was in the conservative direction; it was to tighten up the bonds of society. Caste was its basic and primary unit. As such, caste rules were to be rigorously enforced; caste integrity was to be maintained at all cost, and no quarter was to be given to waverers and deserters. In regard to inter-caste relations, salvation lay in adhering to tradition and custom.

Alien and profane ideas, customs and practices were to be rigorously eschewed. There was a distinct trend towards insularity, an attempt to escape evil by keeping away from it. These developments, reflected in the Smriti literature of the times, are regarded by many as having been in the way of social integration and intellectual development, and as such highly regressive. It should, however, be noted that the very survival of Hindu society was at stake. Caste proved to be the biggest hurdle the missionaries had to surmount. This was because caste was a close-knit unit, and change of faith involved a host of one's relationships: right to property, marital relations, control over children, and even normal social relations with the members of the family and friends. The effectiveness of these bonds in blocking the conversion of individual members of a caste is to be seen in certain measures taken by the British in India, measures which the Muslim rulers had refrained from taking. Despite its supposedly neutral stand in religious matters, the Government of India adopted certain legislative measures, ostensibly to safeguard the personal freedom of converts but helpful to Christian missionaries in the work of proselytization, in the teeth of Hindu opposition: Bengal Regulation VII of 1832 and the Caste Disabilities Act (No. XXI) of 1850, the latter gaining the appelation "Hindu Black Act", to secure inheritance and property rights to converts on their conversion, and the Christian Marriages Act of 1866 and the Converts Remarriage Act of 1886 to protect their interests in respect of marriage.[61] It was necessary to tighten the socio-religious bonds of caste as they existed. U.N. Ghoshal observes that the systematization of the Smritis was a supreme intellectual effort of the Hindus to meet the challenge of Islam; the restrictions imposed "helped her (India) and (herein lay their principal historical justification) to salvage much of her ancient cultural heritage from the imminent danger of wreckage by a relentless and determined foe."[62]

THE BHAKTI MOVEMENT AS THE PRESERVER

Closing the doors in the face of the enemy and holding the community together through compulsive and regulatory

measures could only be a part of the solution. What was most
needed at the time was the strengthening of the sense of
attachment towards ancestral religion, traditional culture and
way of life. The role and importance of the Bhakti saints
lie in their accomplishing this with greater or lesser success.

How far was the Bhakti movement a direct response to
the challenge of Islam and what was the extent of Islam's
influence over it? Islam held out two concepts as being basic
for man and sought their universal acceptance with fanatical
zeal: unswerving faith in monotheism and uncompromising
opposition to idol worship in any form; and assertion of the
brotherhood of man and social equality. As pure concepts or
goals set, these were a part of the Hindu tradition from Vedic
days. But, in Hinduism, there was a sharp line drawn between
those who were gifted or of exceptional merit, able to
comprehend and live up to the ideal set, and the common
humanity. Hinduism accepted the spiritual and social equality
of man in principle, but upheld the Dharmic laws regarding
varna and caste as socially beneficial, being based on
differences found between man and man and the needs of
a well-ordered society. It accepted monotheism as grounded
on ultimate truth, but entertained polytheistic ideas, holding
its many gods to be manifestations or symbols of the one
God, and believing in all the associated mythology. It was
a syncretization of the ideal and the practical, and the Hindu
lived in both the worlds. Islam, on the other hand, rejected
the distinction made in Hinduism between those of exceptional
merit and the common man. It ignored the distinction between
the ideal and the practical, and called upon all men to rise
up to the ideal or the goal set. Its clarion call was on par
with the slogans of Liberty, Equality and Fraternity raised
during the French Revolution, exhibiting the same zeal and
excessive fanaticism during the early phases.

In this confrontation, there was no significant dialogue
between men of religion in the two camps and the scope for
mutual influence at intellectual and elitist levels was very
limited. The impact of Vedanta on Sufi thought or of Islam
on Hindu religion and theology was minimal. The reciprocal
influence was environmental and of a general kind; it was
more sentimental, arising out of the needs of common living.
Of Kabir, Aziz Ahmed writes that his knowledge of Islam

was superficial; his was only "a popular and revolutionary restatement of the essence of Hinduism, with a conciliatory gesture of syncretic assimilation for Islam."[63] The same could be said of the other radical Bhakti saints, not excluding perhaps Guru Nanak.

As stated earlier, the Bhakti movement was already there with a hoary tradition as an active force when Islam appeared on the scene. It did not originate primarily in response to the Islamic challenge as is often made out. However, it could be said that the challenge evoked religious fervour and renewed activity among the Hindus to an unprecedented extent. Further, the concepts to which Islam attached the highest importance came to be central to the teachings of the radical wing of the Bhakti saints. It is this class that was respectful towards Islam and gave clear expression to syncretic sentiments. With all this, their teachings emanated from the Hindu religious tradition and bore no alien touch — they were very much Hindu. For this very reason, as Aziz Ahmed noted, Muslim historiography ignored Kabir,[64] and also all men of his class.

The Bhakti movement ran in two streams, the radical and the moderate, and their respective role and importance have been examined earlier. To restate the position briefly, the radical saints were like meteors leaving no permanent following behind, save for small groups; the Sikhs were the only exception. As R.C. Majumdar observed, "The medieval mysticism, like Brahmaism of later days, hardly effected any breach in the citadels either of orthodox Hinduism or orthodox Islam."[65] It would, however, be wrong to play down the role and importance of the radical saints in Hindu religious history. They commanded general respect, and their teachings came to be on everybody's lips from generation to generation. The stream of orthodox tradition itself became purer because of them, and this was a greater gain than if each of them had left a sizable sect behind.

The Bhakti movement as a whole brought about a new awareness among the Hindus and instilled a sense of commitment to their own religion and culture. The masses had been reached and their hearts won over as never before in a short period. Before the movement could gather momentum, large-scale conversions had already taken place.

The success of the movement lay in halting the wave of defections, and saving Hindu society from incurring further damage. Though not consciously proselytizing with a view to gain converts, the Bhakti saints were able to attract many individual Muslims, and this created an environment favourable to the return of caste groups marginally converted and inadequately Islamized back to Hinduism. It was this that gave an impetus to the emergence of the Muslim revivalist movement from the close of the sixteenth century.

In this religio-cultural confrontation, certain characteristics of the Bhakti movement stand out. The movement was pacific and imbued with the spirit of tolerance. Though the radical saints were anti-caste, their teachings did not provoke or promote inter-caste strife. Though the saints of the orthodox group wanted their religion and culture to remain unimpaired, they did not lead or give a call for even a minor crusade against Islam or Muslim political dominance. The Bhakti movement was not only politically sterile, as Tarachand observed,[66] it was also sterile socially from the point of the radical. But, in this very failure lay its success, for which it is best known. Its was the healing touch all round — inter-caste and inter-religious.

How far did these Hindu responses to the challenge of Islam succeed? If the emergence of Muslim India constituting more than a fifth of the country's population was a measure of the failure, that India did not go the way of Western and Central Asia and other countries was a measure of the success. Further, though large numbers embraced Islam, the converts retained most of their Hindu ideas and way of life. The success of the process of Islamization was only partial and proceeding slowly, and even the immigrant class went native in no small measure. Referring to the devolopments in the Mughul times, M.L. Roy Choudhury writes, "We would call this period the growth of Indianism in Islam. Wherever Muslims went, they influenced the culture of that country by imposing Arab script, language, manners and social ideas, but in India the influence of Hindu culture was most prominent on Islam during this period."[67] The indigenous colouring gained was so deep and marked that Indian Muslims came to be a class by themselves in the world of Islam. In the opinion of Aziz Ahmed, M. Mujeeb and others, conversions to Islam were much less than elsewhere, and the process of Islamization of the converted tardy and partial, because those who conquered and ruled India did not have the fanatical zeal of the early Arabs, and their attitude towards the Hindus was on the whole tolerant. U.N. Ghoshal, R.C. Majumdar, K.M. Panikkar and others lay stress on the dogged Hindu resistance at the local or 'little world' level, and also the tenacity of the Hindu social order with all its failings. We get a feel of the Hindu tenacty in K.M. Panikkar's interesting query — it should cause no surprise that so many members of the depressed classes left, whether it be for Islam or Christianity; but what charm or hold did Hinduism have over them which made the major part of the community to remain within the Hindu fold?[68]

The Mission to Islamize and Its Course

THE AGE OF CONVERSIONS

As stated earlier, most of the mass conversions took place prior to the time of the Mughuls. Of the two wings of the religious elite, the Ullemas were by temperament and training unfit to be good preachers. The Sufis had all the qualities required for success which the Ullemas lacked. Living an austere and simple life, with deep sympathy for the poor and the neglected, evincing the proverbial zeal of the Jesuit monks and intent on spreading the message of the Prophet and saving souls, not much concerned with meticulous observance of the rules of Shariah and as such tolerant towards indigenous traditions and customs, they came to be the chief instruments for the spread of Islam. There was a marked difference between the attitude of the Bhakti saints and that of the Sufi saints. The former had their message and preached with fervour; but theirs was not a proselytizing mission committed to gaining converts. They did not go to the people; those who were attracted flocked round them. As such, their followers came from the progressive, intelligent, upper and middle classes as was happening from the time of the Buddha. The Sufi way was different; it was the same as in the case of the Christian missions. The Sufis went to the doorsteps of those caste groups considered low and kept at arm's length by their coreligionists. The sense of self-importance of these groups was roused when the Sufis approached them; the spiritual hunger to be found in all men made them pay heed to their call with avidity. While *Turkanah Tariqah* (the Turki way of effecting conversions by force) failed, *Sufianah Tariqah* (the Sufi way) succeeded. The work of the converting Sufis was made very easy by the deep fissures in Hindu society. Also, the Sufis made no exacting demands of the prospective converts. Change of faith involved no change in customary life or habits. Caste and old contacts remained within the new circles formed. Ensuring meticulous observance of the Shariah and Islamization of the converted came to be the chief concern of the Ullemas and zealous Sufis in later years.

THE IMPACT OF MUSLIM REVIVALISM

The phenomenal success of the Sufis in gaining converts on a large scale gave an impetus to the Bhakti movement and led to the rise of its radical wing, as stated earlier. The Bhakti saints were able to halt the spread of Islam, and it looked as though the wind had started blowing in the other direction. It is true these were non-proselytizing and sought no converts in the Islamic way. But their syncretic ideas were more insidious and dangerous than attempts at outright conversion. With his eclectic tradition, the syncretic attitude came naturally to the Hindu. But it was otherwise with the Muslim. Endorsement of the syncretic concepts in the air meant equating Islam with Hinduism; this amounted to a virtual confession of absence of faith in Islam. The orthodox were deeply perturbed. Where would this eclecticism take them? Would Indian Muslims be swallowed by the quicksands of Hindu society and transformed into one of its many caste groups? Would they at all be able to maintain their identity as a religious group and continue to be members of the world of Islam? As Aziz Ahmed observes, the issue which the Muslim community faced was "whether to merge syncretically into Hinduism, or to preserve its identity through a reorientation towards orthodox formalism and religio-political particularism."[69] This was the issue over which Dara Shukoh and Aurangzib fought. Interestingly, Christian missions were faced with the same problem over and over again — whether and how far Christianity in India could compromise with the system of caste and Hindu ways without ceasing to be Christian.[70]

The fears of the Muslim fundamentalists were not groundless. But for Muslim political predominance, Indian Islam might have been in a tighter spot. From the time of the Mughuls, instead of marching forward, it was on the defensive. In this situation, the traditionalists and the old guard reacted in the same way as their counterparts among the Hindus did when first confronted by Islam. The need of the hour was to cleanse the house within — Hindu survivals and accretions were to be eliminated; the Shariah was to be enforced strictly; deviations from the Islamic way of life were to be banned; closer links were to be forged with the Islamic communities outside; the ideal of the Indian Muslim was to be "to resemble his Arab archtype as closely as possible."[71] Shaikh Ahmad of Sirhind (1563-1624) was the father of the religio-political movement of orthodox Islam in India, and he belonged to Naqshbandia school of Sufis, closest to orthodoxy. The Muslim revivalist movement threw up many leaders and was an important force down to the present century. The activities of Shaikh Waliullah (1702-62), Wahabism initiated by Saiyid Ahmad of Rai Bareilly (1786-1831) and the Khilafat Movement of the twenties of the present century were among its outstanding landmarks. The revivalists achieved their primary objective — welding Indian Muslims into one community, distinct and separate from the Hindu. The Ashraf were made to shake off much of their aloofness and claims to superiority; the converted Muslim masses were brought into the main stream of 'Islamic' society to a great extent; and the spirit of pan-Indian Muslim consciousness was roused among all sections of the community. The solidarity that could not be achieved when the Muslims ruled was attained during the period of distress in the eighteenth-nineteenth centuries. The political wilderness itself proved to be a great unifying and cementing factor. This new-found unity was clearly reflected in the attitude of the Muslim masses during the Revolt of 1857 and the Khilafat Movement.

During the process of cleansing the house within and achieving solidarity, the revivalists often came to be markedly anti-Hindu. They sought to recapture the old proselytizing and converting zeal; they laid stress on the maintenance of Muslim political predominance to achieve Islam's goal. Shaikh Ahmad of Sirhind told Jahangir that the religious law thrived best under the sword, and reiterated the duties of a Muslim ruler in the matter of proselytization.[72] Shaikh Waliullah exhibited the same spirit in the eighteenth century; he went about exhorting Muslim rulers to join against the Marathas, and not satisfied with the response, invited Ahmad Shah Abdali to rescue the land from the hands of the unbelievers. About his objective, I.H. Qureshi writes, "Waliullah did not want Muslims to become part of the general milieu of the sub-continent; he wanted them to keep alive their relations with the rest of the Muslim world, so that the springs of their inspiration and ideals might ever remain located in Islam and the traditions of the world community developed by it."[73] The same attitude and zeal were exhibited by the Wahabis when Hindus and Muslims were under common subjection to the British. They were as much anti-Hindu as anti-British. Discounting attempts to dub them as nationalists, S.A.A. Rizwi observes, "At no stage in the eighteenth and nineteenth centuries did the so-called Wahabbists, Reformists or Mujahids play a healthy or progressive role in the development of the country, but only pandered to the fanatical sentiments of the credulous believers."[74]

As regards the actual influence wielded by the Muslim revivalists in political matters, Satishchandra and others have emphasised that their role and importance should not be exaggerated.[75] With all their fanaticism and fulminations, they could not take the country back to the early years of Muslim rule, or force the Mughuls to deviate from their tolerant policies. But the little anti-Hindu tiltings often upset the delicate balance that had been attained. We are told that Aurangzib's one great desire was to rule according to the Shariah. But his only major anti-Hindu acts were reimposition of Jizya and destruction of a number of temples on the ground they were newly built or for other reasons. In an earlier age, these would have been viewed as minor happenings by the Hindu. But with the new awareness, there was political upsurge all round, and the decline of the Mughul empire began. Again, in the eighteenth century, it is stressed that Muslim rulers had developed a secular outlook and religious considerations did not weigh much with them. But they banded together to fight against the Marathas in the battle of Panipat (1761), forgetting the implications of supporting Abdali. Their zeal for Muslim solidarity evaporated when it came to support the Mughul in his distress and sustaining his authority, the pillar on which Muslim political predominance over the whole land rested. When it came to a choice between the Marathas and the British, they joined the British by signing treaties of Subsidiary Alliance — that was well before the British inflicted their fatal blows on the Marathas. All these happened because the revivalist upsurge had nipped in the bud the incipient syncretic and unifying trends of the fifteenth-sixteenth centuries. The loss of the spiritual cement was the greatest loss. Thereafter, the process of integration had to depend for success only upon compulsions of common living, political pragmatism and the heritage of tolerance native to the soil. One can only speculate what the course of history in general and the Hindu-Muslim relationship in particular would have been if the revivalists had been less anti-Hindu, and allowed the syncretic spirit to blossom. From the point of the orthodox, "although the empire was lost, religion was saved," as Tarachand observes.[76] The question is whether both could not have been saved by moderation.

THE DUAL ROLE OF THE SUFIS AND THE MIXED HERITAGE

It has been usual to equate the Sufis and the Bhakti saints as messengers of peace striving for accord between the two communities. The view is inaccurate and much too facile as it does not take all the facts into account. As regards the Bhakti saints, as noted earlier, those deeply influenced by Islam placed the two religions on par and had followers among Muslims too; theirs was syncretism in the true spirit. The orthodox wing of the movement did not look towards Islam for inspiration of any kind or was influenced by it; even so, it never exhibited an anti-Muslim attitude. In the case of both the moderates and the radicals, adherence to peace and tolerance, based on traditional values, was near total.

The Sufis, on the other hand, were often in a dilemma. They were in principle not bound by the Shariah, had an open mind in religious matters, and were tolerant towards those who held opposite views. But many of them had a deep sense of commitment towards Islam; spreading the message of the Prophet and making converts were a passion with them. There was an inherent contradiction between the two attitudes, and the attitude of individual Sufis was not the same. Aziz Ahmed is right when he observes that the role of Sufism has been "overestimated and over-idealized as eclectic and as a bridge between Hinduism and Islam", and "in fact, the relationship between Sufism and Hindu mysticism is multi-positional and ranges from polemical hostility through missionary zeal to tolerant coexistence." Again, he notes, "All the major Sufi orders in India, the Chishti, the Qadiri and the Naqshbandi show a similar approach to Hinduism, which begins with hostility, passes through a phase of coexistence and culminates in tolerance and understanding." While Waliullah was noted for his anti-Hindu attitude, his son and successor, Abdul Aziz regarded Krishna as a saint (*Awliya*) because of the impact the *Gita* made on his mind. While the Naqshbandi order was anti-Hindu under Sirhindi, it became tolerant and even eclectic under Jan-i-Janan (1699-1780) who regarded the Vedas as divinely inspired. It is this multi-positional attitude of individual Sufis that makes it incorrect to equate them wholly with the Bhakti saints.[77]

Despite the ambivalence or hostility of individual Sufis, it was only the Sufis as a class that tried to understand the Hindus, developed respect for Hindu religion and culture, and strove for accord and peaceful coexistence. This has rightly earned for them the reputation of having been lovers of peace and bridge builders. In the long run, it is the Sufis of this class that gained the upper hand. Two macro facts go in support of the view: the vast majority of the Sunnis in India being attached to the Hanafi school of Islamic jurisprudence, which alone granted Hindus the status of Zimmis; and the Qadiria order, more deeply influenced by Hindu thought than any other Sufi school and also generally known for its tolerance towards Hindus, becoming "the most widespread in the sub-continent in modern times".[78] Maulana Abul Kalam Azad's signal contribution lay in his synthesizing this trend in traditional theology and showing that there was nothing in Islam coming in the way of showing respect for other religions or living in harmony with persons of other faiths.

Notes

1. M. Mujeeb, 21. R.C. Majumdar, *The Maratha Supremacy*, 730.
2. Tarachand, Vol. I, 87.
3. In 1911, of the twelve million Muslims in the Punjab, ten million were shown under caste heads — Rajput, Jat, Araia, Gujar, Mushi, Turkan and Teli, and this was indicative of their Hindu origin. Those who described themselves as Pathan, Baloch, Shaikh, Saiyid and Mogul were less than two millions. As such, it was estimated that not more than 15 per cent of the Punjabi Muslims could have been of foreign origin. — E.A. Gait, *Census of India* (1911), Vol. I, Part I, Report, 128.
4. M. Mujeeb, 22. A. Ahmed, *Early Turkish Empire*, 8.
5. R.C. Majumdar, *The Struggle for Empire*, 469, 497. S.C. Misra, 13, 54-59.
6. Mohammad Yasin, 3.
7. Claims to superiority of this type were common enough. Buchanan noted that in the Purnea District of Bihar, there were seven hundred families of Sayyads, about hundred of whom were ranked as pretenders. —*Purnea*, 196.
8. Ghaus Ansari, 30.
9. For instance, Kaye, the noted historian, discreetly omitted making any mention of Charles Metcalfe's Indian wife and of his three sons by her. — F.G. Hutchins, 23.
10. *Seir Mutaqherin*, Vol. I, 235.
11. A. Ahmed, *Early Turkish Empire*, 8.
12. Tarachand, Vol. I, 105. Also, Satishchandra, xxx.
13. M. Mujeeb, 20.
14. Moncton-Jones, 3. Buchanan, *Mysore, Canara and Malabar*, Vol. II, 422.
15. George Forrest, Vol. I, 37. Kirmani, 147-51. Also, Mohibbul Hasan, 181-2.
16. Buchanan, *Mysore, Canara and Malabar*, Vol. II, 422. Mrs. Meer Hasan Ali (P. 4) observed, "The Sayyids are the Lords of Mussulman society, and every female born to them is a Lady (*Begum*)", and "The Sayyids are very tenacious in retaining the purity of their race unsullied, particularly with reference to their daughters."
17. Ghaus Ansari, 9-11, 30, 64. Tarachand, Vol. I, 103. Also, M. Mujeeb, 20.
18. S.C. Misra, 131.
19. S.N. Sen's Introduction — M.L. Roy Choudhuri, iii.
20. *Seir Mutaqherin*, Vol. II, 356.
21. Mohammad Yasin, 12.
22. Satishchandra, 257-8.
23. V.K Bawa, 4-5.

24. S.C. Misra, 134-5.
25. *Ibid.,*134, Ghaus Ansari, 50.
26. S.T. Lokhandwala in *Quest*, No. 73 (Nov.-Dec. 1971). Hamid Ali in *Islamic Culture*, July-October 1937. S.C. Misra in *Medieval Indian State*, 50. Also, Noel J. Coulson, 50.
27. Aziz Ahmed, *Intellectual History of Islam*, 20.
28. R.C. Majumdar, *The Delhi Sultanate*, 462.
29. Mohammad Habib — Chisti Records of the Sultanate period, *Medieval India Quarterly*, Vol. I, No.2 (October 1950), 1-2.
30. Aziz Ahmed, *Islamic Culture*, 137-8.
31. Tarachand, Vol. I, 201.
32. W.C. Smith, 38.
33. Aziz Ahmed, *Intellectual History of Islam*, 3, 35.
34. M.W. Mirza in R.C. Majumdar, *The Mughul Empire*, 665. 'Be-Pir' (without a spiritual guide) came to be a word of strong reproach or abuse. — *Ibid*, 677.
35. *Bengal, Past and Present*, Vol. XXVIII, Sl.No.55 (1924), 42-53.
36. *Seir Mutaqherin*, Vol. I, 206-22.
37. S.C. Misra, 14, *et seqq.*
38. Tarachand, Vol. I, 142-3.
39. Satishchandra, Presidential Address (Medieval India Section), *Progs. of the Indian History Congress*, 1966 (Mysore), 133-4.
40. Buchanan, *Mysore, Canara and Malabar*, Vol. I, 124; Dinajpur, 91. Also, A. Sterling, *Cuttock*, 56-9.
41. D.R. Gadgil, 23.
42. Washbrooke, 41-8.
43. K.G. Saiyidain in Nanavati and Vakil, 37.
44. R.C. Majumdar, *The Delhi Sultanate*, 617.
45. *Ibid*, 628, 661.
46. S.N. Sen, *Studies in Indian History*, 166.
47. M. Mujeeb, 21.
48. Muslims are said to have constituted one-fifth of the population of Malabar before it became a part of Tipu's kingdom. They occupied an important position in the region all through. Barbosa even claimed that but for the coming of the Portuguese, the whole of the coast would have become Muslim. — C.K. Kareem, 86-97.
49. S.C. Misra, 14.
50. *Qanun-i-Islam*, 3.
51. S.N. Sen, *Kanhoji Angria*, 188-90.
52. R.C. Mitra, 82.
53. *Ibid.* 149.
54. M.T. Titus, 44-5.
55. R.C. Majumdar, *The Maratha Supremacy*, 734.
56. Buchanan, *Dinajpur*, 92. This view gains further support from the fact that the proportion of the Scheduled Castes to total population is much lower here than elsewhere.
57. R.C. Majumdar, *The Maratha Supremacy*, 732.
58. Aziz Ahmed, *Islamic Culture*, 82.
59. M.L. Roy Choudhury, 274. According to Jadunath Sarkar, under

Aurangzib, Qanungoship was often offered making it conditional that the recipient should embrace Islam. This is clear from many of the Letters Patent issued and the News Letters. — *Aurangzib*, Vol. IV, 314-5.

60. Khushwant Singh, Vol. II, 119, and note at 146.
61. S.V. Desika Char, *Centralised Legislation*, 314-5.
62. U.N. Ghoshal, 530.
63. Aziz Ahmed, *Islamic Culture*, 146.
64. *Ibid*.
65. R.C. Majumdar, *The Delhi Sultanate*, 555. It is interesting to note that there were only 5,504 Brahmos, mostly in Bengal and Calcutta, according to 1911 Census. Also, Aziz Ahmed, *Islamic Culture*, 152.
66. Tarachand, Vol. I, 149.
67. M.L. Roy Choudhury, 103.
68. K.M. Panikkar, *The Foundations of New India*, 50, 56.
69. Aziz Ahmed, *Islamic Culture*, 191. See also pp. 35-6 above.
70. The nature of the struggle may be seen in the bitter conflict between the foreign missionaries and the Indian Christians in Bengal in the last quarter of the last century over the issue of early marriage among converts. The missionaries were dead set against this surviving 'Hindu' practice, but the converts wanted no intervention in their customary life. They went to the extent of asserting that they were 'Hindu Christians' — Christians by faith and Hindu by tradition and culture. — G.A. Oddie, *Social Protest in India*, 87 *et seqq*.
71. Mohammad Yasin, 2.
72. Aziz Ahmed, *Islamic Culture*, 185-6.
73. I.H. Qureshi, cited by Karandikar, 127.
74. S.A.A. Rizwi in Bisheshwar Prasad, 106.
75. Satishchandra, Presidential Address, Medieval History Section, *Proceedings of the Indian History Congress*, 1966, 135-9.
76. Tarachand, Vol.I, 205.
77. Aziz Ahmed, *Islamic Culture*, 134-9; *Intellectual History of Islam*, Chap. IV.
78. Aziz Ahmed, *Intellectual History of Islam*, 42.

CHAPTER 3

Administration of the Plural Society

The Problem as Faced by the Hindu Rulers

By the end of the thirteenth century, the Muslims were emerging as a parallel community and both the Hindu and the Muslim rulers were faced with the problem of administering a society that was no longer homogeneous. The issues posed were broadly similar. But, as they were differently placed politically, and their tradition and cultural background were not the same, their approach and policies were different, though there were things in common.

For the Hindu rulers, the presence of Muslim communties posed no great problems in magnitude or complexity. In most cases, Muslims were numerically small, and the local converts came from the lower stratas of society. They had no counterparts of Hindu zamindars and trading communities. Their cultural ties were more with the Hindu ruling classes than with the immigrant Muslims, despite commonness of religion. They did not suffer from a sense of alienation; they posed no threat to the existing social order or create major security problems. There were few instances of the converts as a community rising in revolt or making common cause with the Muslim invaders, despite the cry of *jihad* in the air. Danger to the Hindu kingdoms came not from within but from without — from the neighbouring Muslim powers who were spurred by ambition. Despite these favourable factors, the Hindu rulers may not have found things easy if they had not been heirs to a strong secularist tradition. To them, the Muslims were just another caste or sect, entitled to protection and even-handed treatment on par with others. It is important to note that this traditional attitude, and pursuit of policies in harmony with it, did not receive a jolt or undergo transformation to any significant extent under the stress of the inimical atmosphere prevailing outside. Indeed, this policy of the Hindu rulers had a wider impact. The general absence of reprisals in the Hindu kingdoms because of the happenings outside had a toning effect in two ways —by cutting the circuit of reprisals, it helped in preventing further fouling of the atmosphere; it had also a sobering impact on the policies of the Muslim rulers within their own kingdoms.

There is plenty of evidence to show that the Muslims lived peacefully and were well-treated in Hindu kingdoms. Besides A.S. Altekar's testimony regarding their position under the Rashtrakutas, and of Mahalingam and B.A. Saletore and others in regard to the kingdom of Vijayanagara, we have vivid accounts as to how they fared in Malabar, where they were an important and sizable community from early times. We have a picture of the position at the close of the sixteenth century from Shaykh Zaynud-Din, a Malabari Muslim:

The Muslims throughout Malibar have no *amir* possessed of power to rule over them. But their rulers are unbelievers. These exercise judicial authority over them by organizing their affairs, by compelling them to pay the debt or fine if anyone is subjected to such payment. Notwithstanding these, the rulers have respect and regard for the Muslims, because the increase in the number of towns was due to them. Hence, the rulers enable the Muslims in the observance of their Friday prayers and celebration of Id. They fix the allowance for *qazis* and *muadhdhins* and entrust them with the duty of carrying out the laws of the *shariaat*. No one is permitted to nelgect the prayer on Fridays. In greater part of Malibar, whoever neglects it is punished or made to pay a fine.

If a Muslim commits a crime punishable by death, they put him to death after obtaining the permission of the elders of the Muslims....

If a Muslim commits a crime, even though it be murder, the unbelievers would not enter his house without permission. But they call upon his co-religionists to expel him from society or starve him or the like.

The unbelievers never punish such of their countrymen who embrace Islam, but treat them with the same respect shown to the rest of the Muslims, though the converts belong to the lowest grades of their society. As a result of such kindly treatment the Muslim merchants of the olden days used to come in large numbers.

And, further, "The Muslims of Malibar lived a happy and prosperous life on account of the benevolence of their rulers, their regard to the time-honoured customs, and their kindness. But the Muslims undervalued the blessings of Allah, and transgressed and disobeyed. So Allah sent them the people of Portukal, who were Christians.[1]

The long quotation covers many aspects, and brings out clearly the general attitude and policy of the Hindu rulers towards their Muslim subjects. That Zaynud-Din was not exaggerating the good treatment received by Muslims is borne out by Ibn Batutah and Barbosa.[2]

We also have a clear picture of the position of Muslims under Hindu rule specially in S.N. Sen's studies on Maratha administration. In the view of the Maratha rulers, Muslims were just another caste, entitled to the same freedom and autonomy as the Hindu castes. They did not disclaim the right to intervene on request or otherwise whenever considered necessary. Hereditary Kazis were appointed by the state to minister to Muslims, and in the opinion of M.A. Karandikar, this was not contrary to Islamic tradition or law.[3] Since customary law was in force in civil matters, there was no room for discrimination in this sector. In regard to criminal matters, the penal law of the Hindus was applicable to all including Muslims. Only the immigrant Muslim classes could have resented its application, as they were heirs to a different system of laws. One other restriction may have been considered a hardship — it was the prohibition of cow slaughter, a matter on which Hindus were very sensitive. In the life of the village communities, we hear of Muslims serving on judicial panchayats, and there having been Muslim patels.[4] As regards public employment, the local converts did not come from classes who were qualified for it or sought such employment. That there was no aversion to employing Muslims as such is clear from Arabs, Pathans, Mughuls and others from outside Maharashtra finding entry into the Maratha army in large numbers. As regards taxation, there is no evidence of any discrimination being practised. On the contrary, there is a reference to Muslims paying *Hashil* at half the rate applicable to Hindus, though the circumstances leading to the concession are not clear.[5] Apart from continuing the grants made towards the maintenance of Muslim religious establishments by previous Muslim rulers, fresh ones were also made, and there were friendly participations in Muslim festivals. While it would be difficult to judge how equitous the distribution of patronage was, it may be surmised that it could not have been munificent or very liberal in the prevailing atmosphere.

In this connection, reference may be made to *Turushka Danda* referred to by scholars. Aziz Ahmed considers that it was a fine levied on Muslims, and also argues that the levy of *Chauth* was "an exaggerated reflection of the aggressive reaction to the former Muslim institution of *jizya*."[6] It may be made clear that there are only some stray references to the imposition of the *Turushka Danda* in the inscriptions of the Gahadavalas of Kanauj dating from 1090 A.D. D.C. Ganguly observes, "Some suggest that it was an impost on the subjects of the Gahadavalas to meet the expenses of resisting the invasion of the Muslims. Others think that the Gahadavala kings realised this tax from the people in order to make annual payments of tribute to the Sultans of Ghazni."[7] It has also been suggested that the impost was a levy on Muslim settlers in Hindu kingdoms.[8] In any case, there is no evidence to show that it had any wide prevalence or was levied in later times.

Major Hurdles in the Path of the Muslim Rulers

ALIENNESS

In magnitude and complexity, the administration of the plural society that had emerged presented no great problem to the Hindu rulers. It was otherwise with the Muslim rulers, and as such requires detailed study. There has been an acute controversy over the nature of the Muslim rule in India —as to how far it was theocratic and how far secular. More than this theoretical and doctrinal approach, what is of importance is the actual state of affairs — the nature of the governing class, how it was situated and had to function. The usual comparisons with the performance of the Hindu rulers of the day, or evaluation on the basis of present-day concepts and standards, would be superficial and wide of the mark. The Muslim rulers are to be judged by the weight of the burden they shouldered and the hurdles they had to surmount. A more sympathetic appraisal of their role than usual seems to be called for.

The first major handicap from which Muslim rulers suffered was alienness, distinct from class, caste and religious differences. Strong objections have been raised against viewing them as 'foreigners', and characterizing their rule as 'foreign rule'. It is to be noted that the Muslims came to India at different times, whether it be as invaders or peaceful immigrants; the in-coming process was on right up to the mid-eighteenth century. The one significant feature was that nearly all those who came chose to stay — after a time, they had no other home. They were not for a brief stay to loot and return like Muhammad of Ghazni or birds of passage like the British, camping only to rule and exploit. As such, Muslim rule was not a case of colonialism or imperialism with the centre of gravity located outside. This view put forward by many modern scholars has not been presented better than by James Mill long ago: "As India was not governed by the Moguls, in the character of a detached province, valued only as it could be rendered useful to another state, which is the idea of foreign conquest; but became the sole residence and sole dominion of the Mogul government, which thereby found its interest as closely united to that of India, as it is possible for the interest of a despotical government to be united with that of its people; the Mogul government was, to all effects and of interest (*sic*), and therefore of behaviour, not a foreign but a native government."[9] It may be added that as each group of foreigners entered, those who had come earlier banded together with the indigenous people to resist the pressure. We see this in the Afghan-Hemu alliance to fight the Mughul, and in the moves to forge a Hindu-Muslim alliance in the wake of the invasion of Nadir Shah. We see it also in the court politics and Muslim social life of the day — the rivalries and conflicts between the newcomers and the 'Hindusthanis', as those settled for long were known. Apart from the continuous process of absorption of newcomers, a matter of utmost signicance was the fact that the Hindus ceased to regard the immigrants and their descendants, the Ashraf, as foreigners; in their eyes, they were as much sons of the soil as themselves.

While the term 'foreign' to describe the Muslim ruling class or Muslim rule would be incorrect, the fact was that the rulers of the day belonged to the dominant immigrant tribes and their descendants only. They kept aloof from all others, whether Hindus or local converts to Islam. The distance separating them was the same as between Europeans and Indians under British rule. Throughout the medieval period, the Ashraf were subject to strong outward pulls. Were they to fuse with the local Indian community or to remain distinct and separate, one with the world of Islam, maintaining Islamic tradition and culture unsullied? This was the problem constantly before them. Their material interests clashed with the call of the heart and the mind. While the former had the upper hand in the final count, the latter queered the pitch often enough. It was only during the travails of the eighteenth century that the barriers separating the Ashraf from the rest of the Muslim community started breaking down, and also a general process of secularization to cover the Hindus began to gather momentum.

In this situation, Muslim rule was the rule of a dominant immigrant racial group, comparable to the white supremacy in South Africa at the present time. No doubt the sharp edges got blunted to a great extent over time, but a large part of the foreignness making for alienation persisted to the end of Muslim rule. This is the general view of many scholars. In the opinion of M. Mujeeb, "Over long periods, this bureaucratic administration (of the Mughals) was dominated by immigrants who had had most of their training and experience outside India, and this gave it much of the character of foreign rule."[10] T.G.P. Spear wrote that, in Aurangzib's time, "The Mughal service in its higher branches was even more foreign than are the services today [1935]"; noting a difference between the two, he qualified that "its outlook and sentiment were Indian."[11] M.A. Karandikar observed more categorically, "The Sultanate and the Mughal governments were basically foreign governments ruled by, not the Muslims as a community, but by different Turkish, Persian and Afghan races who were jealous about their own position as distinct ruling classes." He further stated that Aurangzib's well-known will and testament reflected this attitude; also, a number of earlier rulers of Delhi "did not look upon the Muslims in India as a single community at all", and "were conscious of the fact that they were foreign imperialists".[12]

FEAR OF THE UNRECONCILED HINDU

Closely linked with and arising from their feeling of alienness, there was the constant fear of the unreconciled Hindu. The Hindu rulers had been overthrown, and most of India had come under Muslim rule. But most of the time and to no small extent, it was a military occupation only; the authority of government was weak beyond the Pargana towns where the armed forces were located. Land, trade and commerce were in Hindu hands. The small chiefs and zamindars exercising hereditary authority were well entrenched and possessed grass-roots strength. Their military resources in the sixteenth and seventeenth centuries were not inconsiderable, as revealed by recent studies. Citing Athar Ali, Satish-Chandra states that in Akbar's time, the forces at their disposal comprised "3,84,558 cavalry, 43,77,057 infantry, 1,863 elephants, 4,260 guns and 4,500 boats."[13] The tussle between the zamindars and the government was "a constant feature of medieval Indian society and powerfully influenced the development of many institutions."[14] Large standing armies had to be maintained "to keep in check a hostile or at least repellent population",[15] and sustain political authority; *mulkgiri* expeditions had to be undertaken to enforce payment of revenue. No doubt there prevailed a general sense of security and permanence under the Mughuls, but at the same time, there was an underlying feeling of insecurity as stressed by Aziz Ahmed. This was on par with a similar trend under British rule as brought out very well by F.J. Hutchins in *The Illusion of Permanence: British Imperialism in India* (1967). The great task before the Muslim rulers was to gain the affection and loyalty of the Hindus, and transform their acquiescence into acceptance.

THE HOLD OF ISLAMIC FUNDAMENTALISM

As stated earlier, the goal of a unified, theocratic, Islamic world-state could not be attained, since the fissures that developed were many. However, the growth of a secularist outlook was slow. In Islamic society, the Shariah could not be repudiated on any count, and the Ullemas, its interpreters, had an important place. Muslim rulers had always to keep in view the hold religion had on Muslim mind in shaping their policies. The position in India was particularly difficult and complicated, because Muslims here, specially the ruling classes, were a very small minority, though politically dominant. The Ullemas were not daunted, or inclined to change their outlook, because of the local situation. According to Dr. Hardy, the bulk of Indo-Muslim writing on government embodied, in essence, "a conception of partnership between the doctors of the holy law and the sultans in the higher interests of the faith — a partnership between pious professors and pious policemen."[16] The Shariah was to be the sole guide in all matters, and Islamic tradition and culture were to be maintained unsullied. Propagation of the faith was to be as much the duty of rulers as men of religion. The distinction between the faithful and the unbelievers was to be maintained without dilution, and the Hindus were to be shown no more indulgence than permissible under the sacred law. To be recognized as Zimmis was the utmost concession Hindus could expect or be accorded. This view of the Ullemas might have been viewed sympathetically by a Firoz Shah Tughlaq and an Aurangzib, but Muslim rulers in India in general could hardly afford to endorse it. Even during the

Sultanate period, the rulers only paid lip service to the Shariah. They made their own laws and governed according to their discretion; their actions were reconciled to dogma on grounds of necessity or public good. As regards the Mughul state, it was considered a 'profanation' of Islam by Wismar. As Tara Chand summed up, "Notwithstanding the fact that throughout the medieval period, the head of the state in India was a Muslim, the state was not Islamic. Neither in its constitutive principles, nor in its basic conceptions, aims and ends, did the state follow the injuctions of the holy scriptures — the Quran, the Hadith, or the laws elaborated in the four schools of the Sunni scriptures. It is a mistake to call the medieval state of India theocratic, for it did not function under the guidance of Muslim theologians." Even Aurangzib, "inspite of his intentions failed to instal the sovereignty of the *shara* (the canon law)."[17]

While accepting the correctness of this broad assessment, we have yet to take note of the running battle the Muslim rulers had to wage against the Ullema fundamentalism. The Ullemas had come to constitute a distinct class and a strong pressure group, at least from the time of Ala-ud-din Khalji. They had a place in the court and the administration, and held judicial and ecclesiastical posts. As theologians, they commanded wide respect, and in particular, their influence was great over the immigrant Ashraf. It is true that they did not enjoy the status of *Omrahs* (high ranking nobles) or have any high place in the Ashraf hierarchy. They were in no position to play the role of king-makers or wield the influence of those holding high military rank. They were held well under check even in the pre-Mughul period by Balban, Ala-ud-din Khalji and Muhammad-bin-Tughlaq. But, in a community in which religious motivations had a big enough place, their day-to-day role was bound to be important. By throwing their lot on one side or the other, advancing flexible theological arguments, they could tip the balance in the game of politics. Akbar had to face their opposition, which had a great impact in the long run; their support helped Aurangzib get the better of Dara Shukoh and gain the throne; their hand was to be seen in the overthrow of the Sayyid brothers, whose policies were too liberal for their taste. None of the Muslim rulers, not even the Mughuls, could dare to deny

openly the authority of the Shariah in its application to
secular matters or turn the Ullemas out of the court or the
administration. Akbar and Abul Fazl were alone in making
an approach towards it — "instead of placing Akbar in the
role of the defender of the Sunni faith, Abul Fazl pleaded
for a universal monarchy over all peoples, and propounded
that if the king does not regard all classes of men and all
sects of religion in the single eye of favour,... he will not
be fit for the exalted office."[18] This view of Abul Fazl only
highlights the predicament of the Muslim rulers of the time.

THE MUSLIM RULERS VERSUS THE NOBLES

The next and most important hurdle confronting the Muslim
rulers centred round their own power base — their principal
followers and the nobility constituting the ruling class. After
every invasion, those who came to power did so with the help
of their own tribal followers. Their closeness and intimacy
with the chiefs of the tribes and the rank and file were a
source of strength as well as weakness. They could not inspire
fear and awe or exercise the glamour of a distant power. When
they were weak or their grip loosened even for a moment,
there was turbulence and turmoil. Generals sent out to
conquer carved out principalities for themselves; those
entrusted with the administration of distant provinces became
independent. The Sultans had to be always on their guard
against their own friends and followers more than their
enemies. It was a particularly tough game as they were in
a hostile country with the people sullen and resentful and
ready to strike back. Broadly, throughout the Sultanate period,
the Sultans were only just above their nobles in status,
holding on precariously. This was reflected in the frequent
changes in the rulers and ruling families, the heavy hand
required for putting down revolts and the free flow of blood.

It is only with the Mughuls that there was a visible and
marked change. Right from the beginning, the emperors came
to command a power and a majesty that distanced them from
the nobles which were not seen earlier. Personal fealty was
insisted upon by strong rulers like Firoz Shah Tughlaq, Sher
Shah, Akbar and Tipu, and the offering of such fealty became

a part of the court ceremonial. The towering position they attained was reflected in many matters. In the view of the outside world, the dropping of the nominal homage paid to the Khalif by some of the earlier Sultans had great significance. Akbar went a step further; he shocked the orthodox by claiming to be the Chief *Imam* and *Mujtahid*, the supreme arbiter in matters religious. In administrative matters, the rulers' will prevailed, whether it was in conformity with the Shariah or not, and the Ullemas had to be very circumspect in making their submissions. Court etiquette and practices also were changed to enhance the stature of the rulers. A defeated king or a humbled nobleman was brought in public view before the emperor as if he was a captive with his hands bound; he then made his submission, was graciously pardoned and restored to noble status.[19] There was then the old Hindu practice of *Tulabhara*, weighing a ruler against precious articles like gold and silver and distributing them in charity. This was revived to project the opulence and greatness of the ruler. In the later Mughul age, even a touch of divinity came to be attached to the institution of the emperor. Members of the small sect of Darshaniyas would not have their breakfast until they had had a glimpse of the emperor in the morning. Akbar II (1806) started the practice of making disciples (*Muriads*), who accepted the spiritual guidance of the king and received a light red handkerchief as a symbol of their status. The *Pirzadas* of Delhi, noted as religious leaders, encouraged the practice, being firm believers in the divine right of kings.[20]

The transformation of the Muslim rulers from being only the first among the nobles to becoming paramount and supreme, exercising unquestioned authority, became possible because of several reasons. One remarkable feature of Muslim rule was that feudalism of the type known to the West was not allowed to emerge. After a country was conquered and a new kingdom was established, the land was not parcelled out among the principal followers to form a hereditary aristocracy, just as the Normans did when they conquered England. Instead, the rulers retained all the land in their own hands, and administered directly through a bureaucracy. Those sent out to govern or conquer new lands held their office entirely at the pleasure of the rulers, and were frequently shifted. There was also the rule of escheat under which the entire property of the nobles passed on to the state on their death; their children and dependents had to make a fresh start invoking royal favour. The well-organized Mansabdari system of the Mughuls was a fruition of earlier trends. As M. Mujeeb has observed, "The Sultanate and the Mughul Empire were not a mixture of bureacracy with feudalism, their administration was bureaucratic throughout."[21] There was another important development which helped in the exaltation of the Mughul emperors. Prior to their time, after every conquest, the dependence of the new rulers on their tribal following in regard to both civil and military administration was almost total. This was an asset in some ways, but it was also a liability and security risk. As such, after a time, every Muslim ruler sought to buttress his position with the support of others outside his own tribal circle. This trend gained great momentum under the Mughuls. It is also attributed partially to their numerical weakness as well as to their having no hinterland to fall back upon. While the Mughuls or Turanis were strong in the army, the Iranis had a bigger place in civil administration. More and more Muslims of other groups too, including Afghans who were considered arch enemies at first, came to be freely employed. The major departure lay in the association of Rajputs; it helped in broadbasing the administration further and also in reconciling the Hindus. The emperor's position came to be exalted beyond measure, as he came to be not dependent on any one section of the nobility for his position.

The Mughuls did not attain their exalted position without facing difficulties. Holding the nobles under a leash was a continuous problem. Court intrigues had a greater place than the open fights that prevailed earlier. As long as the strong hand of the ruler was there, everything went off well. With the slightest appearance of weakness, old maladies again cropped up. This happened at the time of every succession to the throne, the nobles taking sides with relish and seeking their own personal advancement. A great weakness of Muslim polity everywhere was the absence of a settled rule of succession: "right of blood, right of sword, right of election and right of nomination equally worked." As Sri Rama Sharma pithily put it, "The right to rule was a personal right, acquire it how one will." Amongst the Timurids, the idea of partition among sons was more current than succession by the eldest son.[22] With this heritage, fraternal struggle over succession was more the rule than the exception even under the Great Mughuls. It was also usual for crown princes to seek to supplant their ageing fathers — Aurangzib imprisoning his father and ascending the throne was only an instance of a revolt that succeeded. With the empire growing and troubles abounding, the idea of partition was mooted in the time of Babar, Humayun, Shahjahan, Aurangzib and his son Bahadur Shah. Hell was let loose after Aurangzib died —the decades following were notable for intriguing, ambitious nobles. The empire lasted only three decades more; after Nadir Shah's invasion, the empire was but a name.

The rapid disintegration of the Mughul empire showed that mere exaltation of the emperor at the expense of the nobles was no solution. Basically, the Mughuls set up a military bureaucratic government centering round the personality of one person, the emperor, and its survival was entirely dependent upon his competence. There was no provision in the system to ensure stability when the rulers were weak. As Jadunath Sarkar observed, the bureaucratic nobles were "a selfish band, prompt in deserting to the winning side in every war of succession or foreign invasion, because they knew that their lands and even personal property were not legally assured to them, but depended solely upon the king *de facto*." In his view, only an independent nobility, having a stake in the preservation of the political system and continuance of the ruling family in strength, would have provided the required stability.[23] Thus, throughout Muslim rule, the management of the nobles was more of a problem than dealing with the Hindus.

The Status to be Accorded to the Hindus

These were the constraints under which the Muslim rulers were to formulate their policies in respect of the different communities and classes under their rule. Central to all else was the position accorded to the Hindus and the way they were treated in general. The Quranic tradition was well set before the Muslims entered India and came into contact with the Hindus. Apart from the Muslims or the faithful, only the People of the Book had a recognized place in the Muslim society — Christians, Zoroastrians Sabaeans and Jews. All others were to be given only the option of "Death or Islam". The conditions under which the People of the Book could be permitted to live among Muslims were laid down by the Covenant of Omar, which was binding. These were designed to emasculate them militarily and keep them as a subject class apart, easily distinguishable from the faithful. They were to be allowed the barest of freedom to practise their religion, and were to be made conscious of their inferior and subject status at every turn.

The initial question was whether the Hindus could be classed under the People of the Book, who were known generally as Zimmis. As mentioned earlier, only one of the four schools of Islamic jurisprudence — the Hanifah — was willing to compromise even to this extent. In the Indian situation, this was inevitable. From Muhammad-bin-Kasim to Aurangzib, all Muslim rulers considered Hindus as Zimmis, entitled to protection; this was the status accorded to them in *Fatwa-i-Alamgiri.* This was rarely questioned except by the ultra-fanatical. The endeavour of the orthodox Ullemas was to ensure that the Hindus were accorded no rights other than those permissible under the Shariah for the Zimmis. Their subject status was to remain firm and clear. It was impossible for Muslim rulers, at any stage, to take such a rigid view in administering a society in which Muslims were a small part. Despite the veneer and appearances, their problem was never one of enforcing the Shariah in letter and, spirit, a point which has been stressed overmuch. Except in stray cases such as imposition of the Jizya, the problems facing them were primarily political, though religious and communal considerations were also there. Granted Muslim political predominance, what were the steps necessary to keep the Hindus under subjection? To what extent was their participation in running the government necessary and was to be availed of? What was the extent of freedom they could be allowed, whether in the religious or the secular sphere, without jeopardizing the security and the interests of the state? To these primary questions asked in the pre-Mughul period, the Mughuls added another — what concessions could be made and what steps taken to reconcile the Hindus to Muslim rule as such and make them loyal subjects?

The Army and the Bureaucracy

THE RACIO-COMMUNAL STRUCTURE

Attention may be focussed upon the system as evolved and perfected by the Mughuls in respect of which we have adequate information. The Mughul Mansabdari was the central piece of both the army and the civil administration. A Mansab was a unit coalescing "into a pair of numbers exact indications of rank, payment, military and other obligations of the holder of a Mansab" —*Zakt* indicated personal (*khalsa*) pay and comparative status, and the *Sawr* the size of the contingent required to be maintained and the money sanctioned for the purpose.[24] The Mansabdari service was divided into 33 grades, the relative rank of each being expressed in terms of the number of Mansab holdings allotted to it. The lowest grade of the Mansabdari had ten holdings, and the highest grades were of 5,000 holdings or more. In 1595, according to the *Ain-i-Akbari* of Abul Fazl, there were in all 3,09,200 Mansab holdings — 1,90,000 were held by those of the rank of 500 and above, 42,000 by those of the rank of 200 and above, and 76,200 by those of lesser ranks.[25] No definite information as to the total number of Mansab holdings in later years is available, but it would be reasonable to hold that with the expansion of the empire, the number would have easily doubled. A Mansabdari rank was only indicative of the status of the holder and of his rights and privileges, and not of the specific duties he was called upon to discharge. In recruiting to higher offices, great value was attached to high birth, specially after the Mughuls came. From the beginning, under the Mughuls, those families which had seen service for more than two generations were known as *Khanzadas*; it is from this class all high-ranking appointments were made. The service was, however, always personal and individual; no hereditary claims were permitted to any office.

Detailed information is available only in respect of the Mansabdari of higher ranks. In Athar Ali's recent book, *Award of Ranks and Offices and Titles to the Mughal Nobility, 1574-1658*, we have a detailed and critical study of the Mansabdari service. Relevant statistical data pertaining to the tribal and communal composition of the service, based upon this study, are given in the tables annexed to the chapter. These have reference only to high-ranking Mansabdars — those of the rank of 200 and above under Akbar, and 500 and above under Jahangir and Shahjahan. Certain aspects of the impact of the policies pursued stand out from a scrutiny of the data. There was first the overwhelming predominance of Muslims over Hindus — they constituted over 80 per cent of the service most of the time. The Hindu position improved from 17 per cent under Akbar to 20.8 per cent under Shahjahan. Muslim predominance was even more pronounced among those appointed as governors of *Subahs* (Provinces). According to computerised calculations based on length of service, the Hindu *versus* Muslim scores were 15.5 : 76 under Akbar, 2.6 : 83.5 under Jahangir and 2.0 : 79 under Shahjahan. While such was the position among the high-ranking Mansabdars, Satishchandra has observed that, in the second half of the seventeenth century, "the proportion of Hindus in the nobility at various levels, from the highest to the lowest, rose to about 33 per cent."[26] This was evidently due to a larger proportion of Hindus gaining entry at lower officer levels. Satishchandra has also stated that the numerical importance of the Hindus did not decline even during the second half of the reign of Aurangzib, a view endorsed by other scholars.[27]

Within the ranks of Muslims, it was the Turani-Irani combine that was dominant all through: 72.4 per cent of the Muslim Mansabdars under Akbar, 58.9 per cent under Jahangir and 64.8 per cent under Shahjahan. As to the relative standing of the two classes, it was more or less even. If any one of them could be said to have had an upper hand, it was the Iranis and not the Turanis. The greater and the growing political importance of the Iranis was reflected in their position among the governors of provinces also —while it was 24 : 42 under Akbar, it rose to 35.5 : 23 under Jahangir, and 45 : 22 under Shahjahan. Irani predominance

was even more pronounced among the central ministers from
Akbar to Aurangzib. Athar Ali observes, "This virtual
monopoly by the Iranis of the offices of central ministers, with
the sole exception of the relatively minor office of Sadr, is
a remarkable fact. It continued under Aurangzib; ... Was it
that the Emperors trusted those who had no roots in the
country; and of such the Iranis happened to be culturally the
most advanced?"[28] Unlike the Iranis, the Afghans, who
constituted a substantial part of immigrant Muslims, were
kept at arm's length. Power had been wrested from them,
and they continued to be suspect. With the Mughuls gaining
stability and relations improving, the Afghan proportion
among high-ranking Mansabdars rose from 4.3 per cent under
Akbar to 8.4 per cent under Shahjahan. Still, their position
was lower than that of Indian Muslims and those classed
as Other Muslims.

Within the ranks of the Hindus, it is the Rajputs who
constituted the charmed circle for conferment of royal favours.
Of the Hindu Mansabdars of higher ranks, 82 to 85 per cent
were Rajputs. Besides, large numbers of Rajput zamindars
all over North India were admitted to lower ranks.[29] The
Bundelas and Marathas were important among the others
who entered the imperial service, the entry of the latter being
late.

No detailed information is available regarding the low-
ranking Mansabdars and the subordinate staff, but a clear
enough picture emerges from travelogues, chronicles and other
contemporary literature. From this, it appears that the
Muslims were predominant at these levels too. The Turanis
tended to crowd into the army, and the Iranis into civilian
posts. One could presume employment of other Muslims,
immigrant and local, in larger proportion at these levels. As
M.L. Roy Choudhury observes, "The Hindu efficiency was
utilised mostly from the converts as in the case of Qanungos
and Karoris."[30] The fact of Muslim predominance at these
levels is also borne out by the position they occupied in later
periods. Sir Alfred Lyall stated that the anti-Muslim attitude
of the British was manifest only after the Revolt of 1857,
and observed, "It is from this period that must be dated the
loss of the numerical majority [enjoyed by Muslims] in the
higher subordinate ranks of the civil and military services."[31]

Even as late as 1900, Lord Curzon's enquiries revealed continued Muslim predominance in the army.

	Muslims	Hindus
Native Army	90,500	48,500
Imperial Service Troops	11,500	5,000
Military Service and Military Police	14,500	9,500
	116,500	63,000

In the memorandum submitted by H.H. the Aga Khan to Lord Minto in 1906, a demand was made for safeguarding this predominance.[32]

Despite this all-round Muslim predominance in the army and the administrative services, there was one important and large field in which the Hindus held their own — revenue administration and finance. Since land and trade were mostly in Hindu hands and the villages were autonomous, administration could not be carried on without large-scale Hindu participation in these spheres. Indeed, Aurangzib and later the Nizam and Tipu tried to dislodge the Hindus from the higher subordinate levels in these spheres, but failed miserably.[33] Within the Hindu ranks, the Kayasthas and Baniya Agarwals in the North, and the Khatris in the Punjab, held a dominant position. Tarachand, R.K. Mukherjee and others have held that they largely replaced Brahmanas. This is very likely because the Muslim conquerors had a particular prejudice against Brahmanas whom they regarded as the symbol of the idolatrous faith, and the Brahmanas in turn had an aversion to serve such fanatical masters. It is, however, difficult to assess the extent of displacement, since we do not know for certain the position the literate non-Brahmanical castes occupied in the ancient Indian officialdom. In the South, Brahminical predominance was pronounced, though Prabhus and other literate classes too had a place.

PERSONNEL POLICY DICTATED BY IMPERIAL AND POLITICAL
CONSIDERATIONS

It is clear from the above that the Mughul army and the civil services were Turani-Irani dominated, and the wider compass of the Mughul power base was Muslim Ashraf and Muslim-oriented. This fact naturally lends itself to a purely communal interpretation. Though the structure bore a communal look, the underlying motivation was primarily materialistic — the pursuit of power. As a historical phenomenon, there was nothing new in this. Like all conquerors, the Mughuls came to power with the help of their tribesmen, and later broadbased the administrative structure by employing others in large numbers in the interest of their own security. The question of public welfare existed no doubt, but it always had a second place. If the Mughul policy in this respect is to be deemed 'communal', it would be difficult to find a ruling class which evinced a different outlook or acted differently.

A comparison with the policies pursued by other Indian rulers would be instructive. The Marathas rose to power with the help of a 'national' army, predominantly Maratha, despite the employment of foreigners, until the time of Baji Rao; the position began to change only with Balaji Baji Rao.[34] Satishchandra states, "Even a casual examination of the composition of the Maratha ruling class would show that it retained its regional character to the end. Hardly any non-Maratha rose to a position of importance in the Maratha states during the eighteenth century."[35] This was equally true of the Sikhs. Though Ranjit Singh employed others freely, including Afghans, it is the Sikhs who formed the bulk of his army, possessing a strong *esprit de corps*. Of the spirit animating it, Fauja Singh Bajwa writes, "An overwhelming majority of the Sikh soldiery was drawn from amongst the Sikhs who were not mercenaries, but who, on the contrary, regarded themselves as co-shareres in the glory which was symbolised in the establishment of Sikh rule at Lahore."[36] The position of Tipu was different. His power rested on a mercenary army, largely comprising outside elements and predominantly Muslim. That he regarded himself to be a Muslim ruler, depending upon the support of Muslims in particular, is clear from his many acts. As regards the public services in Tipu's Mysore, M.H. Gopal writes, "Of the *diwans* or provincial revenue heads in 1792 only one was a Hindu. Of the 65 *asafs* and deputy *asafs* and almost all the principal *mutasaddis* even were Muslims, while of the 26 civil and military officers captured by the British in 1792 and demanded back by Tipu only 6 were Hindus, and even they were petty clerks."[37] Also, in Tipu's army, a Hindu horseman was paid Rs. 40, while a Muslim was paid Rs. 5 more.[38]

The crux of the issue stands out when we compare the problem of Hinduization under the Mughuls with the Indianization of the army and the administrative services under the British rule. The British made no bones about the need to maintain the predominance of their own nationals. At the beginning of the British rule, Cornwallis said, "Without a large and well-regulated body of Europeans our hold of these vulnerable dominions must be very insecure", and in moments of crisis, "it would not be wise to place great dependence upon their countrymen who compose the native regiments to secure their subjection."[39] Speaking a century later, Curzon put forth the same view in a more polished way: as a general rule, the I.C.S. and the Imperial services were to be manned for the most part by the British — "the rule of India being a British rule... the tone and the standard should be set by those who have created and are responsible for it."[40] In his time, 90 per cent. of the civilian posts carrying a salary of Rs. 1,000 and more were held by Englishmen. In the British view, Indianization of the army and the general administration was necessarily linked with the transfer of power, a view reiterated again and again in the constitutional discussions between 1917 and 1935.

The point is that, in all these cases, the motivation was for the most part political — pursuit of power, though the administration bore a strong racial or communal look. If Indianization of the army and the civil services at the higher levels was linked with the question of transfer of power to Indian hands under the British, Hinduization of the same under the Mughuls and other Muslim rulers was linked with the normalization of the Hindu-Muslim relationship at socio-cultural levels and integration of the two communities. Viewed from this angle, it is significant that the level of Hinduization achieved under the Great Mughuls was twice or even three times the Indianization attained at the height of British power under Curzon.

GROWTH OF HETEROGENEITY IN THE SERVICES
AND PREVALENCE OF MERCENARY SPIRIT

The fact that the Turanis and Iranis in particular, and the
Muslims in general, constituted the power base of the
administrative structure did not make the army or the civil
services homogeneous and compact. These were as
heterogeneous as the society outside, whether Muslim or
Hindu. The problem of the heterogeneity of the ruling class
was already there in the Sultanate period and was of no small
importance. Under the Mughuls, no one community was in
a dominating position numerically. The Mughuls, the ruling
tribe, were no more than a sizable minority among the high-
ranking Mansabdars surveyed by Athar Ali — 32.8 per cent
under Akbar, 19.8 per cent under Jahangir, and 23.7 per cent
under Shahjahan. Others were worse off, except for the Iranis.
The pre-eminence attained by the Mughul emperors was the
result of this very factor. Their interest lay in not allowing
any one group to become too powerful. Satishchandra writes,
"The principle of balancing the various ethnic and regional
groups was also sought to be applied by Akbar to the
contingents that the *mansabdars* were required to maintain.
In the initial phase, the contingents of a large number of
the *mansabdars* consisted of tribal levies, or their clansmen
and fellow-countrymen. Gradually, definite rules and
conventions were developed regarding the composition of a
noble's contingent. While some Mughals and most Rajput
nobles continued to maintain contingents exclusively of
Mughals or Rajputs, mixed contingents seem to have become
the usual feature."[41] According to *Mirat-i-Ahmedi*, cited by
C. Irvine, in the case of cavalry, one-third was to be Mughul,
one-third Afghan, and one-third Rajput.[42] The policy could
not be implemented fully, because of the resistence of the
Mansabdars — it was easier for them to recruit from among
their own clansmen or countrymen and also these were likely
to be faithful to them under all circumstances.

Another significant factor was that the old-time tribal and
communal prejudices and antipathies were vanishing rapidly
as years rolled by, and there was no bar on employment
merely on grounds of race, community or creed. This was
reflected in the large-scale employment of the Hindus and

other non-Muslims by the Muslim rulers and of Muslims by the Hindu rulers, though may be only when it suited their interest; such employment covered sectors involving a security risk too. A number of facts may be cited to give a picture of the changing spirit of the times. Within the Muslims' own ranks, the rise of the Iranis who were Shias as co-sharers of power with the Mughuls — that in a Sunni state and a predominantly Sunni society — was a remarkable fact, if we keep in mind the intensity of the antipathy and strained relations between the two sects outside India. As regards the rise of individuals to high positions of trust and responsibility, apart from the well-known cases, reference may be made to Purniah, Krishna Rao and other Brahmana officers of Tipu Sultan, who were in his service to the very end. Indeed, prior to his appointment to the high office of the Dewan of the new Mysore state, Purniah espoused the cause of Tipu's son, Fateh Haidar, to succeed to the vacant throne, instead of supporting the claim of the Hindu ruler for restoration. He said that "Muslim interests were so much blended with every department of the state that any other arrangement could not reconcile the troops and powerful class of inhabitants."[43] Also, the employment of Rajputs as guards of the Mughul seraglio, and five hundred Pathans forming the nucleus of the private army of Guru Govind Singh, show how far the trust could go.[44] In recruiting to the armed forces, it would appear that every ruler had an eye on professional competence and availability of suitable men than wholly on race and community. This was clearly reflected in the composition of the armed forces as a whole and the position in the different sectors. Just as the Rajputs had an important place in the Mughul army, the Marathas figured large in the armies of the Bijapur, Golconda and Ahmadnagar rulers in the south. The Arabs were much in demand all over the country, and every substantial power engaged them.[45] It is said that Ranjit Singh set high store by the Gurkhas.[46] Shivaji had a Pathan regiment of Deccani Muslims, "who were children of the soil and opposed to the Mughuls".[47] In the later Peshwa period, the policy of Career Open to All caught hold of the administration, and S.N. Sen gives a graphic picture of the position resulting from it. The Marathas as a class preferred to serve in the cavalry, and were also generally unwilling to serve the whole year away from home. Therefore, to meet the needs of the growing empire, Balaji Baji Rao enlisted men from all parts of India — "Sikhs, Rajputs, Sindhis, Karnatakis, Rohillas, Abyssinians, and Portuguese". "In the Peshwa's personal force, the Arabs and other foreigners outnumbered the Marathas; in Holkar's army, the Pendharis preponderated over the paid mercenaries; and in Sindhia's armies, there were more Purvias than Maratha soldiers." Because of the Maratha reluctance to serve in the infantry, this wing came to comprise entirely outsiders. When Baji Rao II faced the British, most of his forts were garrisoned mainly by Arabs and non-Maratha Indians.[48] With the sprawling empire of the Mughuls, their armies were in no better state. Tipu's army was avowedly mercenary: "Among the Hindus, only the Rajputs and the Marathas were enlisted, while among the Muslims, the recruitment of Sheikhs, Sayyids, Mughals and Pathans was encouraged."[49] Ranjit Singh raised a picked professional army, and in terms of race and community, it was highly composite. His cavalry was almost entirely Sikh; his infantry was a mixture of Muslims and Hindus with a sprinkling of Sikhs; and the heavy artillery was manned largely by Muslims. Of the East India Company's forces, Cornwallis noted that in the Madras Presidency, the cavalry regiments were generally, and in the Bengal Presidency almost entirely, composed of Muslims, and in all the Presidencies, the infantry was mainly Hindu, with a few Christians on the coast of Coromandel and a few Jews in Malabar.[50] From this broad survey, it would be clear that, in the matter of recruitment to the army, tribal, racial, regional and communal considerations were severely subject to professional competence, the *de facto* needs of the state and other secular considerations. The army of almost every power in India in the eighteenth century was in fact a mercenary one devoid of faith or ideology, except in the case of the Sikhs. As Moncton Jones observed, "It was this mercenary character of the troops all over India that made English conquest comparatively easy."[51]

HURDLES IN THE WAY OF GREATER HINDUIZATION OF THE SERVICES

From what has been stated above, it is clear that there was

as such no aversion to employing Hindus, but their association with the higher ranks of the Mughul administration was limited mostly to Rajputs, wherever they could be found. By way of explanation for this singular fact, Satishchandra has suggested that in other areas the ruling or politically-oriented classes were not distinct and organized like the Rajputs.[52] Also, Tarachand has observed that the Mughuls had "anticipated the policy of employing only martial races", a policy adopted later by the British, and the Rajputs were the only recognized martial race at the time among the Hindus.[53] These explanations seem to be inadequate and unsatisfactory. Initially, the motivation behind the association of the Rajput rulers was primarily politico-military. The diplomatic way of subjugating them was to permit them to retain their regal power and authority as subordinate rulers, and the next step was to utilise their services in administering the empire by appointing them as high-ranking Mansabdars. This policy also helped in reconciling the Hindus as a community. The success of the policy at the higher levels gradually led to a wider participation of Rajputs at lower levels in many parts of North India. In areas where there were no Rajputs, the situation was different. Except in the tribal areas, Hindu resistance had vanished and princely families had been totally liquidated before the Mughuls appeared on the scene. There was no strong enough group left that had to be bought over. If the primary motivation had been reconciliation of the Hindus and not politico-military, there was enough material in the ranks of rich zamindars and chiefs all over the country to be inducted as high-ranking or middle-level Mansabdars. The Martial Class argument valid to some extent should not also be overstressed. The Marathas and the Sikhs did not belong to this class until the seventeenth and eighteenth centuries; the Telangana soldiers had not hit the headlines until the British employed them in large numbers. These observations do not apply to Akbar as his vision had a sweep of its own; his many acts show that reconciliation of the Hindus was at the forefront of his policies. After him, there was a clear lack of interest; under Aurangzib, there was a positive disinclination. The activities of the Muslim revivalists who emerged in opposition to Akbar's liberalism would have acted as a damper. That there was no

decline in the proportion of Hindus in the higher echelons
or that there was even a marginal improvement should in
itself be considered significant and progressive. This apart,
there is one aspect of the question which is rarely taken into
account. In politics, nothing is conceded until it is fought for.
Indianization of the services under the British was a product
of the national movement and the political struggle.
Hinduization under the Muslim rulers too was necessarily
linked with the rise in political importance of the Hindus,
the fight they put up and the needs of the state.

The Communal Factor in Fiscal and
Administrative Policies

THE LAWS IN FORCE AND THE ADMINISTRATION OF JUSTICE

Under Islamic law, the provisions of the Shariah were binding,
and these were to be enforced by all Muslims rulers; the latter
had no inherent power to legislate. None of the Muslim rulers
of India had the courage to question this. In practice, however,
as Ibn Hasan succinctly put it, "both Islamic law and the
Hadis ceased to be the code of government."[54] The Hindus
were left unhindered in the enjoyment of their personal laws
and customary life relating to marriage, inheritance,
functioning of caste, etc. As mentioned earlier, even the
converts to Islam continued to adhere to old-time caste laws
and customs. The attempts to wean them from their Hindu
ways were by ecclesiasts at the social level only and not at
the political level.

There was also no attempt by the Muslim rulers to effect
radical changes in the indigenous system of administration,
whether in principles or practices. They engrafted their own
revenue-collecting and peace-keeping machinery over the
indigenous setup, as W.H. Moreland has brought out very
well in his studies. S.N. Sen states, "While the Hindu
monarchies disappeared, the Hindu institutions survived."
Also, "The old institutions... continued to exist under the

Muhammadan rulers and so powerfully did they influence the administrative policy of Muslim kings that even the most careless comparison will be enough to establish beyond doubt the close affinity between the revenue regulations of Tipu Sultan of Mysore, a zealous follower of the Prophet of Mecca, and those of the Peshwas, the Brahmin defenders of the Hindu faith."[55] As a result, there were no revolutionary changes in the substance of the revenue or administrative laws. However, the adoption of Persian as the official language and its wide use in diplomatic transactions gave the administrative system a strong Islamic veneer.

As regards administration of justice, most of the cases, whether civil or criminal, were disposed of by panchayats or zamindars. When a person felt aggrieved, he could approach the state authorities, or even appeal directly to the ruler. The absence of a graded system of courts and well-regulated system of appeals, as introduced later by the British, was a major lacuna; but this acted as a check on litigation, a known evil under the British system. Muslim rulers took great pride in keeping the door of the hall of justice always open and in hearing cases personally. Writing in the early days of British rule, *Seir Mutaqherin* comments caustically on the aversion of the East India Company's officials to receive petitioners, compared with the easy accessibility of the Indian rulers. H. Raymond, the translator and a contemporary of the author of the *Seir*, observes, "There are no princes and no ministers on the face of the earth so accessible, and none so inclined to put up with the murmurs, the reproaches, and even the foul language of their disappointed suitors."[56]

In civil disputes in which both the parties were Hindus, the jurors were Hindus, knowledgeable in the Dharmasastras and local tradition and customs. A typical case was a dispute over customary honours in a temple at Srirangam (Tamilnadu) which came before the Nawab of Carnatic in 1792. The disputants were both of the Srivaisnava caste. The plaintiff claimed that it was his customary right as per inheritance to receive the holy water (*thirtha*) first before all others, and this right the respondent's ancestors had usurped. The Nawab first took an assurance from the parties that they would abide by his decision. Then, he associated with himself eight jurors coming from different Hindu castes who were knowledgeable in the affairs of the temple. The jurors supported the claim of the plaintiff holding that his claim was far anterior to that of the respondent. The Nawab, however, ruled that both the parties should enjoy the right alternately, one on the ground of earlier established right and the other on the ground of long usage going back to the days of Vijayanagara.[57] No great difficulties could have arisen when both the parties to a civil suit were Hindus. Where, however, one of the parties was a Muslim, the state courts stood by the Muhammadan law. This was on par with the application of English law to all persons resident in the Presidency Towns, whether Indian or European, with a view to ensure the enjoyment of their own laws by the British-born subjects living in India.

As regards the administration of criminal justice, the law enforced was the Muhammadan law as modified to suit local circumstances. This was on par with the application of the Hindu Criminal Law by the Peshwas.

We have no clear picture of the hardship caused and the extent of inequity suffered by the Hindus because of the application of the Muhammadan Law. That the issue was very much there and would have been of no small magnitude cannot be doubted. This would be clear from what happened during the first half of British rule, when a similar situation arose. Just like the Muslim Ashraf being attached to the Shariah and the Muhammadan Law as evolved in India, Englishmen in India were attached to their own laws and wanted them to be applied even in regard to their transactions with the local inhabitants. This was ensured by making English Law the law of the Presidency Towns applicable to all the inhabitants; only the Personal Laws of the Hindus and the Muslims were specifically saved. Special Crown courts were also established to handle cases in accordance with that law. These arrangements were considered to be opposed to Indian interests even in government circles, but the vested interest acquired by Englishmen in India could not be wholly eliminated until the passing of the Indian High Courts Act of 1861. The partiality for the English Law went so deep that there was a persistent attempt to make it the *Lex-Loci* or the law of the land where no other law was applicable until the idea was finally given up as being impracticable.[58] In one sector, they succeeded — the Indian Penal Code, which replaced the Muhammadan criminal law, was largely fashioned according to British concepts. It is interesting to note that a person like C. Rangacharlu, Dewan of Mysore (1881-83), who was nurtured in the British administrative system and held it in high esteem, felt that it was much at variance with native concepts of justice.[59]

TAXATION, REVENUE CONCESSIONS
AND PUBLIC PATRONAGE

There are innumerable references to acts of discrimination arising out of communal bias in the matter of taxation, revenue concessions and public patronage; it is not easy to piece them together. In the early years of his reign, Akbar fitted out a fleet of hundred ships for the Haj pilgrimage and gave each of the pilgrims Rs. 600. Under Aurangzib, the Hindus had to pay customs duties, while Muslims were exempt; also, they "had to pay land revenue and other taxes at double the rate that the Muslims paid."[60] Buchanan refers to the many concessions to the Ashraf and holy men in different parts of the country. Under Tipu in Mysore, Muslims were exempt from paying the whole of the house-tax and half the assessment on land; they were also exempt from taxes on grain and other goods meant for personal use and not for trade. In the army, a Hindu horseman was paid Rs. 40 a month, while a Muslim of the same rank was paid Rs. 5 more.[61] Haidar Ali was charged with taking over half the *Inam* lands while his son seized upon what was left.[62] Hindu scholarship and religio-cultural activities languished for lack of patronage, as mentioned earlier. In contrast, Islamic scholarship, architecture, painting, music, etc. centered round court life, and flourished with state support. Such discriminative measures could not but have been resented.

CURTAILMENT OF RELIGIOUS FREEDOM
AND OPPRESSIVE MEASURES

More than discriminatory financial policies, it was the specific

measures curtailing religious freedom and open attacks on
the religious life of the Hindus that did the greatest harm,
though the liberals had gained the upper hand under the
Mughuls. Of these, the imposition of Jizya, a capitation tax
levied on non-Muslims, was the most important, and it
attracted the widest attention. Strict conformity to the Shariah
required its levy. But there were loopholes if one was keen
on giving it a wide berth. It was a tax levied in lieu of military
service, which was compulsory for Muslims. Many Hindus
were in the service of the state and in the army, and not
all Muslims rendered military service. Further, under the
Shariah, *Zakat*, a tax collected for the benefit of the poor,
was to be paid by Muslims. In India, the tax was "seldom
collected by the state and for the purpose of public finance,
it was practically non-existent."[63] All through, the question
of Jizya was as much a political as a religious issue. For
the fundamentalists, its levy was a symbol of orthodoxy; its
payment in all humility in the prescribed manner was an
assertion of the power and glory of Islam. They could not
conceive of an Islamic state without the tax being levied. For
that very reason, the Hindus considered it to be extremely
humiliating and oppressive. With reference to the Sultanate
period, I.H. Qureshi has urged in extenuation that monks
and priests, the aged and helpless, were exempt, and there
was good enough evidence to show that cultivators did not
pay the tax.[64] It was not the financial but the psychological
and sentimental aspect that was most important. When Akbar
abolished it in 1564, he acted with great courage. In the words
of Lawrence Binyon, "It was an assertion of Akbar's will and
conscience against a tradition of all the Muslim conquerors
of India, sanctioned by centuries of custom, against all his
advisers."[65] Mughul liberalism in the subsequent years
centered round the tax being not resurrected. According to
Satishchandra, in the course of over two centuries of Mughul
rule, it was levied only during 57 years.[66] In his fanatical
desire to govern in conformity with the Shariah, Aurangzib
reimposed the tax in 1679, and raised a ghost that could not
be easily laid. Referring to the impolitic nature of the step
taken, a later-day Muslim chronicler observed, "Since the
death of the Prophet and his Khalifas, it had never been heard
that any of the kings of Iran, Turan, Rum or Shan,

notwithstanding their zeal for Islam, had imposed a poll-tax on unbelievers."[67] The strongly worded protest from Shivaji and the resistance put up by the Rajputs who were close to the Mughuls against its levy showed how much the emperor had alienated the Hindus by this one single act. After Aurangzib, the diehards were marked off from the liberals by their attitude towards this tax. While the Sayyid brothers won over the Hindus by their liberalism, Nizam-ul-Mulk wooed the diehards through his efforts to reimpose the Jizya.[68] It was only with the collapse of the empire following Nadir Shah's invasion that the controversy ended.

Compared to the Jizya, the pilgrim tax levied at major Hindu religious centres was a minor irritant. A. Sterling, in his account of Cuttack, states that the rulers of Orissa had been glad to pay the tax levied at Puri to the Mughuls to avoid harassment in other ways.[69] In any case, Akbar abolished it in 1563. Shahjahan reimposed it, but withdrew it on the representation of a renowned Hindu scholar of Benares. It does not appear to have been imposed by Aurangzib, perhaps because it was not mandatory under the Shariah.[70] In any case, the tax was being levied at Allahabad, Gaya and Puri in the nineteenth century, and it was abolished by the Government of India under Act X of 1840.[71]

Cow-slaughter was always an explosive issue. Under the Peshwas, there was a total ban. Views were expressed that it was not a religious necessity for a Muslim and could be avoided.[72] During the Revolt of 1857, when Hindu-Muslim accord was of paramount importance, Bahadur Shah forbade cow-sacrifice during the *Id* festival, and was anxious that nothing should be done to cause trouble.[73] This could not be the normal attitude at the height of Muslim power. Even when the Muslim chips were down, Malhar Rao Holkar could not persuade the Rohilla chief, Najib-ud-Daulah, with whom he was friendly, to ban cow-sacrifice even for a few days — "The practice is one of the religious commands (*amar-wa-nahi*) and I shall never give it up.", he said.[74] Opposite trends could be seen at the mass level, and very likely, the general position was not very different from what it is now. *Seir Mutaqherin* refers to a quarrel among two neighbours of opposite communities leading to cow-slaughter, followed by the murder of a Muslim boy and a general riot. The author felt that the local authorities had been too partial towards Hindus in handling the unsavoury situation. From the general narration of this and other events, it appears that the Hindus were able to hold their own at such times.[75] Again, reflecting the trend towards mutual accommodation, Buchanan writes with reference to the Dinajpur District in Bengal, "By far the Hindus are able to exert their influence to prevent it [cow-slaughter], and beef is not much consumed."[76]

There is then the question of destruction of temples and the ban on building new ones. For the Hindu, a temple is not merely a place of communal worship as in the case of a mosque or a church; in the theology of idol worship, it is a house of the living god. The ruins of temples all over the land stand mute witnesses to the havoc wrought. Trying to minimise its importance, Aziz Ahmed writes that any war with the infidels was considered to be *jihad*, and "the lip-service to *jihad* is occassionally accompanied by a minor demonstration such as the destruction of a temple, the panegyric of the court poet or the compliment of the court historian."[77] This assessment is hardly convincing. But, as stated earlier, it may be readily conceded that most of the havoc wrought was in the early years of Muslim rule and a by-product of wars waged. The Muslim rulers were generally pragmatic enough not to desecrate or destroy temples within their own kingdoms. Even so, the performance of rulers like Firoz Shah Tughlaq, Muhammad Adil Shah of Bijapur and Aurangzib hardly justify the view that destruction of temples was not there in peace time, in a conspicuous way if not on a large scale. Providing for exaggeration, the following account of the construction of the tomb of Murshid Quli Khan, Subahdar of Bengal, a favourite and apt disciple of Aurangzib, who died in 1727, cannot be wholly discounted: Murad, entrusted with the construction, "pulled down all the neighbouring Hindoo temples, and used the materials for raising the new work; the zamindars and other Hindoos would have preserved their temples at any price; but no intreaties or bribes could prevail; not one was left standing in Moorshidabad, or at the distance of four days journey from it."[78] Bewailing the havoc wrought by Aurangzib, a Muslim chronicler commented with acidity in 1817, "In the twenty-two *subahs*, wherever there was a Hindu temple, he erected a mosque over it, and appointed Imams and Muazzims."[79] Though temple destruction during peace time was a rare occurrence, it helped to sustain the *idee fixe* of the Hindus that Muslims were idol breakers. During the third Mysore War, when Tipu's forces attacked Tiruvannamalai, a famous pilgrim center of the south, Forrest writes, "The Hindu inhabitants, collecting the arms of the vicinity, prepared to defend the shrine from the usual foul Mohommadan desecration."[80] Nothing of the type envisaged happened. Indeed, there are few references to Tipu's forces indulging in such vandalism. On the contrary, the only major attack on a place held sacred as reported at the time was the one by the irregular troops of the Marathas under Parashuram Bhau at Sringeri, one of the four famous pontifical centres set up by Sankaracharya. Tipu expressed shock at what happened, and offered help to the pontiff, while the Marathas expressed deep regrets and offered reparation.[81]

Construction of new temples had to assume a low profile, since it came under the ban of the Shariah in a specific way. The policy of the rulers varied. Under the Mughuls, while Akbar lifted the ban, Shahjahan is said to have reimposed it.[82] The theoretical policy of the Muslim state, Aziz Ahmed observes, was to withhold permission for building new temples; this was "aimed at a gradual and tactful elimination of idol worship". He states further that "the policy seems to have been seldom enforced", since an extremely large number of temples have survived from medieval times.[83] From the point of numbers, the statement may be true; if it is so, it would be in accord with the general policy of the Muslim rulers not to interfere too much with the socio-religious life of the Hindus. But even a cursory survey would show that no big temples that could match the grand mosques of the day were constructed. This could not have been merely the result of lack of private patronage; the fear of the Sword of Damocles hanging overhead would have surely been an inhibiting factor.

The subject of Islamic proselytization has been discussed earlier. As regards the specific role of the state, Quranic society was, in theory, a missionary society, and it was the duty of the state to propagate the faith. The directive could not be taken seriously by the Muslim rulers in India. Of the Mughul times, M.L. Roy Choudhury writes, "Akbar refused to do so, though Jahangir made a few conversions, and Aurangzib a still larger number. ... On the whole, the spirit of the Mughul political philosophy had a changed outlook."[84] However, it has to be admitted that the proselytizing divines derived great help from several factors — Muslim political predominance, the state's recruitment policy in regard to the army and the public services, fiscal policy favouring Muslims, the generous state patronage to Muslim religious institutions, etc. The Hindus were handicapped in all these matters. This apart, there was a specific ban on proselytization by non-Muslims. Criticism of Islam in any manner was blasphemy; any attempt to wean away a Muslim from his faith was punishable with death. Sultan Zayn al-Abidin of Kashmir and Akbar were perhaps the only rulers who had lifted the ban openly.[85] It is clear that there was considerable laxity in practice. Otherwise, we cannot explain the activities of the Christian missionaries in Jahangir's court or the success of the many Hindu reformist saints, notably Chaitanya, who was not of the radical group, but attracted many Muslim followers. Also, it is known that Muslim ecclesiasts had a hard time in preventing reversions and holding the flock together. When complaints came from influential quarters, the state intervened. Abdul Rashid refers to one such case in the time of Shahjahan when he writes, "Prohibition of conversion to Hinduism and Christianity was justified as a defensive measure; enquiries made in Bhambar, an adjoining area, revealed that 4,000 Muslim women had been converted to Hinduism. Laws against blasphemy were made more stringent."[86]

Forced conversions fall into a different category. As stated earlier, this had no place after the early years of Muslim rule to any significant extent. There was, however, a persistent practice of forcible conversion of solidiers taken captive on the field of battle. Akbar had called a halt to this. But, Shahjahan went on record as having resorted to it while extirpating the Portuguese at Hooghly. Haidar Ali had recourse to it while subduing the Bedas of Chitradurga, and Tipu in reducing Malabar. As stated earlier, some have been inclined to view such actions as only an extreme form of punishment sanctioned by the spirit of the age, but the view makes light of their impact on the mind of the vast Hindu population.

Besides these matters concerning religious freedom, there were acts of discrimination designed to stress the inferior and subject status of the Hindu in vogue, with or without official sanction — that a Hindu should not dress like a Muslim, or ride a horse, or go by a palanquin, or have an umbrella carried over one's head as a mark of respect, etc. To what extent these and such other restrictions could be enforced and constituted a serious disability, it is difficult to say. As opposed to this, there were also conscious efforts on the part of the rulers and the Ashraf to tailor court life and develop closer social relations to reconcile and win over the Hindu. Such opposite trends were necessary parts of the process of integration.

LIBERALS VERSUS REVIVALISTS

The policies pursued in regard to the several issues considered above varied from one ruler to another. What we are concerned with here is the general trend. The thawing in Hindu-Muslim relationship could be seen well before the coming of the Mughuls. The Bhakti saints and the liberal Sufis prepared the ground. The response of the rulers was favourable, but had to be subdued and convert; they were in no position to antagonise the strong fundamentalist clique. The entire credit for lifting the state out of the quagmire and putting it firmly on a secularist path goes to Akbar, the one and only 'statesman' of medieval times, and the little band of his advisers. Free from communal prejudice, eclectic and appreciative of the merits of other religions and social systems, aware of the great responsibility resting on his shoulders as the ruler of a composite society, predominantly Hindu, he saw at a glance that the future of the Mughuls and the prosperity of the country lay in bridging the communal abyss, and building upon the affection and abiding loyalty of all his subjects. In his view, in the words of Abul Fazl cited earlier, "if the king does not regard all classes of men and all sects of religion in the single eye of favour...

he will not be fit for the exalted office."[87] In one clean sweep, he did away with the discriminatory laws and galling restrictions hurtful to the Hindus: the Jizya and the pilgrim tax were abolished; enslavement and forcible conversion of prisoners of war were stopped; the ban on construction of new places of worship was lifted; proselytization by non-Muslims was permitted; those converted to Islam by force or under abnormal conditions like drought or famine were allowed to revert to their ancestral faith; Hindu women forcibly married to Muslims were ordered to be restored; to crown all, even the law prescribing death penalty for being critical of Islam or the Prophet was abrogated.[88] His Din-i-Ilahi creed and the inter-religious meet at the Ibadat-Khana proclaimed his genuine respect for all religions. Nothing more could have been done to assuage the hurt Hindu feelings, and to assure them that they were completely free in the matter of religion. On the political front, his policy was no doubt expansionist, but he won over Rajputs more through his conciliatory policies than by force of arms. The place he gave them in the higher echelons of administration assured them and the other Hindus that they could look forward to becoming equal partners in the governance of the empire along with Muslims. Politically, it was as much a landmark as the Announcement of 1917 under which the British assured Indians that the goal in view as they demanded would be Responsible Government or Swaraj and they would be trained for the purpose. The promise Akbar held out was as important as the concessions he made. As the eminent historian Freeman observed, in catholicity of outlook and liberalism, "In his age, he stood alone, not only in Islam, but in the whole world; Catholic and Protestant Christendom might have both gone and sat at his feet."[89]

With Akbar, a non-communal and secular outlook had come to its own. It was no longer a force operating under necessity; it had a clear cut philosophy and outlook. This was as much reflected in *Seir-Mutaqherin* of the late eighteenth century as in Abul Fazl's *Ain-i-Akbari* earlier. But the one great shortcoming was that Akbar's ideas and policies did not find good enough support from any influential section of theologians and religious men. On the contrary, they provoked a sharp fundamentalist reaction, and there was an unabated succession of movements inclined towards orthodoxy and separatism down to the present century — Shaikh Ahmad of Sirhind and the Naqshbandi movement in the sixteenth and seventeenth centuries, Waliullah in the eighteenth, the Wahabis and Deoband in the nineteenth and the Khilafat in the present century. In comparison, the forces of liberalism were throughout weak, ill-organized and lacking in charismatic leadership, whether it be on the religious or the political front.

This weak spot made vigorous pursuit of Akbar's policies by his successors difficult. Jahangir and Shahjahan had a broad outlook, though instances of bigotry on their part too are cited. They could just maintain the *status quo* in the field of public employment and general policies. With Aurangzib, the position came to be different. As a ruler and administrator, he was the ablest of the Mughuls. Only, his religious fervour, his desire not to flout the known provisions of the Shariah, led to his reimposing Jizya and destroying temples. Several other acts of his relating to fiscal and general policies smacked of communal bias. It is well known that Hindu political resurgence was a direct outcome of his religious policy. Despite these happenings, it is important to note that Shias continued to hold most of the ministerial posts, and their strength as well as that of the Hindus in the bureaucracy improved rather than show a downward trend. This is a point going in support of the view sometimes expressed that Aurangzib did not in fact allow his views on religious and theological matters to affect his administrative actions and public policies. The available evidence points both ways and cautions us against dogmatism in evaluating his policies. Whatever the limitations, Aurangzib's religious policy ended with him. But the struggle between the liberal forces and orthodoxy continued. With the loss of political power, there was a sea change in the position of Muslims.

DIFFICULTY IN EVALUATION

One can easily pile up instances of racial and communal discrimination, and also of acts to the contrary. Motives and compulsions behind any policy or action are always multiple, and it is not easy to determine whether and to what extent racial and communal bias could have played a part. For instance, there is the common charge that Muslim rulers expropriated *Inam* and rent-free lands of temples and Brahmanas. In the Patna District, Buchanan noted that 37.5 per cent. of the land was claimed to be *Inam*. He observed that the claim was untenable, because under Muslim rule, "no grants of land were tolerated for the support of idolatory or of a pagan priesthood", no doubt an extreme view.[90] Again, as mentioned earlier, Haidar and Tipu were accused of taking away all *Inams* granted to temples and religious men. While acquiring the lands of the Brahmanas of Nanjanagudu in Mysore, Tipu gave them a monthly pension of hundred pagodas.[91] Who could say if this was not a fair enough compensation? As against the wide-spread charges against Tipu in this respect, we have this opinion of Sir Thomas Munro, who was in a position to judge: "It does not appear that the Hindu princes were much more scrupulous than Tipu in resuming *Inams*, ... for, if almost every prince gave away and none resumed, the whole country would in a short time have been converted into *Inam*."[92] Further, Tipu abolished rent-free land tenures of officials also and substituted cash payments, and this seems to have been the general state policy.[93] From these, it would be clear that a purely communal interpretation of his policies in this respect would be untenable. To take yet another instance, Aurangzib, the Nizam and Tipu tried at one stage to replace Hindu or Brahmana revenue officers by Muslims.[94] Were the steps they took due to communal reasons only or were they part of a policy to gain control over revenue administration dominated by Brahmanas and thereby improve the finances of the state as contended? As regards social disabilites such as restrictions on riding a horse or going by palanquin, Aziz Ahmed has a point when he says that these reflected a medieval attitude much more than merely communal bias.[95] All these caution us not to reach hasty sweeping conclusions in this sensitive sphere.

THE IMPACT OF THE COMMUNAL POLICIES ON SOCIETY

In our evaluations, it is important to remember that the impact of communal bias on the life of the people was far less than it appears. This was due to the fact that Muslims had failed to break the inner ring and their authority did not penetrate deep enough on the countryside. Village communities, castes and guilds, zamindars and chiefs, enjoyed a considerable degree of independence. This provided a thick-enough shell for protecting the people from communal excesses. No doubt they were helpless when the state brought in its superior force to enforce any policy or order. Taking a total view, such occasions were infrequent, because Muslim rulers were generally pragmatic in their approach. So long as the taxes were paid and there was no danger to the security of the state, they left the Hindus alone.

The rigour of the communal bias was experienced mostly by the Hindu elite, middle and higher, and in urban areas, the pivotal centres of Muslim power. Loss of political power, non-association in any big way in the administration of the country except at lower levels, drying up of state patronage to scholars and religious and charitable institutions, etc. left the elite weak and bankrupt. This has led some scholars to characterise the communal problem of the day as being primarily elitist. This was so to a great extent. But we should not forget that this could be said generally of all imperialisms. *Pax Romana* and *Pax Britannica* ensured peace and relative prosperity, and people were contented; it is the elite that felt the pinch, protested and revolted. On this ground, the contentment of the masses need not be dismissed as of no account.

Judged by contemporary standards the position in India does not seem to have been very different or particularly unsatisfactory. The Zimmis in Muslim countries outside fared much worse than the Hindus in India. We have a picture of it in the travels of Mirza Abu Talib Khan during 1799-1803. Of the Greeks under Turkish rule, he writes, "Even the most oppressed subjects in India are princes, when compared with these. The Turks adhere strictly to the Mahomedan regulations, of exalting the subjects of their own religion, and of depressing those of any other. The spirits of the Greeks are entirely broken, and they appear to have given themselves up to despair."[96] More than such accounts, the very survival of the Hindus, retaining most of their religio-cultural heritage and social institutions, unlike what happened elsewhere, is a decisive macro evidence to show that they fared relatively well. As regards Western Europe and the Christian world, it is well known that Roman Catholics in Protestant countries and *vice versa* fared badly and could well be classed as second class citizens. The French Revolution marked only the dawn of secularism. The fight with fundamentalist forces and vested interests went on for decades before it could take root. The sectarian fight among Christians at home was reflected in the policies of the colonial powers in India. The Regimental History of the Presidency of Bengal reveals that the East India Company had a bitter dislike for Roman Catholics. There was a ban on their employment which lasted well into the nineteenth century. Any officer or solidier who married a Catholic, or whose wife had become a Catholic, was to be transferred to the Infantry. Despite the popular jibe 'India was won by Irishmen under English officers for the benefit of Scotchmen', the British army in India was no more than ten per cent Irish at any time, and in 1881, there were only eight Irish batallions as against a total of 146.[97] It is generally held that religious neutrality and tolerance of native social institutions characterized the policy of the East India Company. Christian missionaries were sore with it. Bishop Heber complained, "We are in matters of religion the most lukewarm and cowardly people of the world."[98] The Company's policy in the early years was primarily governed by commercial and political considerations. With growing stability, particularly after the enactment of the Charter Act of 1813, the Company's attitude came to be not so neutral. While generally the Company's governments did try to keep out of the fray, the missionaries went hammer and tongs against native religions. The fanatical spirit in the air is clearly reflected in the Private Papers of the Company's administrators, let alone in the writings of the missionaries engaged in proselytization. The French in India were no different. Their attitude is clearly reflected in the pages of the Diary of Ananda Rangam Pillai, the *Dubash* of Dupleix — the pressures brought to bear on Pillai to persuade him to become a Christian, the efforts of the priests to get a native Christian appointed as *Dubash* instead of Pillai, Madame Dupleix's bigotry and close links with the priests, the fight over the Iswaran temple at Pondicherry between the Christian priests and the Hindus, etc.[99]

Taking all aspects into account, it would appear that the day-to-day life and material prosperity of the mass of the Hindus were not affected much by the inimical communal policies pursued by the Muslim rulers from time to time. Taxes were not oppressive; land being plentiful, it put a limit on exactions. The real harm done was in the realm of higher values. As pointed out earlier, Muslim domination over six centuries left the Hindus pathologically broken; the springs of their development and progress were choked. Subject to the qualifications made, Jadunath Sarkar's judgement, no doubt harsh and strongly worded, lays bare the essential weakness of the policies pursued: "With every generous instinct of the soul crushed out of them, with intellectual culture merely adding a keen edge to their sense of humiliation, the Hindus could not be expected to produce the utmost of which they were capable; their lot was to be hewers of wood and drawers of water to their masters, to bring grist to their fiscal mill, to develop a low cunning and flattery as the only means of saving what they could of the fruits of their own labour. Amidst such social conditions, the human hand and the human mind cannot achieve their best; the human soul cannot soar to its highest pitch. The barrenness of the Hindu intellect and the meanness of spirit of the Hindu upper classes are the greatest condemnation of Muhammadan rule in India. The Islamic political tree, judged by its fruit, was an utter failure."[100] This is a judgement, it should be noted, that is valid in respect of all imperialisms and also of all governments with narrow class support and not concerned enough with general welfare. The degeneration that had crept in was reflected in the social behaviour of the upper class Hindus: in the early decades of the last century, as illustrated by G.S. Mundy: "The Muslims were distinguished by the polish and suavity of their manners, a mixture of aplomb and reserve, while the Hindus clearly betrayed their feelings of insecurity."[101]

The Mughul Charisma as an Indicator of Relative Success

The rapidity of the collapse of such an empire as that of the

Mughuls was something astounding. Just thirty years or so passed between the death of Aurangzib and the invasion of Nadir Shah, after which the empire was but a name. None sought to topple it; it just crumbled since there were none strong and wise enough to sustain it. Several reasons are given for the decline of the Mughuls, which it is not necessary to go into here. It needs only to be stressed that the communal policy of the Mughuls cannot be considered the prime or even a major cause for the disintegration of the empire. Aurangzib's anti-Hindu policies died with him; their reversal by his successors did not save the empire, as clearly brought out by Satishchandra.[102] There was no doubt Hindu resurgence arising out of Aurangzib's policies. This was not so much a religious revival as a revival of militancy — the Hindus trying to come to their own in the political field. If it were otherwise, as Michael Edwardes rightly observed, "The Hindus should have been able to work together and establish a united Hindu dominion on the ruins of the Mughul empire."[103]

The best way of evaluating the success of the Mughul communal policy is to enquire into the respect, affection and loyalty the Mughuls evoked among the different sections and in the community as a whole, both at the height of their power and in the years of decline. At the zenith, while sovereignty was naturally confined to their possessions, the Mughuls had attained a pre-eminent position in the whole of the subcontinent; they commanded a high degree of deference and compliance to their wishes even from rulers not subject to them. Their power was considered to be irresistible, permanent and everlasting; they stood for peace and stability over the whole land. They were overlords in a way. This was reflected in the deferential tone of Shivaji's letter to Aurangzib protesting against the imposition of Jizya. It was seen in Sahu issuing directions that the Delhi Darwaja at Poona should not face north, since "a gate facing the north would mean defiance and insult to the *Badshah*." It came naturally to the Maratha Sardars to refer to the Mughul emperor in their own personal correspondence as *Sarvabhauma* (Supreme Ruler); Nana Phadnis referred to him as *Prithvipathi* (Ruler of the World) in his autobiography.[104]

The decline of the Mughuls did not merely create a power vacuum. Supplanting ruling dynasties when they lost their vigour and assertion of independence by subordinate rulers were nothing new. What was without any precedent was the widely prevalent consciousness of the need for a central authority. The Mughuls had concretised the concept of India's political unity with their expansionist policies and the highly-centralized bureaucratic system of administration they had set up. Fights and political manoeuvers following the death of Aurangzib should be viewed as conscious or unconscious efforts to ensure that this unity was not lost, and not merely as a fight for the central plum.

An outstanding fact was that none of the Indian powers, be it Hindu or Muslim, entertained the idea of eliminating the feeble Mughul, and stepping into his shoes. Only a Nadir Shah or an Ahmad Shah Abdali, uninhibited by local traditions and sentiments, could think of doing so. The Sayyid brothers had an emperor murdered, but felt constrained to find a successor among the members of the royal family. A heavyweight like Nizam-ul-Mulk retired to his Subedari in the south to stabilise his power there rather than continue to dabble in Delhi politics. The Marathas were not bound by old-time political ties and loyalties; they were also not inhibited by racial and religious sentiments like some others. They raised the cry of a Hindu empire, but they knew their own limitations. Instead of displacing the Mughuls openly, they sought to entrench themselves within the framework of the empire in diverse ways step by step. At the time of the invasion of Nadir Shah, the need of the hour was to save the empire. Baji Rao proposed to the Vazir of Oudh and others that "all the nobles, high and low, should join together with their armies in a kind of confederation as it were to reduce the affairs of the Timurid line to a better order, and to oppose 'the enemy', i.e., the foreign invader." As Satishchandra observed, "Carried to its logical conclusion, this new approach implied the establishment of a kind of confederation under the overall direction and control of the Peshwa, with considerable autonomy for the various 'powers' constituting it, and the retention of the Timurid monarchy as a symbol of unity and a rallying center in case of foreign danger."[104] Mahadji Sindia took a big step forward to achieve the same objective when he accepted the office of *Vakil-i-Mutlaq* (Regent Plenipotentiary), and hoped to revive the empire with Maratha arms and the Mughul's prestige. Tarachand characterized Mahadji's action as the purchase of "a worthless bubble at a very high price." It did not appear to be so to contemporaries. Major Browne, the East India Company's envoy to the Mughul at Delhi, reported to Warren Hastings, "This office being superior even to that of the Vizier, Sindia by this step raised the Maratha power above every other in the empire."[106] Even as late as the Revolt of 1857, the Mughul and the Peshwa were the only two rallying points for the rebels; neither could be ignored.

The charisma of the Mughuls in the years of decline is comparable to the halo of the Roman empire when it was fading out. This was not merely a question of the happy memories of bygone times. What was of significance was the value still attached to the Mughul empire as an institution, as a vital reality that could take the country out of the morass it had fallen into, and make it unified, strong and prosperous again. Percival Spear rightly observes that there was for the Mughul's authority "something of the reverence and spirit of acceptance which exists in Britain for Parliament," and this persisted.[107] Even at the close of the eighteenth century, the charisma was great. Of this, Wellesley and his council wrote in 1804, "Notwithstanding his Majesty's total deprivation of real power, dominion and authority, almost every state and every class of people in India continue to acknowledge his nominal sovereignty. The current coin of every established power is struck in the name of Shah Aulum. Princes and persons of the highest rank and family still bear the titles, and display the insignia of rank which they or their ancestors derived from the throne of Delhi, under the acknowledged authority of Shah Aulum, and his Majesty is still considered the only legitimate fountain of similar honours."[108] Of all the rulers of the day, Tipu Sultan was alone in forswearing allegiance to the emperor openly, and in claiming to be a *Padshah* and having the *Kutba* read in his own name. Even he took this step only after his attempt to get the Mughul's recognition was thwarted by the Nizam, according to I.H. Qureshi.[109] The Nizam's action in having the *Kutba* read in the emperor's name again on the fall of Seringapatam was to set right the wrong done.[110]

In this background, knowing the depth of the Indian

sentiment, the British acted with great circumspection in dealing with the emperor's claims to allegiance and acts of fealty. The East India Company began its political career as a servant of the Mughul in accepting the *Diwani* of Bengal, Behar and Orissa at the hands of Shah Alam, when it could have claimed the provinces to be British territory by right of conquest. Later, when it was toying with the idea of taking the Mughul under its wings, Shah Alam switched over to the Marathas for support. This gave the Company a convenient excuse for not rendering the customary acts of fealty, and also for not seeking recognition in respect of the new territories it acquired. There was, however, no open defiance or denial of allegiance. The matter was left vague deliberately. In 1797, Sir John Shore visited the Begum and the sons of the late emperor, paid the usual *Nazars* and accepted the robe of honour conferred. In 1804, Wellesley persuaded Shah Alam to come under British protection, since the possession of his person and control of his activities were considered to be of great political value. While acts of fealty indicative of subordination were resolutely dropped, the emperor was not deprived of his title and many of the ceremonial privileges right upto 1857. A categorical assertion of the sovereignty of the British crown was made only in 1813, that under the Charter Act and the Treaty of Paris of that year; at the same time, the superscription 'Servant of the Emperor' was omitted from the official seal.

The British were even more circumspect in seeking to terminate the sentimental ties subsisting between the Indian princes and the emperor. In 1818, the ruler of Oudh was persuaded to assume the title of Nawab dropping the title Vazir, which he was proud of bearing hitherto, but denoted subservience to the emperor. A similar attempt in the case of the Nizam did not succeed, for the rulers of Hyderabad were always proud of their unswerving loyalty to the Mughul and the Mughul tradition. At the time of the Revolt of 1857, the coinage of most of the Princely States bore the name of the Mughul. It was not until 1872 that all the princes and chiefs of the country were persuaded to drop it, those of Sind still constituting an exception. The name of the British Queen was inscribed only by a few.[111] While the Company's rule ended and the direct administration of the country was taken

over by the Crown in 1857, it was only in 1877 that Queen
Victoria assumed the title Empress of India.

This persistence of the Mughul charisma and .its impact
on socio-political life for more than a century after the death
of Aurangzib constitute the best macro evidence we have for
the relative success of the Mughuls, evaluated in terms of
loyalty evoked. It should, however, be noted that there was
a significant difference in the responses of the Muslims and
the Hindus. To the former, Mughul rule had symbolised the
glory of Islam, and the power and solidarity of the Indian
Muslims. Further, as a community, they had enjoyed special
socio-political privileges. It was only natural that the eclipse
of the Mughuls touched a more tender chord among them.
Apart from the attitude and conduct of the Muslim elite, the
charisma was reflected at the level of the masses in 1857.
The British considered the Revolt, not without reason, more
of a Muslim affair than Hindu. At the same time, it would
be wrong to think that sentiments of loyalty had not been
evoked in great measure among the Hindus. The tolerant and
liberal administration of the Mughuls had brought in a breath
of fresh air for the Hindu, and also raised in him high hopes
as to the future. It is the thwarting of this very hope that
had given rise to the Hindu political resurgence under
Aurangzib. Despite this regress, it is clear that under the
Mughuls, acquiescence was changing to acceptance, and a
spirit of genuine loyalty developing. This is evident from the
attitude of the Rajputs during the trying years of Aurangzib's
reign and also in the after years when the Mughul affairs
were in shambles. This is reflected in the poor response to
the Maratha slogan favouring *Hindu-pad-padshahi*. This also
finds expression in the high hopes and despair of the common
man who had a high opinion of *Pax Mughaliana*, as seen
from contemporary records. Broadly, it could be said that the
Muslim response was overt, positive and enthusiastic, while
that of the Hindu was subdued, tending to be neutral. It is
clear that the Mughuls had not wholly succeeded in welding
the two communities politically, and could not evoke an equal
degree of affection and loyalty in each of them. If it were
otherwise, the British would have had no place in India. On
this score, it would not be right to underrate the positive
achievements of the Mughuls.

APPENDIX

Racial and Communal Composition of the Higher Ranks of Mansabdars in Mughul India

Note: 1. The statistical information is taken from Athar Ali's *The Apparatus of Empire: Award of Ranks, Offices and Titles to the Mughul Nobility, 1574-1658.*

2. The data furnished refer to the following years: 1595 A.D. (Akbar); 1621 A.D. (Jahangir); and 1656-57 A.D. (the last year of Shahjahan's reign).

3. The Mansabdars have been categorised under the Highest, the High and the Medium on the basis of the number of Mansab holdings held by them, the Princes forming a separate class. The criteria adopted under the three Emperors were as follows:

	Highest	High	Medium
Akbar	3,000 & above	500-2,500	200-450
Jahangir	5,000 & above	1,000-4,500	500-900
Shahjahan	5,000 & above	1,000-4,500	500-900

TABLE - A

Mansabdars — Highest, High and Medium

	1595	1621	1656-57
PRINCES	4	4	8
Iranis ...	75	68	139
Turanis	93	48	123
Afghans	10	15	34
Indian Muslims	36	35	59
Other Muslims	18	31	49
Rajputs ...	40	34	87
Marathas ...	—	1	12
Other Hindus	7	6	7
TOTAL	283	242	518

TABLE - B

Racial Composition within the Ranks of Muslim Mansabdars (Exclusive of Princes)

	1595	1621	1656-57
Iranis	75 (32.3%)	68 (34.5%)	139 (34.3%)
Turanis	93 (40.1%)	48 (24.4%)	123 (30.4%)
Afghans	10 (4.3%)	15 (7.6%)	34 (8.4%)
Indian Muslims	36 (15.5%)	35 (17.75%)	59 (14.3%)
Other Muslims	18 (7.7%)	31 (15.7%)	49 (12.1%)
TOTAL	232	197	404

TABLE - C

Relative Position of Hindus and Muslims among High Ranking Mansabdars (Exclusive of the Princes)

	Highest	High	Medium	Total
1595				
Muslim	17	80	135	232 (83%)
Hindu	4	18	25	47 (17%)
1621				
Muslim	17	120	60	197 (82.8%)
Hindu	3	28	10	41 (17.2%)
1656-57				
Muslim	13	171	220	404 (79.2%)
Hindu	4	52	50	107 (20.8%)

TABLE - D

Racial and Communal Composition of Governors of Subahs on the Basis of the Length of Service

	Akbar	Jahangir	Shahjahan
Iranis	24	35.5	45
Turanis	42	23	22
Afghans	0.5	3.7	2
Indian Muslims	8.5	21.3	10
Muslims Race Unknown	1	—	—
Hindus	15.5	2.6	2

Notes

1. *Tuhfat-al-Mujahidin*, 51-2, 60.
2. U.N. Ghoshal in R.C. Majumdar, *The Delhi Sultanate*, 653-4.
3. S.N. Sen, *The Maratha Administrative System, 475.* Karandikar, Chapter II.
4. H.G. Franks, 35. S.N. Sen, *The Maratha Administrative System*, 216.
5. S.N. Sen, *ibid*, 475.
6. Aziz Ahmed, *Islamic Culture*, 81.
7. D.C. Ganguly in R.C. Majumdar, *The Struggle for Empire*, 51.
8. Lallanji Gopal, *Journal of Indian History*, Vol.43, No.129 (1965), 933-5. It may also be noted that *Jizya* was called *Turushka Danda*. — S.A.A. Rizvi in G.A.Oddie, *Religion in South Asia*, 34.
9. James Mill, Vol.II, 429. Also, Satishchandra, xxx; Bipin Chandra in Romila Thapar, 46-7; and J.S. Grewal, *The Medieval Indian State*, 9-10.
10. M. Mujeeb, 36.
11. T.G.P. Spear, 16.
12. M.A. Karandikar, 118-9.
13. Satishchandra in *The Spirit of India*, Vol.II, 79.
14. Satishchandra, xix.
15. Mohammad Yasin, 27.
16. J.S. Grewal in *The Medieval Indian State*, 11.
17. Tarachand, Vol.I, 127, 129.
18. M.L. Roy Choudhury, 148.
19. For a vivid description of the scene of the submission of the renowned Durga Das to Aurangzib, see Jadunath Sarkar's *Futuhat-i-Alamgiri* of Isardas Nagar, 168f, 181-2—Mss. in the National Library, Calcutta.
20. Percival Spear, 74. At the time of the Mutiny, Bahadur Shah claimed that the Timurid empire was "an imperishable religious institution and as such was not subject to dissolution." — Roy Choudhury, p. 118.
21. M. Mujeeb, 36.
22. M.L. Roy Choudhury, 88. Sri Rama Sharma in *The Medieval Indian State*, 26-7.
23. Jadunath Sarkar, *Mughal Administration*, 53-4.
24. Athar Ali, xi-xii.
25. *Ibid*, xiii.
26. Satishchandra in *The Spirit of India*, Vol.II, 79.
27. Satishchandra—*Proceedings of the Indian History Congress*, Presidential Address, Medieval Indian Section.
28. Athar Ali, xxiii.
29. Satishchandra, xxviii. It would seem that the policy of roping in Rajputs had been initiated in good measure by the Gujarat Sultans in their career of expansion earlier.— U.N. Dey in *The Medieval Indian State*, 68.
30. M.L. Roy Choudhury, 274.
31. Tarachand, Vol.II, 349.
32. *Ibid.*, Vol.III, 402-3.
33. Aurangzib—Tarachand, Vol.I, 155. Tipu and Nizam — M.H. Gopal, 71; Nikhilesh Guha, 32-3.

34. S.N. Sen, *Maratha Military System*, 62-3.
35. Satishchandra, in Bisheshwar Prasad, 173-4.
36. Fauja Singh Bajwa, 349. All the Muslims taken together in the irregular cavalry were 1,029 out of 10,795 under Ranjit Singh and 2,431 out of 19,754 under Jawhar Singh. In the regular infantry, they formed only a small minority. That there was no aversion towards Muslims or hestitation in employing them on a large scale whenever necessary could be seen from their constituting more than half the total strength of the artillery. *Ibid.*, 143.
37. M.H. Gopal, 71.
38. Nikhilesh Guha, 79-80.
39. George Forrest, 29-30.
40. S.V. Desika Char, *Readings in Constitutional History*, 390.
41. Satishchandra, xxviii.
42. William Irvine, 9.
43. Mohibbul Hasan, 320-1.
44. Khushwant Singh, Vol.I, 78.
45. S.N. Sen, *Maratha Administrative System*, 451.
46. Fauja Singh Bajwa, 140-1.
47. S.N. Sen, *Maratha Military System*, 61-3.
48. *Ibid.*, 62-5, 94.
49. Mohibbul Hasan, 351.
50. George Forrest, 149. N.K. Sinha, 167. Sitaram Kohli, Vol.I, 7-8. Khushwant Singh, Vol.I, 209.
51. Moncton-Jones, 26.
52. Satishchandra, Introduction.
53. Tarachand, Vol.I, 144.
54. Ibn Hasan, 61.
55. S.N. Sen, *Maratha Administrative System*, 486.
56. *Seir Mutaqherin*, Vol.III, 158 and note 118.
57. Hari Rao, The Carnatic Nawab's Decision over *Thirtha* Honours— *Proceedings of the Indian History Congress* (1966), 342-6.
58. S.V. Desika Char, *Centralised Legislation*, 194-7.
59. Dewan Rangacharlu's *The British Administration of Mysore* (1874). -Reprinted in the *Quarterly Journal of the Mythic Society*, January-June 1988, pp.20-22.
60. Jadunath Sarkar, *Aurangzeb*, Vol.IV, 313. M.L. Roy Choudhury, 189-90, 225. J.N. Chaudhuri in R.C. Majumdar, *The Mughul Empire*, 235. A.L. Srivastava in *ibid.*, 542.
61. M.H. Gopal, 68, 91. Nikhilesh Guha, 79-80.
62. Read's letter to Harris, Commander-in-Chief, 2 July 1797, para 10—Mss. Record, G.No.18156, Madras Record Office. Crisp's opinion— M.H. Gopal, 91. Also, Buchanan, *Northern Parts of Kanara*, 50; *Mysore, Canara and Malabar*, Vol.I, 57.
63. Tarachand, Vol.I, 135.
64. I.H. Qureshi in R.C. Majumdar, *The Delhi Sultanate*, 450
65. Lawrence Binyon, 63. R.C. Majumdar, *The Mughul Empire*, 115.
66. Satishchandra, 261-2.
67. William Hoey, Vol. I, 151.

68. Yusuf Hussain Khan, 153. Also, Satishchandra, 176.
69. A. Sterling, 133.
70. Aziz Ahmed, *Islamic Culture*, 81.
71. S.V. Desika Char, Centalised Legislation, p. 311.
72. Tarachand, Vol.II, 370-I.
73. Percival Spear, 207-8.
74. Jadunath Sarkar, An Original Account of Ahmed Shah Durrani's campaigns in India and the battle of Panipat — *Islamic Culture* (1933), 433-4.
75. *Seir Mutaqherin*, Vol.I, 72-5.
76. Buchanan, *Dinajpur*, 76.
77. Aziz Ahmed, *Islamic Culture*, 79.
78. F. Gladwin, 121-2.
79. William Hoey, Vol.I, 151.
80. George Forrest, 63.
81. B.A. Saletore, Tipu Sultan as a Defender of the Hindu Dharma— *Medieval India Quarterly*, Vol.I, No.2, October 1950, pp.43-55.
82. M.A. Karandikar, 115.
83. Aziz Ahmed, *Islamic Culture*, 88.
84. M.L. Roy Choudhury, 151.
85. Aziz Ahmed, *Islamic Culture*, 86-7.
86. Abdur Rashid in R.C. Majumdar, *The Mughul Empire*, 213.
87. M.L. Roy Choudhury, 148. Ibn. Hasan, 61.
88. A.L. Srivastava in R.C. Majumdar, *The Mughul Empire*, 539-40.
89. *Ibid.*, 139.
90. Buchanan, *Patna and Gaya*, Vol.II, 561.
91. Buchanan, *Mysore, Canara and Malabar*, Vol.II, 148.
92. Mohibbul Hasan, 342.
93. Regarding acquisition of rent-free tenures of the police and the watch and ward by Tipu, see Report of the Magistrate of Canara, 30 March 1812—Mss. Vol.8 A, No.33, pp.1983-4. (Madras Record Office).
94. Vide note 33 above.
95. Aziz Ahmed, *Islamic Culture*, 90. Alexander Hamilton, p.158, regarding such practices in the Hindu kingdom of Keladi.
96. C. Stewert, *Mirza Abu Taleb Khan's Travels*, 242 *et seqq*.
97. Major Hobbes, Scrap from Fort William Regimental History—*Bengal, Past and Present*, Vol.LIII, Sl. No.105, January-March 1917, 7.
98. O' Malley, 322.
99. *Ananda Rangam Pillay's Diary*: attempts at conversion and appointment as *Dubash*—Vol.II, 62, 157-8, 210, 215, 244-52; Madame Dupleix's bigotry and links with priests—Vol.VIII, 248-51; the Iswaran temple episode, Vol.V, xii, 299-315; overbearing priests—Vol.III, 249 and Vol.VIII, 334.
100. Jadunath Sarkar, *Aurangzeb*, Vol.III, 296-7.
101. G.C. Mundy, 247.
102. Satishchandra, 266 *et seqq*.
103. Michael Edwardes, 5.
104. S.N. Sen, *Maratha Administrative System*, 185-6.
105. Satishchandra, 189, 238.

106.   Tarachand, Vol.I, 165-6. R.C. Majumdar, *The Maratha Supremacy*, 390.
107.   Percival Spear, 9.
108.   S.V. Desika Char, *Readings in Constitutional History*, 133.
109.   Aziz Ahmed, *Islamic Culture*, 53.
110.   K.M. Panikkar, *The Foundations of New India*, 66.
111.   Surjit Singh Randhawa, Change of Superscriptions on Coins in Native
       States, 1858-72—*Proceedings of the Indian History Congress*, 1966,
       pp.396-404.

CHAPTER 4

Patriotism — Resistance to Foreign Aggression and Rule

In **popular perception**, patriotism is associated only with armed resistance to foreign invasion and rule. But it has a much wider connotation — it is the love of hearth and home and of all the cherished institutions of the community one lives in, and the sacrifices people are prepared to make in their defence when they are in jeopardy. The fight put up could be of various kinds and conditioned by the socio-ethical values cherished and other factors. The term would cover overt submission when resistance is futile, but covert resistance holding up the progress of the aggressor or acting as a brake on the exercise of his authority; sullen acquiescence, waiting for an opportunity to revolt; and also getting into a shell, keeping away from the path of the aggressor in social and public life and cultural matters to the extent possible. Finding safety in flight could be another solution — the Quakers, opposed to war and armed resistance, left for the New World, and the Parsis found refuge in India; the wandering Jews cherished the memory of their homeland in exile. It is necessary to have a wider view of patriotism than the conventional one. The form patriotism took in India was different at different times, conditioned as much by tradition and cultural heritage as by changing historical circumstances.

Loyalty to Rulers in Ancient India

Patriotism is often evaluated in terms of loyalty towards the state as constituted, and the readiness and zeal evinced towards its protection. There were two factors on which it depended, both equally important: identity of interest and sentimental attachment between the rulers and the ruled; also, whether a change in rulers spelt danger to cherished institutions. In Ancient India, the first factor was very much there, but the second was conspicuously absent. Changes in ruling dynasties hardly affected the life of the people. The new rulers received taxes based on custom, and the elite of all categories found sure patrons in them. Even the defeated rulers were not driven to the wall; mostly they continued in power occupying a humbler status. Changes in socio-economic institutions were few; custom and tradition ruled as of old. The eclectic tolerant atmosphere that was very much there in socio-religious life permeated political life as well. No doubt a different situation presented itself whenever there was an influx of foreigners like the Sakas and the Hunas. Even this posed no great challenges; the aliens were rapidly indigenized and absorbed before long. We have no knowledge of the many tensions and conflicts that should have been there. Macro evidence is, however, clear on there having been no crises of any magnitude. In the absence of serious threats to cherished institutions, and life proceeding on an even keel, there was little scope for sanguinary manifestations of patriotism. From this it would be wrong to conclude that the people had no sense of loyalty towards the rulers or the royal families. The 'true to salt' spirit evinced by a bureaucracy and an army and all those who enjoyed royal patronage was bound to be there. Also, there was no gulf separating the rulers from the ruled; the people were attached to the rulers unless they had been antagonised by bad government. This is clear from the fact that the states were longlived, their life extending over a couple of centuries. For a continent like India, there were not too many of them, and the subnational factor also played its part providing a measure of unity at the level of the individual states. Many scholars have dismissed manifestation of patriotism in ancient India as expressions of dynastic and personal loyalty and no more.

It is only in the works of B. Subba Rao and Y.A. Raikar that we have a good appreciation of its role and importance. That patriotism did not find expression more intensely as we view it today was due to the simple fact that there was no need for it.

Hindu Resistance to Muslim Invaders and Muslim Rule

It is only with the Hindu resistance to the Muslim invaders and Muslim rule that the issue of patriotism assumes real importance; later, it is a question of Indian resistance to the establishment of British rule. There is one marked difference in the nature of the struggle on the two occasions. British rule was alien from the beginning to the end; it was a plain question of fighting imperialist domination. In the case of the Muslim invaders, as long as they retained their alien outlook and were regarded as aliens, the problems were one and the same. But the invaders were soon indigenized and became a part of the Indian community. Thereafter, patriotism as an issue got transformed into a class and communal struggle — the Hindus fighting the entrenched dominant Muslim Ashraf for their rights and privileges. The crux of the issues was, however, the same in either case: Why did the Hindus succumb to the Muslim invaders? How is it that they put up with Muslim rule, oppressive and discriminatory as it was in many ways, for so long? What was the level and character of the community consciousness, whether as a nation or as a religious community fighting for its rights? Similar questions are to be answered in regard to India falling a prey to the British.

GROWTH OF MUSLIM POWER: PACE AND LIMITATIONS

Because of the ease with which the Hindu kingdoms were overthrown and the fact of six long centuries of Muslim domination, there has been very inadequate appreciation of the resistance the Hindus put up and the extent to which they were able to hold their own in different sectors. This is partly due to the fact that we have hardly any Hindu version of the events; most of what we know comes from Muslim chroniclers and foreign travellers who visited India. There is first the fact that the pace of conquest was slow. The forces of Islam swept like a tornado, conquered the whole of Western and Central Asia, Northern Africa, and several parts of Southern Europe, within sixty-seventy years of the Prophet's passing away (632 A.D.). Nothing like that happened in the case of India. The conquest of Sind in 712 A.D. by the Arabs under Muhammad-ibn-Kasim amounted to nothing more than gaining a precarious foothold over two frontier towns, Multan and al-Mansurah. The several invasions of Muhammad of Ghazni between 1000-1027 A.D. were primarily for loot, though the inclusion of Afghanistan and the Punjab in the kingdom of Ghazni gave a good foothold for the Muslim expansion later on. It was only two centuries later, with the Ghurids, that the Muslim conquest of India began in earnest. What the Ghurids began, Ala-ud-din Khalji and Muhammad-bin-Tughlaq completed. Muslim arms penetrated deep into the South, and the progress was halted only by the rise of Vijayanagara. By the mid-fourteenth century, Muslim political predominance in the country as a whole had been fully established. There was further expansion under the Mughuls; but their real achievement lay not so much in acquiring new lands for Islam as in consolidating the gains made and establishing a strong centralized empire. What the Muslims achieved in the course of a century and a half, the British achieved at much less cost in men and materials within about fifty years with much better results.

Besides the slow pace of conquest, Muslims were never able to establish their authority over several parts of South India and Orissa, and also over the forest and inaccessible regions of Madhya Pradesh, Chota Nagpur, Rajputana and Maharashtra. Besides, even where they planted their standard, their success lay primarily in overthrowing the rulers at the top, and not in establishing their authority effectively over the whole country-side. The resistance offered by the little worlds with their autonomous villages, chiefs and zamindars proved to be too much for them. We have a vivid account of what was happening in a contemporary account of the early thirteenth century, the biography of

Dharmasvamin, a Tibetan pilgrim monk: the Hindu and Buddhist kings of Bengal and Bihar were leading a precarious existence, "too weak to oppose the Muslim forces, but strong enough to emerge from their forest retreats and re-establish their rule when the invading army had passed away."[1] Bengal was never at peace till 1613 A.D., when it was completely subjugated by Jahangir.[2] As to the final outcome, S.B.P. Nigam writes, "it is now clear that the Turkish arms constituted by the nobility having failed to disturb the inner ring of the Hindu society, concentrated mainly in developing an urban civilization with military strength as its nuclear power."[3] As described earlier, in the socio-economic setup that emerged, landed wealth, trade and commerce remained mostly in Hindu hands. While a large chunk of the Hindu population got converted to Islam, the Hindu society as a whole was able to weather the storm, and retain its religion and cultural identity intact. This is well exemplified by a random fact — outside India, wherever Islam spread, the Arabic script came to be imposed, displacing local scripts; in India, it was only Sindhi and Kashmiri that adopted the script, apart from Urdu.

Two different explanations are offered for the slow progress of Muslim arms and the survival of the Hindu society in strength unlike others. The Arabs and the later Muslim rulers, it is said, did not take the conquest of India seriously for long. By the time they did, the fanatical spirit of *jihad* or holy war had cooled down. The Turks were after power and wealth, not converts. The roots of their pragmatism, their willingness to make peace with the Hindus, lay in their indifference to religious considerations. This view has considerable merit, and cannot be brushed aside. But, there was, at the same time, the innate political and cultural strength of the Hindu society and the stubborn resistance offered, the aspects stressed by U.N. Ghoshal, R.C Majumdar, P.V. Kane, K.M. Panikkar and others. In their career of conquest, those invading India may not have had the fanaticism of the Arabs, but a good bit of the *jihad* spirit was surviving in them. In the politico-military struggle, the invaders won the first round with top honours, but clearly lost the second. There is no need to attribute any spirit of benevolence to them. If they could have displaced the chiefs

and zamindars easily, they would have done so, and parcelled
out the land among their followers, just as the Normans did
when they invaded England. The political wisdom and relative
tolerance which they exhibited should be considered to have
been due as much to the strength of the opponent as to the
cooling down of the zeal for religion and their limited
resources.

THE HINDU MILITARY DEBACLE

It is not the slowness of the progress of Muslim arms that
should cause surprise, but the ease with which big, ostensibly
strong, kingdoms were toppled. Of the success of the Ghurids,
Aziz Ahmed writes that their regime had become "the
laughing stock of Muslim Asia for its intrigue, lack of
discipline and morale, and military inefficiency", their home
land was trampled by hostile troops, their economic resources
were nil, they had no constitutional virtues; yet, "the mules
succeeded where the war horses had floundered." Of the whole
series of events leading to the success of the Turks, R.C.
Majumdar writes, "It is puzzling, nay almost baffling, to
explain the almost complete collapse of Northern India, within
an incredibly short time, before the onslaught of invaders
whose power and resources were hardly equal to those of some
of the bigger Hindu states, not to speak of a combination
of them." S.N. Sen observes that the collapse of the Yadavas
"at the first attack delivered by an external foe does not argue
well for its military capacity."[4] In most of the cases, it was
a matter of a pygmy laying low a giant.

Several explanations are offered for the Hindu failure on
the military front — intrinsic superiority of the invaders; the
power of the Muslim cavalry against the Hindu elephants;
the rapidity of movement and the blitz-kreig tactics adopted;
the use of canon and firearms from the time of Ala-ud-din
Khalji; the false sense of chivalry for which the Rajputs were
noted; the Hindu tradition of viewing a battle as a tournament
for one to exhibit his fighting capacity and personal prowess;
etc.[5] Puzzling as it may be, the fall of the kingdoms at the
first blow must be attributed to military weaknesses — in
weaponry, techniques and organization. But some more

puzzling facts of no less significance call for an explanation. Why was there no attempt to re-form troops and fight a guerilla war in the plains as much as in the hills and inaccessible regions? Why did the Hindus acquiesce so easily and so quickly to alien rule and live as a subject people for centuries? Why did they not avail of their overwhelming superiority in numbers and the other advantages they had to assert themselves, that in the face of the gravest challenge ever posed to their religion and culture? In essence, why did Hindu patriotism reach such a low ebb?

DECENTRALIZED POLITICAL SYSTEM IN THE WAY

OF EFFECTIVE RESISTANCE

While the crushing defeats on the battle fields can be explained in military terms, the inability of the Hindus to organize an effective defence system was due to several general factors of great significance. The most important of them as a proximate cause was the inherent weakness of the political system. The Hindu system of government was basically decentralized, both in conception and structure. There were no doubt big kingdoms and empires. But, as Tarachand has said, they were "conglomerations of more or less autonomous units."[6] The vivisection went deeper. As would be explained later, the centre of gravity of the Hindu political system, its vitality and strength, lay primarily in the villages and towns. Highlighting this aspect, K. Satchidananda Murty observes, "The state as a union of autonomous towns and villages was a great and unique political contribution of India."[7] Whatever be the virtues of the system, they were not conducive to united action against the invaders. There were no strong bonds holding the rulers and their subordinate chiefs together based upon politico-economic inter-dependence, making reciprocal cooperation a vital necessity for survival. This was far less in evidence than in feudal Europe. As a result, whenever a ruler at the top was overthrown, those below were more concerned with safeguarding their individual possessions and interests than on restoring the ruler or getting the ruling family back to power. They transferred their loyalty to the new ruler much too quickly and easily. This weakness in the political heritage did not prove catastrophic in pre-Muslim India. The contestants belonged to the same religio-cultural milieu; a change in rulers had only political consequences affecting individuals at the higher rungs of the political ladder; it posed no challenge to the community as a whole affecting adversely its economic and cultural interests.

It was an altogether new situation that was created when the Muslims invaded. Traditional attitudes die hard, and overhauling established institutions is by no means easy. The Hindu chiefs constituting the second line of defence did not realise the immensity of the danger ahead, and the paramount need for unity and concerted action if the danger was to be countered. This is the best explanation that can be offered for single battles proving decisive, and the absence of prolonged guerilla wars, excepting in deserts, forests and other inaccessible regions. When Clive entered Murshidabad with 200 Europeans and 500 sepoys, he is said to have remarked that "the inhabitants if inclined to destroy the Europeans might have done it with sticks and stones."[8] The position was not altogether different earlier. The Hindu chiefs failed to realise that their real stength lay in the people, and in mobilizing their support in all possible ways to fight the enemy. If they had risen to the occasion and provided the necessary political will, better defence could have been put up, and the invaders worsted.

The shortcoming arising out of this factor, the decentralized political system, was very much in evidence in later times too. After the disastrous battle of Rakkasa-Tangadi (Talikota) and the sack of Vijayanagara, the Muslim rulers who had joined hands just for the occasion had fallen out. All had not been really lost. If the subordinate chiefs had banded together and acted cohesively, the position could have been retrieved, and the empire set on its feet again. It is the spirit of localism ingrained in the Hindu political system and the absence of a wider, secure loyalty-base that stood in the way. In the case of the Marathas too, Shivaji had held under check the self-centeredness and spirit of independence of the *Watandars* and founded a kingdom that could face the might of the Mughuls. Later, the Maratha state came to be loose knit, following the traditional Hindu pattern. Outside *Swarajya* or the Maratha homeland, the conquered chiefs retained their autonomy, paying *chauth*; the Maratha generals sent out to conquer carved out autonomous principalities for themselves, with limited allegiance to the central authority at Poona.[9] The Marathas had not learnt from the Mughuls, who had set up a strong centralized administration based upon bureaucratic principles.

THE MYTH OF THE KSHATRIYA CLASS

The strong hold the varna and the system of caste have on our minds has led to the presumption that there was a strong organized warrior class in the Kshatriyas at the time of the Muslim invasions, and it failed to rise up to expectations. Tarachand talks of wars being "the business of princes and kings and of the caste whose vocation was fighting."[10] M. Mujeeb writes that because of the caste system and the position of the Kshatriyas in it, the total resources of the state were never involved, and "in times of need even no conscription of members of the non-military castes could be made, nor would military service normally be open to them."[11] It has been explained earlier that this view is incorrect. The Hindus had no martial class or caste at the time except in theory. Though they may have had a martial political tradition, the Rajputs came to be regarded as Kshatriayas of blue blood and honoured only because of their heroic struggle in fighting the Muslim invaders; otherwise, they were regarded as *vratyas* and not of the pure breed. Satishchandra is appreciative of the point when he says that the Mughuls were handicapped in the appointment of Mansabdars of high rank outside the Rajput clan, because the politically dominant or ruling classes were not distinct or organized.[12]

THE CHARGE OF GENERAL POLITICAL
AND CULTURAL BREAKDOWN

There have been many attempts to link the political and military collapse of the Hindus with the several weak spots in their socio-cultural life. Some have gone to the extent of holding that there was an all-round breakdown which helped Islam and Muslim arms to force an entry with such success. Speaking of the clash between "the two degenerate and decaying social systems — the Turkish and the Rajput," Aziz Ahmed writes, "in this clash, the former proved itself to be decisively superior, for in war as in peace, success depends upon comparative merit."[13] Many others, less forthright, have hinted at it while dwelling on particular shortcomings. A general survey of the times would show that there was no such breakdown as could justify the expressions used. If there was regress in one sector, there was progress in another; if one region lagged behind, another forged ahead. As regards the political map, the Gurjara Pratiharas, with an empire as large as that of Harsha, had faded out, the power of the Palas of Bengal was on the decline, and the North was in a state of relative disarray; but further south, the Later Chalukyas and Kalachuris of Kalyani, the Yadavas of Devagiri, the Hoysalas and the Great Cholas were strong and powerful. In the field of religion, Buddhism had declined, but its place was taken by resurgent Hinduism all over the country. With the change in faith, Buddhist art and architecture had given place to remarkable developments in temple architecture and sculpture. Sanskrit had lost its classical flavour, but the cultivation of the language and the literary output had not declined. Indeed, Kashmir was a great center of Sanskritic learning just prior to the invasions by Muslims; in South India, contributions to metaphysical speculations by scholars and divines who attained eminence were of the highest order. If there was any shortfall, it was amply made up by the emergence of the several vernacular languages and their growing literary output. It is said that there was an increase in caste rigidity, a sign of degeneration. Apart from this being a natural defensive reaction, the view itself is based upon the dicta of the Smritis, and not on the life as lived, about which we have such scanty information. The several religious movements preceding and succeeding the Muslim invasions exhibited clearly the Hindu capacity for resilience; if it were not so, the Hindu society would not have survived. As U.N. Ghoshal says, the Hindu collapse was "not due, as has been held, to a wholesale decadence of her civilization, or even to a marked degradation of her social life in comparison with the earlier times."[14] The correct appreciation would be that at the time of the Muslim invasions, the Hindu society was as healthy as it was earlier; it was unfortunate that it was subjected to a severe viral attack and the anti-bodies proved powerless.

THE ROLE OF THE HIGH AND LOW AND RIGIDITY OF CASTE

Of the particular aspects of the Hindu religion and culture which could be construed to have militated against effective Hindu resistance, it is the system of caste that is generally put in the dock, both by Hindu and non-Hindu scholars. The restrictions and taboos regarding commensality and free social intercourse, it is said, came in the way of the effective functioning of the army, and also prevented many of the higher castes from joining the armed forces. Aziz Ahmed writes, "The Indian army overridden by caste system could not be anything but a display of soul-racking taboos. May be, a tenth part (or less) of the whole population was in arms, the remaining nine-tenths serving as menials in the fields and sleeping in the distant villages." Even R.C. Majumdar writes that foremost among the causes for the downfall of the Hindus seemed to be "the inequitous system of caste and the absence of contact with the outside world."[15] As stated earlier, the view that the Kshatriyas survived as a varna and constituted the main fighting force in medievial times is erroneous. Hindu armies were from very early times sufficiently broadbased without reference to varna or caste. Also, the functioning of castes was sufficiently flexible when it came to adjustments in the matter of social behaviour to meet the needs of army life. In his in-depth study of the military system of the Marathas, S.N. Sen has pointed out that the Maratha empire was born and flourished when the caste system was there, strong and virile. Rejecting the assessments of M.G. Ranade and Jadunath Sarkar, he says, "The caste system has beeen responsible for many evils in India, but for the real cause of the downfall of the Marathas, we must look elsewhere."[16] Again, if caste rigidity has not been much of an impediment in the functioning of the army under British rule and at the present time, there is no reason at all for attaching a higher value to it in regard to the earlier periods.

Apart from caste rigidity, there is the question whether the feeling of high and low of caste and inter-caste rivalries and jealousies undermined the loyalty of the army and of the people in general to any significant extent. Stray cases of treachery and crossing over could be cited; these were bound to be there. The adverse impact of this factor does not appear to have amounted to much, if we go by the detailed scrutiny and assessment of the Maratha administration by S.N. Sen. A.L. Srivastava, who is highly critical of the caste system in general, observes, "Caste might have been a powerful cause of weakness and lack of solidarity; but there is no recorded or unrecorded evidence to show that at that time any group or section of the people refused to cooperate with their rulers in the time of war or of an invasion, or there was any desertion from their armies for reasons of caste. Baneful though the castes were, they had not acquired the political values they possess in the present democratic setup in the country."[17]

There is, however, a theory advanced that at the time of the Ghurid invasion, there was a social revolution, the disfranchised lower castes in urban areas embracing the new faith in large numbers, and helping the invaders to conquer their fellow countrymen. Advancing this view, Muhammad Habib wrote, "This was a turnover of public opinion — a sudden turnover, no doubt, but still one that was long overdue. The Indian capacity for fighting was there, but it had not been simply called to play — people will not fight for their chains. The so-called Ghorian conquest of India was really a revolution of Indian city labourers led by the Ghorian Turks — under the new regime the army became a function of the new working class."[18] The strength of the theory rests on two facts — the rapidity and ease with which the Ghurids and later rulers effected their conquests, and the concentration of Muslims in urban areas. That the invaders could overthrow only the rulers at the top but were unable to pierce the inner ring goes against the view that the disfranchised lower classes among the Hindus welcomed and supported them. The large proportion of Muslims to be found in urban areas can be easily explained by the towns having been the focal points of Muslim power and the beneficiaries of the state and Ashraf patronage congregating there. Further, there is no evidence of any wide-spread social disaffection arising out of caste differences or of social conflicts of magnitude at the time, whether in urban or in rural areas. No doubt one may refer to the anti-caste aspect of many of the contemporary religious movements. But this, as noted earlier, had no significant bearing on the political and military happenings of the day.

HINDU TOLERANCE AND ABSENCE OF A WAR CRY

In the search for an explanation for the failure of the Hindus, it is only the rigidity of caste, its high and low, and other deficiencies that have attracted attention. Hardly any attention has been paid to the possible adverse impact of Hindu tolerance and eclecticism and the flexibility of caste, presumably because they are taken to be progressive and always for the good. Surprising as it may seem, it is these very factors that contributed most to weaken Hindu resistance.

Muslim invasions and Muslim rule provided the greatest possible provocation to the Hindus — they lost political power; their religion and cultural life were in jeopardy. Yet, there was the strange phenomenon of the saints and religious leaders of the day not raising a war cry. The only exception was the mild remonstrance of Guru Nanak on the pusillanimity of the Lodis at the time of Babar's invasion, according to U.N. Ghoshal.[19] When the third Sikh pontiff, Guru Amar Das, was asked to rise against the tyrannical acts of the local Muslims, he said, "It is not proper for saints to take revenge."[20] This was the characteristic and general attitude of the Hindu religious leaders. When, later on, there was a touch of militancy, they always talked of safeguarding the Hindu Dharma, never of an attack on the opponent's faith or institutions in retaliation. Ramdas urged, it is said, "A man should pay attention to *prapancha* (worldly or temporal demands) first, and then *paramartha* (the fruit of spirituality) will follow." His message was directed against too much of passivity. He wanted people to rise against Aurangzib, because of his brazen attacks on the Hindus as a religious community.

He did not condemn Islam or brand Muslims as a class as enemies.[21] Hindu militancy reached its peak when Guru Govind Singh gave the Sikhs two swords — *phakiri* (spiritual) and *amiri* (temporal). Even then, it was only in self-defence, directed against the Mughul authority, and not against the Muslims.[22] It is significant that this was by a sect that went farthest to be the bridge-builder between Hinduism and Islam, and not by the orthodox and conservative wing of the Hindus.

Not only was there no war cry raised in self-defence, it was remarkable that the oppressive and discriminatory treatment often accorded to the Hindus in regions under Muslim rule did not provoke retaliation in those under Hindu rule. Shivaji no doubt founded a Hindu kingdom; he proclaimed that it was for the restoration of the Hindu Dharma. But his concept of a Hindu state did not envisage persecution of Muslims or denial of equal rights to them. He is said to have maintained mosques at state expense, and even Kafi Khan praised him for venerating Muslim saints.[23] As explained earlier, this was the general attitude of the Hindu rulers, despite the happenings elsewhere. In the long history of Hindu-Muslim relations, K.G. Saiyidain states, "Except when prejudices of others awakened their emotional wrath, the Hindu has never desecrated the Holy shrine of another, be it a mosque or a church." He further observes with great perception, "With rare exceptions, Hindu religions have not exploited political and economic life for the material gains of religious groups," and "if Hinduism had played the role that the Christian church played in Europe, the history of India would have been different."[24] This Hindu tolerance appeared very strange to foreign travellers — while they saw many temples desecrated or destroyed by Muslim fanatics, they rarely came across a tomb or a mosque ravaged by the Hindu. The Oriental Memoir of 1838 noted, "A conscientious Hindoo would esteem it a crime to deface a Moslem place of sanctity or a Christian church, and would anticipate retribution for such an offence" — it was a sin according to the *Sastras* or dictates of his religion.[25] While armies fought many a battle, it is seen from contemporary records that inter-communal clashes at the mass level were rare; the prairie on the countryside where the Hindus had the upper hand did not catch fire.

Hindus were not also perturbed by the large scale conversions to Islam that were going on. While Islamic proselytism was always there, though varying in intensity, it is significant that conscious effort to stem the tide came only with the rise of the Arya Samaj at the close of the last century. No doubt the Bhakti movement had halted effectively the spread of Islam. But, as Tarachand noted, it was "politically sterile".[26] It lacked militancy; it did not carry the battle into the enemy's camp. On the contrary, the teachings of the syncretic Bhakti saints like Kabir who appeared early on the scene watered down whatever militancy the Hindu could command — one could not hug an enemy and fight him at the same time.

For a valid explanation of the enigma presented by the Hindu attitude, we have to think in terms of the values developed right from the Vedic days. Nurtured in an eclectic and tolerant religion and culture, the Hindu could not be intolerant towards other faiths, however alien they were. Islam could not be viewed otherwise than with respect; Muslims could not be hated or fought with only because they professed another faith. Besides, there was the ingrained belief that non-violence was superior to violence; while those attached to worldly life could have recourse to violent means to achieve justifiable ends, those devoted to God were to avoid it. Hatred and recourse to violence, whatever the provocation, were reprehensible. There is a well-known episode in the life of the Maratha saint Eknath — the saint took a bath 108 times in the river, each time after a Muslim rowdy spat at him, insulting him and trying his patience; in the end, the rowdy became an ardent disciple of the saint.[27] Eknath has always appealed to the Hindu heart much more than Shivaji mounted on a horseback with a flashing sword. On the whole, the tolerance exhibited towards Islam and the Muslims as a community all through and the absence of a war cry in defence of religion by religious leaders deprived the Hindu of much of the zeal required to fight the enemy.

CASTE FLEXIBILITY AS AN IMPEDIMENT TO EFFECTIVE RESISTANCE

There is another factor of psychological importance that

impaired Hindu resistance. As stated earlier, caste rigidity and
rivalries were not of that consequence as often made out. On
the contrary, in the sequence of events, it is the very flexibility
and adaptability of the system of caste that helped the Muslim
rulers in a big way, an aspect that has received hardly any
attention. Most of the Muslims in India were local converts.
On conversion, they came to constitute just another caste in
the Hindu style. The Hindu was accustomed to changes in
sectarian beliefs and emergence of subcastes grounded on faith.
Conversion to Islam was many steps removed from changes
within the Hindu fold and was out of the ordinary. But that
was no reason why tension was to be allowed to build up.
The needs of the Hindu castes and the requirements of the
local community were adequately met when the converts
formed their own groups and did not infringe upon the rights
or interfere with the lifestyle of others, including those of the
parent stock. Indeed, as and when Muslims emerged as a group
in a locality, invariably retaining much of the Hindu
characteristics, they were neatly fitted into the structure of
the local community. There was no doubt a period of stress
and strain, but that was passing. Along with this development,
the immigrant Muslims also came to be indigenized. In the
Hindu eyes, they too constituted just another caste like the
local converts. When we survey the pre-Mughul scene, we
should be impressed by the rapidity with which adjustments
were taking place. The employment of Muslims by the
Vijayanagara rulers and of Marathas by the Bahmani Sultans,
Hemu heading an Afghan-Rajput force against the Mughuls,
and such other events showed that the initial antipathy was
wearing off. Much more significant was the rise of the syncretic
Bhakti saints coming close on the heels of the Muslim
conquests. The Hindu, true to his own tradition, was accepting
the Muslim, whether convert or immigrant, as an equal
member of society. The process no doubt helped in maintenance
of peace and furthering the cause of integration, but the
militancy of the Hindu in fighting the Muslim got undermined.

OTHER FACTORS FAVOURABLE TO MUSLIM SUCCESS

In contrast to the Hindus whose will and capacity to resist

were undermined by the several factors considered above, Muslims, both as invaders and rulers, were in an advantageous position in a number of ways. There was first their religious zeal and determination to carry the message of the Prophet to the ends of the world. Success on the field of battle was considered to be a success for the faith. Political ambition and the will to conquer were never wholly divorced from religious fervour. Muhammad of Ghazni was twice honoured for his *Jihad* against India by the Khalif. Apart from zeal, both as invaders and rulers, Muslims had the advantage of being one integrated solid community as compared with the Hindus. When they belonged to the same tribe, the bond of unity was at the highest. Even when they came from different tribes, the bond of unity arising from common religion and cultural traits held them strongly together. They were marked off sharply from the indigenous population — they were the ruling class, devoted to arms and the profession of ruling, true Kshatriyas in the classic sense, united and strong. The Hindu had *de facto* no warrior class to match, excepting for the Rajputs in a small way. Besides, they set up a strong militaristic centralized administration with a well-organized bureaucracy; without this, they could not have retained their power that long. Despite the promptings of fanatics, they exhibited a good measure of worldly wisdom and spirit of pragmatism which made for success. Their primary and only weakness lay in their being small in numbers, almost microscopic, in an alien land.

Once the alienness of the immigrants wore off and Muslims as a class came to be regarded as being members of a common society, from the point of view of the Hindu, the Muslim rulers had as much right to govern as any others in the non-democractic setup of the day. As G.S. Sardesai observed, "The Hindus always attached greater importance to the preservation of religion than to political freedom," and the causes for the Hindu revolts leading to the rise of Vijayanagara and of Shivaji were more "cultural than political."[28] On sentimental grounds, the Hindu, specially the elite who stood to benefit, may have preferred a Hindu *raj*. But what people craved for most was a just and good government. This was not merely the attitude of the Hindu in the situation he was in; it is a universal phenomenon, often overlooked, as Ernest Gellner has brought

out very well in his study *Thought and Change* (1964).[29]
Peace and good government, the Mughuls provided in good
measure. Under their beneficent rule, the sullen acquiescence
of the Hindu was getting transformed into genuine acceptance
of Muslim rule, and the progress registered was more than
halfway.

A GENERAL APPRAISAL OF HINDU PATRIOTISM

To sum up, the common and generally expressed view is that
the patriotism of the Hindus in their confrontation with the
Muslims was at a very low ebb, even touching the nadir, since,
inspite of the overwhelming superiority in numbers and the
other advantages they possessed, they allowed themselves to
be a subject race for nearly six centuries. How this happened
is an enigma. The Hindu was not wanting in personal courage
or readiness to sacrifice. His love for the land he knew and
the local community he lived in was great; he could not be
easily uprooted. He had pride and stubborn attachment to his
religion, culture and way of life. Al-Biruni, with his liberal
outlook, was critical of his claim to "exclusive superiority"—
"The Hindus believe that there is no country but theirs, no
king like theirs, no science but theirs."[30] It is clear that the
Hindu was not wanting in natural patriotism. It is this that
enabled him to weather the storm — he could retain much
of his local independence, and also his religion, culture and
way of life. This was no mean achievement when we see how
others fared. The failure was at the higher political levels
wherein the confrontation proved cataclysmic. The causes for
it stemmed ultimately from the nature of the Hindu religion
and culture, from the tolerance and eclecticism ingrained in
them. These qualities were no doubt beneficial under certain
circumstances, but in the present case they proved to be focal
points for cracks to develop. Lack of homogeneity and social
solidarity arising out of caste came in the way of concerted
action to some extent, but the weakness arising out of this
factor was much less than often made out. This was because
the Hindu social system as a whole had found general
acceptance, and there was no room for tensions and conflicts
of the type and order that existed between Shias and Sunnis,

and Roman Catholics and Protestants, in other countries. As such, inadequate social homogeneity does not appear to have been a major factor for the Hindu debacle. Of greater consequence was the heritage of a decentralized political system. As would be seen later, the bottom layers of the political pyramid were firm and strong, but the superstructure was weak — this was reflected in the difference in the resistance offered at the two levels. The most seminal and determining factor was the weakening of the will to resist, because of the perspectives and ideals developed. The spirit of 'live and let live' that was generated and permeated the whole of the Hindu thought and society all through history did not permit anyone to be regarded an alien or as an enemy for long. Besides, there was the readiness to compromise at every step, a willingness to accommodate the intruder or the rebel much too soon. These factors did not prove catastrophic in meeting the challenge of the earlier invaders, the Sakas and the Hunas, as the attitude of the latter was entirely different. The present conflict was with a fundamentalist, militant community that was intent on imposing on all its own religion and socio-political order with fanatical zeal. The Hindu approach may have made for peace and helped in the process of integration, but it could be of little help in stemming the Muslim tide, either on the politico-military front or in the field of socio-religious life. Hindu patriotism had a particular blend that accounts both for its successes and failures. There was an intense attachment to land, religion and culture. May be, in the face of the challenge posed, it was less liberal, cosmopolitan and progressive in outlook than in earlier times. But it was at no stage chauvinistic, intolerant or aggressive. The patriotism of the Hindu was an expression of his particular brand of nationalism, which was not narrow in outlook.

Indian Resistance to the Rise of British Power

THE BRITISH CONQUEST OF INDIA AS A DIPLOMATIC ACHIEVEMENT

The issue of loyalty and patriotism is common to Hindu

resistance to the Muslim invaders and their rule and the Indian resistance to the rise of the British power. But the circumstances and the general nature of the problems encountered were not similar.

An outstanding fact was the rapidity with which the British extended their power and stabilized their authority over the whole subcontinent. To say that the British 'conquered' India would be inaccurate; all that they did was to shake the tree lightly and the fruits fell into their laps. For the vast empire acquired, the battles fought and won were not militarily of any great significance; the achievement was mainly in the field of diplomacy. India was conquered with Indian money and Indian forces, helped by the neutrality, connivance or active support of Indian rulers.

The Great Mughuls had achieved much, but the Mughul system depended too much upon the personality of the emperor, for achievements as much as for survival. When the strong hand of Aurangzib was removed, the empire came to be at a loose end. The absence of a central authority was felt keenly. The nobles, however highly placed, were only bureaucrats; they could not command the traditional loyalty and prestige attached to hereditary rulers. There were frantic efforts to sustain the authority of the emperor and bring the affairs of the empire to order. But these ceased to be of significance after the devastating invasion of Nadir Shah and the sack of Delhi in 1739. The Subedars placed in charge of the different provinces became virtual rulers, proffering only nominal allegiance to the emperor. Everyone was after salvaging what he could. None had the stature or competence required to rehabilitate the fallen Mughul or to step into his shoes.

In the years of confusion that followed the demise of Aurangzib, the Marathas rode to power rapidly, and became the chief contenders for the imperial mantle. Shivaji had founded his kingdom on the basis of *Swarajya* and *Swadharma*. It was a national state of the Marathas; nothing more ambitious could have been contemplated at that time. After Aurangzib, the position was different. Establishment of a Hindu empire replacing the Mughuls came within the realm of possibility. The Marathas held out a vision of the *Hindu-pad-padshahi* before the country. When it came to political matters, the religious fervour of the Hindu was weak. The Rajputs were the only powerful and organized group among the Hindus outside Maharashtra. They could not contemplate with equanimity the dissolution of the old order of the Mughuls in which they had been accorded a specially honoured place. If a change was inevitable, they were in favour of regaining their lost independence. Even the Jats who had risen to prominence during the troubled years were not willing to yield to the Marathas. It was a singular fact that the Marathas had no other Hindu power to back them up in their policies. As for the new Muslim rulers, the loss of Muslim political predominance ensured by the empire was most galling, and they could not reconcile themselves to it. In this situation, the Mughul, helpless and in distress, was still the most acceptable to all to be the emperor. The Marathas had perforce to pursue a dubious policy. They entrenched themselves gradually within the Mughul political setup. Instead of collecting *Chauth* from the Mughul territories as an act of defiance, they received it as a grant; they became Subedars assuming responsibility for administering provinces, just like the East India Company receiving the Diwani of Bengal and Behar at the hands of the emperor; the crowning act was while at the zenith of their power — the acceptance of the office of *Vakil-i-Mutlaq* (Regent Plenipotentiary) which made Mahadji Sindia the supreme arbiter of the affairs of the empire.

The Maratha manoeuvres deceived none. The Muslim ruling classes could not reconcile themselves to what was happening. When the efforts to rejuvenate the empire was proving futile, some looked for outside help. The invasions of Nadir Shah and Ahmad Shah Abdali were in tune with what always happened when there was power vacuum at Delhi. The help that came was found to be disastrous even by those who sought it. There was a stalemate in the Afghan-Maratha fight for supremacy, but the Marathas were having decidedly the upper hand over the whole country excepting the North-West. As H.G. Keene observed, the British did not wrest India from the Muslims — they had been defeated everywhere when the British appeared on the scene; if they were not there, the fight for supremacy would have been among the Marathas, the Rajputs and the Sikhs.[31] The Muslim spirit was at a

very low ebb; they had to accept the overlordship of the
Marathas or find some other source of support to sustain their
authority and independence.

It was fortuitous for the British that they were there on
the scene at the time, fully conversant with Indian affairs.
They extended a hand of lasting friendship on terms that
were enticing — permanent protection from all external foes
with their possessions and powers as rulers fully secured
internally. It was manna to those who had nowhere else to
look for help. One after the other of the Muslim rulers, the
erstwhile Subedars of the empire, fell into the net — the
Nawab of the Carnatic, the Nawab of Murshidabad, the Vazir
of Oudh and the Nizam of Hyderabad. The emperor himself
accepted British protection in 1803. The depth of their sense
of insecurity and anxiety was seen in the keenness they
exhibited to secure British support and protection. The historic
grant of the Diwani of Bengal and Behar is itself an instance.
Mir Jafar was not in favour of it; the Company was not keen
on receiving it; but the emperor served it on a plate to
subserve his own ends. *Seir Mutaqherin* bemoaned that an
affair of such magnitude, which at other times would have
required "good deal of parley and conference with the
Company and the King of England, ... was done and finished
in less time than would have been taken for the sale of a
jack-ass or a beast of burden, or a head of cattle."[32] The
Nizam, foremost among the Muslim rulers, was persistent
in his efforts to ally himself with the British and obtain their
protection, and felt he scored a success when he got it.[33] The
only ruler who held aloft the Islamic standard without
compromising at any stage, and fought and died rather than
yield, was Tipu Sultan, whom the Mughul Ashraf had looked
down upon as not belonging to their class. After all the
Muslim rulers were roped in, the position of the Marathas
became untenable. Besides the power of arms, the dangling
of the carrot of Subsidiary Alliance did its trick in their case
too. The process of empire building was near complete with
the conclusion of the Treaty of Mandasor in 1818.

Scholars have been very critical of the Maratha
performance. They could secure no friends outside their circle,
Hindu or Muslim. They were too grasping; the burden of taxes
they imposed upon conquered provinces was much heavier

than under the Mughuls with little in return.[34] The excursions for collection of *Chauth* outside their homeland made them particularly unpopular, and earned for them the appellation of freebooters. Without questioning the validity of the charges, it may perhaps be observed that this aspect has received overemphasis because of the Maratha failure in the final count. It has to be remembered that the Hindu-Muslim divide among those fighting for power was a fact. The Muslim rulers of the day could not reconcile themselves to the loss of their predominance, or countenance Maratha overlordship, however cloaked or sweetened. The Rajputs had the tradition of royalty ingrained in them; in their view, the Marathas, though Hindus, were upstarts, and they struck for their independence. To win them over, the Marathas should have offered something more tempting than the British. They were not unfamiliar with the ploy which the British were using to win over native powers. M.G. Ranade compared the levy of *Chauth* to the system of Subsidiary Alliance; but, as S.N. Sen pointed out, a *Chauth*-paying state entitled to military protection was not required to give up its diplomatic independence, an essential requirement under the latter. In any case, at a later time, the Marathas themselves had entered into an arrangement fully on par with the Raja of Bundi.[35] However, there is no evidence to show that the Marathas appreciated fully the long-term potentialities of the system or sought to apply it extensively. On the contrary, in 1791, it is said that Nana Phadnis himself asked Cornwallis why the British were not willing to conclude a Subsidiary Alliance treaty with the Marathas as they did in the case of the Nizam, and he was told that there had been a change in the British policy.[36] From this, it would appear that the Marathas, like the others, regarded the system to be no more unsafe than hiring of foreign troops or conclusion of treaties of amity that could be broken at will. On the whole, the ambivalence and cunning for which the Marathas were noted according to Orme and Wilks[37] could not prevail over the diplomatic astuteness of the British. The British had one great advantage over the Marathas in their political dealings. Being in India primarily for purposes of trade and small in numbers, they did not rouse the fears or the antipathy that the Marathas did. While making their choice, the native powers would have all felt that these foreigners could be dealt with and disposed of easily if they proved troublesome when the circumstances improved, a thing not possible in the case of the Marathas. In the end, it was the dark horse that won the race.

VICTORY FOR AN EFFICIENT BUREAUCRACY

The main credit for British success should go to the essentially bureaucratic setup of the administration of the East India Company, a point to which not much attention has been paid. The Company's affairs in India were in the hands of civilian and military employees deputed from home. In the days prior to steam navigation, it took more than three months for letters to reach. Home control could be exercised only in respect of general policies in the widest sense. The men on the spot enjoyed great powers and wide discretion. But home control was a reality. Those who served in India had to return home after service, and they could be called to account any time — Clive, Warren Hastings and Elijah Impey had to stand trial at the bar of Parliament. It was a well-organized bureaucracy with the headquarters at London that conquered India, consolidated the gains and set up a sound administration. As regards the rise of Muslims to power, there was a good element of zeal — the will to conquer, the passion to convert. In the case of the British, we do refer to the zeal for empire-building, the mission to civilize, etc. These no doubt provided a sense of commitment to higher values. But the element of personal gain to those actively engaged in empire-building was negligible when compared with what the Muslim invaders acquired by way of riches, land and power. There was another significant difference between the Indian rulers and the British. In the case of the former, the fate of the army and future of the state centered round one person. As Tarachand observed, "The state was incorporated in the person who held the army. His failure implied the collapse of the state."[38] This was not so in the case of the Company. There were frequent changes in the persons at the helm of affairs, and nobody was indispensable. There was steady teamwork and continuity in policies. The Company's records reveal the thorough discussion and systematic planning that went behind every policy decision, and the freedom with which the officers at all levels expressed their views. Also, there was the element of detachment in the examination of issues, for not much personal was involved, except in the service sense. Small in number, far removed from home with no hinterland to fall back upon, the British could not have profited by the situation in India if the administrative system and the procedures were not up to the mark, ensuring efficient functioning of both the engine and the brake.

FAILURE ON THE MILITARY FRONT

The British could not have benefited if they had not the capability required, but India's fall must be almost entirely attributed to domestic factors. As stated earlier, the British conquest of India was more of a diplomatic achievement than military. But the battle-front was not unimportant, for victory in battle always clinched matters. With regard to the Mughuls, William Irvine said, "Military inefficiency was the principal, if not the sole, cause of that empire's collapse. All other defects and weaknesses were as nothing in comparison with this."[39] The view underlines the importance of the factor. The defects from which the Mughul army suffered were common to the forces of the other Indian rulers too.

The most glaring defect was the failure to acquire proficiency in the manufacture and use of the latest type of firearms, and become self-sufficient in this respect. Most Indian rulers bought firearms from others, and also employed Europeans and non-nationals in large numbers in their artillery wings. They were there not merely to teach and train in the art of manufacture and use of firearms. They were often a part of the permanent fighting establishment. Of the Marathas, S.N. Sen observes, "They were quite satisfied with the weapons rejected by their rivals as useless, their factories turned out a number of antiquated guns of a type hopelessly out of date. ... They were compelled to fight their English rivals on their own terms, in their own fashion and with inferior weapons."[40] The permanent employment of non-nationals, particularly Europeans, in large numbers was a security risk and had serious consequences. Irvine refers to extensive employment of Europeans and Muslims from Constantinople in the Mughul army, and explains that the absence of many references to the former was due to "the slight consideration with which Mahomedan nobles treated Europeans, even those of the same position, upto the middle of the eighteenth century."[41] The Marathas were more culpable than the Mughuls in this respect.

Gaining control over the seas was another grossly neglected field. Europeans in India could not be held under check without it as the coastline was vulnerable. The weakness on the Indian side was frequently exhibited in the handling of the Portuguese and the British by the Mughuls and the Marathas, and the continued defiance of Maratha authority by the Siddis of Janjira. Naval power was closely linked with external trade. Indian rulers were indifferent to development of trade as such, and failed to encourage Indian merchants to carry on trade with other countries in their own ships. Even on the coast of Malabar, the dependence on Arabs and Europeans was near total. The rulers were satisfied with the *status quo*, since the foreigners brought in gold and silver and paid the prescribed taxes without their having to exert in any way. India had enough of the naval tradition surviving from the Chola days to build upon if there had been economic compulsions and the political will. This is clear from the fact that the ships of the East India Company were built in Indian dockyards by Indian craftsmen in large measure even in the early nineteenth century.

Despite these weaknesses, Indian rulers may have held their own, if theirs had been a professional army, trained, disciplined and well organized. A large proportion of the soldiers did not wholly depend upon army service for their livelihood. Sir Thomas Munro observed that "of the whole [of the] horsemen normally employed under the southern Jagheerdars", only one-tenth served whole time. The desire to be near enough to their villages to attend to agricultural chores made Marathas generally unwilling to serve outside their home provinces.[42] Not being trained, disciplined and professional, the armies were only a 'rabble' or 'a motley crowd', as many contemporary writers sarcastically observed. Speaking of the Oudh army, Warren Hastings writes, "The

Nabob's own sepoys, rabble as they were, were more than adequate against a worse rabble of any that could be opposed to them" on the northern frontier.[43] According to *Seir Mutaqherin*, the forces that faced the British at the time of the battle of Buxar were "not an army, but a whole city in motion; and you could have found in it whatever could be had in former times in Shah-djehan-abad itself, whilst that city was the capital and the eye of all Hindostan."[44] These inadequacies were compounded by irregular and partial payments. As a contemporary wrote, "They [the soldiers] are never paid one-third of the stipulated sum by the princes of Hindostan which renders them mutinous and discontented, but they would most certainly approve themselves obedient, faithful and brave, in the services of a power who should pay them regularly."[45] Even Haidar and Tipu were charged by Orme and Wilks with not paying the contracted sum always, though the general contentment of their troops suggested that their performance was much better than that of others.[46]

We have a clear picture of where the British scored in the observations of Lt. Col. Fitz-Clarence: "It is discipline, together with a quick firing of the flintlock and fieldpieces, which has given us the striking superiority over the natives. It is the steady fire of these that the troops of the native princes cannot face: that regularity of movement, quickness of evolution, and strict and unerring obedience in action, giving union and combination, opposed by confusion, clamour, distraction and insubordination, must ever secure a commanding ascendancy."[47] The British superiority in this respect came out best in the hour of defeat. *Seir Mutaqherin* was all praise for the conduct of the East India Company's troops supporting Ramnarain as against the Shahzada when they suffered defeat: "It must be acknowledged that this nation's presence of mind, firmness of temper, and undaunted bravery, are past all question. They join the most resolute courage to the most cautious prudence; nor have they their equals in the art of ranging themselves in battle array and fighting order."[48]

The British conquered India mostly with the help of local recruits — "mere junglewalas (quazi denizens of the wood) requiring instruction in everything, profoundly ignorant of all the arts of life."[49] With training and discipline, they came to be superior to the troops of the native rulers. It is clear that the failure on the Indian side was primarily due to lack of leadership and vision. Haidar and Tipu and Ranjit Singh had created strong, well-trained and well-equipped armies to match those of the British with limited help from Europeans, and contemporary western observers had a high opinion of them.

The political setup and the economic situation also proved to be detrimental to the Indian cause. In the case of the Mughuls, with an able emperor at the top, the Mansabdari bureaucratic setup could function efficiently and bring prosperity; but with a weak one, it lacked purpose and direction and was at a loose end. There was no second line of defence such as a hereditary nobility or a strong middle class to absorb shocks. Tarachand has pointed out that numerically the Mughul nobility had a very narrow base for such a vast populous empire — even the Czarist Russia had a much broader base with 1,30,000 members of the landed aristocracy to provide support.[50] Costly wars and the needs of the growing empire had led to the emergence of the Jagirdari system, which undermined political and economic stability. This, according to Satishchandra, was a major cause for the decline of the Mughuls.[51] In the case of the Marathas, Shivaji had founded his kingdom, checking effectively the spirit of local independence of the Watandars. But the Peshwas gave too free a hand to the generals while expanding the empire. This weakened the authority of the central government at Poona very much. What emerged was not a well-knit empire but only a confederation of warlords bound together by racial affinity and limited political links; to present a united front at hours of crisis or evolve a common policy was by no means easy.[52] In the case of both the Mughuls and the Marathas, the absence of strong centralized governments and financial crises and want of money at the time the challenge from the British came led to their defeat.

NEGATIVE SECULARISM AND THE SPIRITUAL VACUUM

With all these political and military limitations, Indian rulers were not badly placed in all cases. Mahadji Sindia's regular army was considered to have been the best that an Indian prince had at any time. At the time of the final showdown with the British, according to Elphinstone, "The Marathas had at their command ample means of waging a successful war — armies, arms, ammunition. Everything was ready. They only lacked a leader."[53] The fighting capacity of Tipu's army was exhibited on the field of battle; Sir Thomas Munro expressedthe view that Cornwallis could not have won against Tipu and crippled him beyond recovery without Maratha help.[54] The greatest shortcoming was not military; it was the spiritual vacuum that prevailed, the absence of an inspiring ideal.

In the earlier struggle between the Hindus and the Muslims, each of the sides was relatively united, and had an ideal to work for. In the case of the Muslims, what made them victorious and politically dominant was loyalty to tribe, zeal for Islam and consciousness of Islamic unity. In the case of the Hindus, no doubt resistance proved futile, and they became a subject race. But their consciousness of oneness and patriotism were strong enough to enable them to preserve their local independence and their religion and cultural identity to a very great extent. Otherwise, Hinduism and the Hindu society would have been wiped out beyond recognition. With the passage of time, the process of integration weakened the bonds based solely on religion and race considerably, and the spirit of 'live and let live' permeated social and public life. This was reflected in the marked heterogeneity of the army and the civil services everywhere as stated earlier, and also in public relations and political dealings. This was equally evident in trade relations and general economic life. These were no doubt good trends. The eighteenth century could well be considered the age of the dawn of secularism in India, a point very well brought out by Satishchandra in the political, D.R. Gadgil in the economic, and Hermann Goetz in the socio-cultural spheres.

The secularism attained at the time was, however, of a negative type. The old bonds that had held together the two communities ranged against each other had lost much of their relevance, and new ones bringing them together infusing common sentiments and ideals had not yet developed in an adequate measure. As Humayun Kabir rightly observed, the synthesis achieved was "largely based on practical considerations or emotional urges", and this could not "prove enduring as it was not supported by the intellectual integration of the philosophies of the two great communties." And, "In the absence of such intellectual articulation, accommodation at the level of practice, emotion and even intution have not been able to withstand the challenge of contrary forces."[55] The old wounds had not healed sufficiently, and it was a divided India, devoid of unifying higher values and ideals, of patriotism in essence, that the British conquered.

SELF-CENTREDNESS, THE MERCENARY SPIRIT
AND THE COMMUNAL DIVIDE

The eighteenth century was the age of mercenary armies contrasted with the armies of the earlier times infused with the spirit of tribal and dynastic loyalties. The new rulers were out to get good recruits from anywhere, without reference to religion, race or nationality, and adventurers and recruiting agents were most active. Buchanan observed that militiamen attached to princes served them well as long as they were regularly paid; if someone paid them better, they switched over, equally willing "to serve a Mussulman or Christian leader or a Hindu prince."[56] Of the fortune that awaited an adventurer looking out for a career, John Baillie wrote enthusiastically, "It is the best (place) in the world for a young man who has nothing to depend upon as he is sure if he behaves himself properly to get what he comes for", and the risk of death was "quite trifling to what it is looked on at home."[57] A number of adventurers, both Indian and European, attained prominence. Murari Rao served Muhammad Ali, Chanda Saheb, Dalvai Nanjaraja Urs of Mysore, the Marathas and the French at different times. Ibrahim Khan Gardi was in charge of the Maratha artillery in the battle of Panipat. Dhondia Waugh, a Maratha, served Tipu and was later imprisoned by him, and then came to be well known for leading a revolt against the British after the fall of Tipu. Of the European adventurers, Ramond was with the Nizam with 14,000 men. De Boigne and Perron rose to eminence and high power under Mahadji and Daulat Rao Sindia, and Aligarh came to be virtually a French principality. However good and useful for the occasion, the adventurers and mercenary troops could not have the zeal of national armies or be depended upon. The historic desertion of Perron and other French officers who quit Maratha service at a crucial moment in 1803 made clear the dangers of such dependence.

Self-centredness and meanness of spirit of the ruling class matched the mercenary spirit of the common adventurers of the day. Of all the native powers, it is the Marathas who had the power and the opportunity to bring the affairs of the country to order. If the Marathas had been sagacious and intent upon making friends than enemies, if a leader of vision had risen among them, the country would have been saved. Right up to 1750 A.D., they had a good enough image. It was only when their policies became blatantly imperialistic that the position changed. Outside their homeland (*Swarajya*), the collection of *Chauth* was regarded as ransom paid by those affected, for nothing was assured or received in return. There was no guarantee of internal peace or protection from external dangers; no non-Maratha rose to high position in civil or military service, or found patronage otherwise. Writing on how the Rajputs were antagonised, Satishchandra observes, "The Mughuls had generally demanded only the supply of an armed contingent. Even this demand had carried with it the possibility of an imperial *mansab* and the assignment of additional jagirs inside or outside Rajaputana. There was no such prospect of gainful service under the Marathas. Default in the payment of tribute implied the threat of the claims of a rival prince being backed by the Marathas, whereas payment exhausted the treasury and led to the growing exploitation of the peasantry. This was the reason why the Marathas, unlike the Mughuls, were unable to win the loyal support of any of the Rajput princes even for a limited time."[58] The attitude of the Jats, Bundelas and others towards the Marathas was no better. At the time of the crucial battle of Panipat, "the Marathas had not a single friend or ally in the North", and it looked as though they were in an enemy territory with the people all around "burning for revenge against the fearful depredations in the past", as G.S Sardesai observed.[59] According to a letter in the Banera archives, the defeat of the Marathas was celebrated with great rejoicing and lighting of lamps in Jaipur.[60]

There is no evidence to show that the Marathas made any special efforts to win over the Muslims either. The treatment accorded to the emperor does not speak well for their diplomatic finesse. Khandoji Holkar in 1753 declined, with marked impoliteness, to receive the *khilats* sent by the emperor telling him that he was no servant of his.[61] We have also the following account of how Shah Alam was received when he passed under Maratha protection in 1771 — "The unfortunate emperor was obliged ... to descend from the throne, and sit on a small carpet to receive them. Bissajee and Holkar, after some interval, helped him to reascend his throne, which he may be said to have received from their hands. The whole of the interview passed in the most humiliating condescensions of the emperor, and the greatest insolence of the Marathas."[62] There were many who saw the writing on the wall beginning with the well-known warning of Alivardi Khan to Siraj-ud-Daulah. After the conclusion of the Third Mysore War, Tipu told the Maratha commander Hari Pant, "You must realise I am not at all your enemy. Your real enemy is the Englishman of whom you must beware." After the last war with Tipu in whose fall he gave a helping hand to the British, Nana Phandnis brooded, "Tipu is finished; the British power has increased; the whole of east India is already theirs; Poona will now be the next victim. Evil days seem to be ahead. There seems to be no escape from destiny."[63] According to the French Cossigny, the Nizam told him in 1787, "The English invasion of India has not given me the same pain as the usurpation of Tipu."[64] Tarachand has compared the condition of the times to the Hobbesian state of nature and observed, "It resembled a jungle in which fierce and beastly men prowled around, animated by intensely selfish and extraordinarily shortsighted passion for power. They were restrained neither by ethical considerations nor any farsighted aims. ... India exhausted and ruined herself in the insensate and virulent struggles of contending personalities and factions, and failed to throw up a leader of sufficiently cammanding stature who could evolve order out of chaos."[65]

In this atmosphere, if contemporary accounts are full of the indifference of people to political happenings and their lack of patriotism, it should cause no surprise. We have a caustic picture of it from Alexander Dow — "They heard of an emperor as the superstitious hear of a guardian angel, whom they never beheld. An indifference for his fate succeeded to his want of power. A peasant, at the end of many months, was informed of a revolution at Delhi. He stopt not his oxen, nor converted his plough-share into a sword. He whistled unconcerned along his field; and inquired not, perhaps, concerning the name of the new prince."[66] The thinking section of the community was not unaffected. The Mughul culture that had blossomed was a wonderful flower, but it had grown on poisoned ground. The opulence and extravagance of the ruling class and the suffering of the masses were there for all to see. Looking at the condition of Oudh, Talib Khan wailed in dismay, "There is no knowing how God's people will obtain release from the wrath of the oppressors."[67] And, *Seir Mutaqherin* said, "They (Englishmen) have been sent by God Almighty to chastise the guilty, criminal races of Hindustanees." Both extolled the virtues and abilities of the new comers, but neither felt sure that they would not prove to be worse than the 'native tyrants'. M. Raymond, in his introduction to *Seir Mutaqherin*, himself a contemporary of its author, describes the dejection, the despair, the feeling of helplessness, that prevailed —"There runs throughout our author's narrative, a subterraneous vein of national resentment, which emits vapours now and then, and which his occasional encomiums of the English can neither conceal nor palliate, and yet he is himself but a voice that has spoken among a million of others that could speak but are silent."[68] There were also some of the type of Raja Ram Mohan Roy who welcomed British rule, for, as Hermann Goetz says with some justification, they were "idealists who preferred a sound and healthy foreign government to a tyranny national indeed but corrupted beyond hope."[69] In any case, the voice of the intellectual of either class was too weak to have any impact on the political happenings of the day or the final outcome.

THE SURVIVING VALUES AND THE BRIGHT SIDE

The picture of India presented above is sombre and depressing, but there were bright spots. While loyalty to the state and country came to be foreign, the doglike loyalty to the master was a relieving feature. Contemporary records are full of this aspect of the Indian character. A Muslim writer of the day observed, "The soldiers of this country are generally faithful, daring, true to their salt, willing to lay down their lives in the employ of their masters, and do not leave their service."[70] And, Elphinstone said, "A subject will take service against his natural sovereign as readily as for him; and has always more regard for the salt he has eaten than to the land in which he is born."[71] We have a thrilling account of the hot pursuit of Muhammad Issaf by a contingent headed by Tajkhan, a commander of Mahadji Bhonsle in 1775, in the Maratha records.[72] We have the classic instance of Ibrahim Khan Gardi in charge of the artillery battalion fighting bravely and dying for the Maratha cause, while his co-religionists were ranged on the opposite side.[73] The major betrayals and desertions we know of were by Europeans, specially the French. The chief beneficiaries of this sense of loyalty to the master were the British, for it helped them to conquer India mostly with the help of local recruits.

Because of the final outcome, attention has been mostly focussed on the foxy dealings of the leaders at the top, their self-centredness and sellouts to garner what they could save. There was another aspect, the courage and bravery exhibited. Lt. Col. FitzClarence has laid stress on the 'natural bravery' of the Indian soliders, and described how they held on in forts when the British expected them to be wise enough to surrender after they were breached.[74] Percival Spear has termed the times the Age of Iron. He writes, "With few exceptions the actors were vigorous and hardy, brave and warlike. There were brilliant feats of arms, there was stolid endurance and desperate courage. There was energy in abundance, and indeed rather too much of it than too little. It was not a case of anaemic courtiers falling before the onset of the northern vigour, but rather of sword clashing upon sword, of fierce men giving and receiving stroke after stroke."[75] We have many instances of how the Maratha solidiers, deserted by the French officers placed in command, elected new leaders and fought on to the bitter end. The personal courage and sense of dedication of individual soldiers, however, proved to be of little avail, because the country was hopelessly divided, and the leaders had no high ideal or sense of values which might have brought them together.

The resentment and the sense of disappointment at the lower levels took some time to find expression. Many of the rulers and the political elite continued to be in ornamental positions of power as minions of British imperialism. The natural leadership of the community, however, passed on to other hands. Among Muslims, the importance of theologians, who had played a secondary role hitherto, increased very much. Muslim revivalism of the times was anti-Hindu, but it was as much anti-British. It is this aspect that has led to the Wahabi and other revivalist movements being considered to be facets of the Indian national movement by many. On the Hindu side, what mattered most was attachment to chiefs and zamindars. When some of the latter suffered at the hands of the British and grew disenchanted, they could rely on the community at large for support. Behind every revolt prior to the great uprising of 1857, there were the hands of Muslim theologians and disgruntled zamindars and chiefs enjoying mass support. We have a detailed study of the happenings in S.B. Chaudhury's *Civil Disturbances during the British Rule in India, 1757-1857* (1955). The Revolt of 1857 marked the climax of the old trends at the level of the masses. It was the spontaneity of the uprising that was most significant. The bottled-up resentment, the patriotism of the common man, came to the open in a volcanic eruption. Though there were leaders, by and large, the movement was leaderless, a major cause for the failure. The secularist trends of the eighteenth century made the revolt national. The British considered it to have been more of a Muslim affair. Strictly viewed, this was a fact. The revolt itself began as a mutiny of the army, and mutinous soldiers played the dominant part. Muslims played the major role as the British Indian army was predominantly Muslim, as explained earlier. Nevertheless, the moving spirit behind the revolt, the sentiments evinced by the rebels, had bridged the communal divide, and the revolt was as such truly secular and national.

The intellectual classes and the Western educated were not actively involved, but it was clear where their sympathies lay. The *Hindu Patriot* wrote boldly in May 1857, "The recent mutinies of the Bengal army have one peculiar feature —they have from the beginning drawn the sympathy of the country. ...There is not a single native of India who does not feel the full weight of the grievances imposed upon him by the very existence of the British rule in India — grievances inescapable from subjection to foreign rule."[76] This class took over the lead, and with the growing acceptance of democratic values, Indian nationalism took a new turn in the modern period.

Notes

1. G. Roerich, xviii, 61-2, 64-5, 94, 98.

2. N.K. Bhattasali, Bengal Chiefs' Struggle for Independence in the Reign of Akbar and Jahangir—*Bengal, Past and Present*, Vol.XXXV, Sl.No.69 (January-March 1929), 30. Also, B.S. Mathur on Mewar's resistance - *Journal of Indian History*, No.134 (August 1967), 509-20.

3. S.B.P. Nigam, ix.

4. Aziz Ahmed, *Early Turkish Empire*, 10-3, 40. R.C. Majumdar, *The Struggle for Empire*, 125. S.N. Sen, *Maratha Military System*, 2.

5. *Seir Mutaqherin* refers to an incident in which Rajputs led enemy soldiers dying of thirst to some springs in the desert, and is all praise for their benevolence. Could wars be fought on such terms?— Vol.III, 316-7.

6. Tarachand, Vol.I, 150.

7. Satchidananda Murty, 66.

8. Bholanath Chunder, 71.

9. S.N. Sen, *Maratha Administrative System*, 170-1; *Maratha Military System* xvii-xviii, 234.

10. Tarachand, Vol.I, 108.

11. M.Mujeeb, 29.

12. Satishchandra, Introduction.

13. Aziz Ahmed, *Early Turkish Empire*, 10.

14. U.N. Ghoshal, 528 *et seqq*.

15. Aziz Ahmed, *Early Turkish Empire*, 45. R.C. Majumdar, *The Struggle for Empire*, 126-7. Also, M. Mujeeb, 29.

16. S.N. Sen, *Maratha Military System*, xiv.

17. A.L. Srivastava, A Survey of India's Resistance to Muslim Invaders from the North-West—*Journal of Indian History*, Vol.43, No.128, p.360.

18. Mohammad Habib in Satchidananda Murty, 72. For a critical review and rejection of Habib's thesis, see S.S.A. Rizwi in G.A. Oddie, *Religion in South Asia*, 26-7.

19. U.N. Ghoshal, 264. Also, Vikas Misra, 89.

20.   Hari Ram Gupta in R.C. Majumdar, *The Mughul Empire*, 307.
21.   N.K. Behere, 164-5.
22.   Hari Ram Gupta in R.C. Majumdar, *The Mughul Empire*, 316-8.
23.   S.N. Sen, *Maratha Military System*, 17-9.
24.   K.G. Saiyidain in Nanavati and Vakil, 37-9.
25.   *Oriental Annual*, 80.
26.   Tarachand, Vol.I, 149.
27.   N.K. Behere, 136.
28.   G.S. Sardesai, Vol.I, 35, 37.
29.   Ernest Gellner, 150-3 *et seqq.*
30.   R.C. Majumdar, *The Struggle for Empire*, 127.
31.   H.G. Keene, 283.
32.   *Seir Mutaqherin*, Vol.III, 9. Also, Mir Jafar and Siraj-ud-Daulah of Fazel Rubbec—*Bengal, Past and Present*, Sl. No.24 (April-June 1916), 244-52.
33.   Mohibbul Hasan, 132, 182, 277-8.
34.   S.N. Sen, *Maratha Administrative System*, 110-22.
35.   *Ibid.*
36.   George Forrest, Vol.II, 198.
37.   Tarachand, Vol.I, 273.
38.   *Ibid.*, 269.
39.   William Irvine, 296.
40.   S.N. Sen, *Maratha Military System*, 108-9, 126.
41.   William Irvine, 152.
42.   S.N. Sen, *Maratha Military System*, 237.
43.   Warren Hastings, 47-8.
44.   *Seir Mutaqherin*, Vol.II, 526. Also, S.N. Sen, *Maratha Military System*, 138.
45.   *History of Hindostan*, Vol.II—The Present State of Hindostan (1764), 507-8.
46.   M.H. Gopal, 45-6.
47.   Fitz-Clarence, 257.
48.   *Seir Mutaqherin*, Vol.II, 341.
49.   Charles F. Kirby, Vol.I, 292.
50.   Tarachand, Vol.I, 152-3. Jadunath Sarkar, *Mughal Administration*, 44-54.
51.   Satishchandra, 268 *et seqq.*
52.   S.N. Sen, *Maratha Military System*, xvii-xviii, 124; *Maratha Administrative System*, 207-8.
53.   R.C. Majumdar, *The Maratha Supremacy*, 513.
54.   Mohibbul Hasan, 269.
55.   Humayun Kabir, Presidential Address, *Report of Seminar on National Integration* (1958), 10. Also, Tarachand, Vol.I, 147.
56.   Buchanan, *Mysore, Canara and Malabar*, Vol.II, 73.
57.   *Bengal, Past and Present*, Vol.XLVII, Sl. No.93, January-March, 1934, 10.
58.   Satishchandra in Bisheshwar Prasad, 185.
59.   Tarachand, Vol.I, 60, 71.
60.   *Journal of Indian History*, Vol.XLVII, Sl. No.139, April 1969, p.214.

According to M. Elphinstone's correspondence, "So much was the Maratha rule detested that when the fort of Sambalpur was taken by the British, the garrison made a distinct understanding that the British troops should escort them beyond the borders of the state and protect them from infuriated peasants."—Sinha and Avesthi, viii. Also, S.N. Sen, *Maratha Military System, 146.*

61. Jadunath Sarkar, *Tarikh-i-Ahmadshahi*, 105-11.
62. Jonathan Scott, *Ferishta's History*, Part V, 254.
63. Mohibbul Hasan, 263, 322.
64. Cossigny's letter to de Casteris, 19 July 1787—Mohibbul Hasan, 115.
65. Tarachand, Vol.I, 52.
66. Alexander Dow, Vol.I, xc.
67. Humayun Kabir, 15-21.
68. *Seir Mutaqherin*, Vol.I—Preface, 6; Vol.III, 29.
69. Herman Goetz, 7.
70. Henry Court, *Araish-i-Muhfil*, 43-4.
71. M. Elphinstone, *History of India*, 214.
72. *Selections from the Peshwa Daftar*, Vol.36, No. 267.
73. H.G. Rawlinson, *The Last Battle of Panipat*, 19-20, 52.
74. Fitz-Clarence, 245, 252.
75. Percival Spear, 10. Also, Tarachand, Vol.I, 52. 74. S.V. Desika Char, *Readings in Constitutional History*, 224.

CHAPTER 5

Territorial Consciousness from the Village to One India

Nationalism — Variety in Manifestation

Love of the land one is born in is but natural — it is patriotism pure and simple. With that is associated love for its people, culture and institutions — that is nationalism. Where the sentiment is broadbased and evinced towards all sections of the community resident in the land, it is, of the 'open type'. Where it is limited to one section, majority or minority, large or small, it is of the 'closed type'. The basic sentiment or the primary bond of union in the case of those of the latter class may emanate from tribal affinity, common racial origin, common religion, common language or any other factor; however, it is always linked to common living in a region or associated with it. There is good room for nationalism and subnationalism to coexist, exhibiting similar or different characteristics. Also, national and subnational sentiments could be very strong and virile in very small communites as in bigger ones, e.g., in the city states of ancient Greece as in England and the U.S.A. In view of the variety of senses and contexts in which the terms territorial consciousness and nationalism are used, it is necessary to keep in mind the great flexibility of the two concepts.

The history of India may be viewed as one continuous

struggle to evolve an open society and attain nationhood covering the whole land — to acculturate and integrate all classes and communities, to fight local and subnational trends and fissiparous forces, to seek greater and greater unity amidst persisting diversities, and to extend the locus of unity to cover the whole land and even stretch it beyond. In this struggle, territorial consciousness was of no less importance than caste and religion. Its manifestation was at three distinct levels, deserving study — the village and the little world one lived in and knew best, the vision of One India embodying the acme of hopes and aspirations, and the in-between regions wherein subnational forces operated and big and small kingdoms flourished.

Manifestation at the Little World Level

THE SELF-SUFFICIENT VILLAGE — VITALITY AND STRENGTH

Prior to the sea changes following the dawn of the modern age, territorial consciousness was most potent at the level of villages and towns, and tended to be sharply weaker at the regional and all-India levels. However much we may talk of centralization and strong governments, the political setup in the pre-modern age was highly decentralized. The village communities of the day were miniature states for all practical purposes and, indeed, "the state as a union of autonomous towns and villages was a great and unique political contribution of India."[1] Despite the vastness of the country, there was broad uniformity in the structure and general pattern of life. The villages were small, with a population of only about 500-1,000 persons. Still, the occupational structure was fairly well balanced to meet all the material needs of the community. While there were craftsmen and those rendering general services, such as the potter, the leather-worker and the priest, agriculture was the primary occupation, and nearly everyone was engaged in agricultural operations. As land was plentiful down to modern times, landless labourers were not many, and transactions in land were few. Land was considered more or less the property of the community.[2] The schedule and pattern of agricultural operations were regulated collectively, and there was periodical redistribution of land for purposes of cultivation. Everyone in the village had a claim on the produce, and received his share at harvest in accordance with custom and general consensus. An appropriate portion was set apart to meet the demands of the state and also recompense village officials. As explained earlier, what one recieved depended upon the services rendered by him and not on caste or social status. Every village had a chief and a council or panchayat in charge of all matters concerning the village, including maintenance of peace, settlement of disputes and award of penalties. There were many instances of villages functioning on democratic lines, specially in South India in the ancient period, but in most cases the orientation was aristocratic or oligarchic. However constituted, respect for elders, primacy of custom, and search for consensus than imposition of the majority view as a matter of course were characteristic of their working.[3] The members of the village were jointly responsible for meeting all fiscal and other claims of the state and for ensuring peace in the countryside.

The strength and vitality of the village communities, the qualities lost as the modern age advanced, came from several factors. Theirs was an open society. No doubt the several castes of which they were composed were closed groups, each of them with its own laws of inheritance, and personal and family life. But this did not prevent the members of a caste group from joining hands with those of others to form a single politico-economic community, and cooperating in all matters of common concern. Though caste rigidity and observance of social restrictions were more pronounced in villages than in towns, the amity and closeness of cooperation in secular matters were something remarkable. "Were it not so," M.M. Nanavati observes, "the villages would have developed into armed camps at an unstable equilibrium and always liable to run into strife and conflict at every turn."[4] This social stability came from economic stability. Self-sufficiency in respect of essential commodities and requirements, shared economic life and resultant interdependence of castes, fair-enough distribution of the products of labour, and absence of sharp inequalities in wealth, these made for

'the decentralized socialism' that prevailed, a term used by
C. Rajagopalachari.[5] Comparing the position with the
conditions in Medieval Europe, Nazrul Karim observes,
"European Manorial system was a much weaker and much
less stable organization than the Indian village community.
There was no room for either serfdom or baronial exploitation
in the Indian village community, and therefore the Indian
village was more firmly entrenched in the Indian social
structure." And, "The social organization of the village
community gave economic security to its members, and
because of that the village organization remained stable and
unchanged."[6] In turn, the social and economic stability gave
the villages remarkable political strength. Comparing the
position with that in later times, Percival Spear noted, "Yet,
the same village, whose institutions were so anaemic in the
nineteenth century, had seemed to be the protoplasm of all
Indian social life. It was at any rate something so tough that
it had survived intact all the wars and revolutions, all the
pestilences, floods and famines of twenty centuries."[7]
Assessing the place of villages in "the pyramid of state-society
relationship in pre-British India", Y.A. Raikar justifiably
observes, "If the apex of the pyramid indicates the national
state, the bottom represents the society. This suggests that
even if the power at the national level ceases to function,
the balance would automatically be adjusted at a lower level
like a provincial state, and in any case the solidarity of the
lowest social structure would remain undisturbed."[8] The
unswerving loyalty of every member of the village community
was assured, since none could survive outside the world of
caste and village.

THE LIMITS OF SELF SUFFICIENCY
AND OUTSIDE RELATIONS

While self-sufficiency and independence of village communities
were major facts of pre-modern India, the point was so much
stressed that until a few decades back they were looked upon
as little cesspools without inlets or outlets. This view has
since been mostly abandoned. M.N. Srinivas and A.M Shah
observe, "While roads, especially inter-village roads, were very

poorly developed, while monetisation of the rural economy was minimal, and while the local dominant class could lay down the law on many matters, the village was always a part of a wider economic, political and religious system. The appearance of isolation, autonomy and self-sufficiency was an illusion."[9] Primary caste groups having close marital and family ties were spread over a number of adjoining villages forming a cluster. In the case of the numerically small groups such as those among the Brahmanas and Vaisyas, which were thinly spread over, the geographical limits of the clusters were wider. Everywhere there were temples, monasteries of religious orders and centres of higher learning of local importance to which people of different villages felt attracted. The weekly fairs often served several villages. The coppersmith, the goldsmith, the *vaid* of higher reputation, etc. living in adjoining bigger villages or small towns catered to special needs. The political links with the outside world were better defined. In most cases, there were hereditary zamindars and chiefs exercising jurisdiction over several villages, with their duties, rights and privileges regulated by custom. Within their own spheres, they settled inter-village disputes, maintained peace in the countryside and regulated common welfare activities such as maintenance of irrigation works, inter-village roads, etc. They represented the villages in all dealings with the rulers of the land — payment of taxes, contribution to feudal levies, etc. Often enough, the rulers regarded the local chiefs to be a part of their own political or bureaucratic setup. With the coming of the Muslims, however, the state bureaucracy stood out distinct and separate from the indigenous hereditary chiefs and zamindars.

THE LITTLE WORLD LOYALTY AND PATRIOTISM

No doubt there were clear limits to village self-sufficiency under ancient and medieval conditions, but we could speak more confidently of the self-sufficiency and localism of 'the little worlds'. These should be viewed as a number of overlapping circles covering a large number of villages and concerned with different matters, but always having a central core, the village itself. Loyalty to the village and the

surrounding little world was deep-seated and mattered most
at all times and under all circumstances. All higher types
of loyalties had to rest on this base. Granite-like, it was the
hardest to overcome. In his study on Warren Hastings,
Moncton-Jones writes, "The tenacity and longevity of these
little village commonwealths would be unaccountable, judged
merely by their strength to resist an enemy. The secret of
it lies first in their producing power as agricultural groups,
and secondly in the Indian's love of the soil, a passion as
great as or even greater than that of the Irish peasant. Wave
after wave of conquerors passed over them, plundering and
even temporarily devastating the village; yet century after
century the same family of ryots are to be found, little water-
weeds, when the boat has passed, working back to their old
places and settling down to their accustomed functions, though
often enough with rights diminished. In them lay India's
vitality." Resistance there was too; the great zamindars "most
constantly treated with the government rather as tributary
princes than as subjects."[10] As C. Rajagopalachari observed
with great perception, a no-government condition that often
prevailed could not have been tided over, except for the
discipline of the joint family, the *jati* (caste) and the
village.[11] As seen earlier, it is this Hindu power at the
lowest levels that acted as a brake on Muslim expansion and
authority. No substantial change was noticeable at the
beginning of the last century. Writing in 1805, the Judge-
Magistrate of Masulipatam in the Madras Presidency
wondered if the criminal law of government would ever
become effective, and if the people would not prefer their own
masters for the state for years to come.[12] That this Little
World condition and the power of the zamindars and local
magnates were far from fading out even by the close of the
last century is seen from Washbrook's important study on
the Madras Presidency during 1870-1920.[13]

Thus, in pre-modern India, it was the village and its little
world outside which constituted the dominant partner in the
political setup, and commanded the affection and loyalty of
the community best. As graphically expressed by B. Subba
Rao, India of the day was an inverted pyramid with the
villages and their little worlds at the top and the state at
the bottom, if the apex represented power, vitality and

strength.[14] To us, at the present time, all this may appear to be just narrow-mindedness and parochialism; but we would be very wrong if we forget that this was the product of the socio-economic conditions of the times, and met the needs of the day best.

One India — the Vision and the Reality

THE HINDU HERITAGE

In this situation, it is really surprising that, side by side, there should have been an all-India consciousness too, strong and vibrant, from the earliest times. One India was not only a vision but a goal towards which all efforts were directed; an unconscious urge, not much of a purposeful movement, nevertheless important and fruitful. Till the coming of Islam, it ran in a single stream; with the deep communal divide, it had to bifurcate; there was again a deep urge for the two courses to converge and form a single stream.

The One India of the Hindu was the product of the Aryo-Dravidian synthesis and the quick assimilation of later-day entrants such as the Hunas and the Scythians. While the process of acculturation and integration in their various facets was a continuous one and its operation may be seen even today, a fairly homogeneous society had emerged by the time of the Buddha. The Mauryan empire was the first concrete evidence indicative of the emergence of political and cultural homogeneity in the country. Deep down in the South, this was reflected in the all-India setting of the great epics of the Sangam Age, *Manimekhalai* and *Silappadhikaram*. "This living unity was observed by Huan Tsang from Kandahar, Kashmir, Khatmandu to Camchivaram, Cape Camorin and Kathiawar even as late as the seventh century A.D."[15] In the eleventh century too, Al-Biruni had not a word to say about the diversity in peoples and languages, much less on their differences and animosities. As G.S. Ghurye observed, "The whole country and the people, despite many political divisions and contending royalties, manifested a unified and homogeneous front to a foreign observer, excepting for its caste system."[16] Such was the position at the time of Islam's entry into India.

Contrary to opinions frequently expressed by eminent scholars,[17] it cannot be said that the expanding Aryans were not conscious enough of being one community with a common religious heritage and culture from the earliest times, though the nomenclature 'Hindu', as applicable to the indigenous composite religio-cultural community that had emerged came into usage only with the coming of Muslims. A clear line was drawn between Aryans and non-Aryans (*mlechchas* or barbarians). Once a person entered the Aryan fold, as it happened with the spread of the Aryan culture, he ceased to be a *mlechcha*. The way of life of the Aryans was *Aryadharma* or *Sanatanadharma* (the path of the ancients); Aryavarta was the land where their religion and culture prevailed.[18] The nexus between the land and the people, the territorial consciousness, was pronounced enough, as reflected in the ancient texts. Their view of their land was not static; it expanded with the spread of the Aryan culture. Originally, it was the region between the rivers Saraswati and the Drishadwati (Brahmarshi Desha). Later, in succession, it was the region between the rivers Ganga and Jamuna (Brahmavarta); then that between the Himalayas and the Vindhyas (Madhya Desha); and finally, the whole of the subcontinent from the Himalayas to the southern seas (Bharatavarsha). Medhatithi, the first commentator on Manusmriti, observed that every region wherein Aryadharma prevailed was a part of Aryavarta, and even Brahmavarta, the most holy part of Aryavarta, would be a non-Aryan land (*Mlechcha Desha*) if *mlechchas* or non-Aryans subjugated it and lived there.[19] At times, their conception of Aryavarta extended over the whole world; this was only a reflection of the desire that Aryan culture should become universal.[20] Despite this elasticity in usage, it was Bharatavarsha or India of old that was the land of the Hindus as generally understood.[21] This concept came to be so deeprooted in Hindu consciousness that it was reflected as much in elitist literature and activities as in folklore and day-to-day life down to modern times, e.g., in the ritualistic *sankalpa* or vow to perform a religious rite, mentioning the place and date of undertaking it. As such, the references to the survival of this tradition of One India all over the country in the writings of Buchanan and other travellers should cause no surprise.[22]

This all-India consciousness of the Hindus was both the cause and effect of the religious and cultural homogeneity attained and the common bonds forged in political and economic matters. It manifested itself in several ways: common religious heritage and every religious and theological trend acquiring an all-India sweep; monasteries and pilgrim centres held in equal veneration being spread over the whole land; the homogeneity of the ruling classes interlinked through marriage and family connections; free movement of people and freedom of trade leading to economic integration, etc. These well-known facts need no elaboration.

There is, however, one aspect which requires further consideration. K.M. Panikkar has observed, "India's unity in the past was based on *svadharma* or of religion and culture and except as a matter of concept involved no sense of a politically united India." And P.V. Kane has stated that the emotional regard for Aryavarta was religious and not political, and the extent of religio-cultural homogeneity attained "did not make for a deep-seated and effective sentiment of nationhood or national unity". This view is shared by many others.[23]

The distinction made between the two aspects, the cultural and the political, does not seem to be warranted, either in terms of aspiration or achievement. The vision of one politically united India had entered the very matrix of Hindu consciousness. Traditionally, India was the land of Bharata, the progenitor or primeval ruler who held universal sway. The spirit animated the South as much as the North; this is reflected in the legendary supremacy claimed by the Tamils over the Aryan kings and over Aryavarta in general, as referred to in the Sangam classics. Every *Sutrakara* or writer on Dharmasastra, down to Rajasekara in the tenth century and later too, described the whole land as a *chakravarti-kshetra*, the region to be brought under one rule by anyone aspiring to the status of *samrat* or *chakravarti* (emperor).[24]

The achievement of Bharata and the proud boast of the Tamil classics were mythical, but Asoka had succeeded in turning the myth into almost a reality. In the historical period, most of the struggles were among small states; but the struggle often released supra-regional forces which turned into a flood. We witness it in the *dig-vijaya* (career of conquest) of Samudragupta, in the Cholas planting their standard on the banks of the Ganga, in the Harsha-Pulakeshi confrontation, and in the struggle among Palas, Pratiharas and Rashtrakutas for supremacy. Stressing "the underlying faith in the fundamental political as well as the cultural unity of India" engrafted in the Hindu tradition, Percival Spear observes, "The unity of the country, however frequently broken, is as natural an Indian conception as the balance of power, however often threatened, is a constant European conception in politics."[25]

This struggle for supremacy has been characterized by some as having been purely political, while others have opined that this ideology only encouraged wars.[26] No doubt the struggles were based mostly on political and mundane considerations; they could not have been otherwise. The Dharmasastras came in handy as they gave moral and religious sanction to them. From this, it would be wrong to conclude that it had the effect of encouraging wars. On the contrary, it served a humanitarian purpose. The Dharmasastras classified the attempts at conquest, which were inevitable, into three categories — *Dharma-vijaya* (acceptance of submission), *Lobha-vijaya* (conquests for gain in land and money), and *Asura-vijaya* (conquests ending in robbery and oppression).[27] Manu advised rulers to win over foes by conciliation and gifts and avoid wars; where a war had to be undertaken, after victory, the victor was to place a relative of the vanquished ruler on the throne after ascertaining the wishes of the conquered, and honour the new king and his chief servants with gifts.[28] Moral sanction was thus for *Dharma-vijaya* only, conquests to unify the land to ensure beneficent rule.

Just as the religious tradition did not stand in the way of political unification, the general situation in the country and the outlook of the people too posed no obstacles. The spirit of localism was no doubt there, but neither the sentiments nor the material interests of the local communities were likely to be adversely affected by change of rulers or modifications in the political setup. The one factor that might have posed a problem was the emergence of subnationalism centering round language. Except in the South, there was no such growth in the pre-Muslim period. The sentiment in favour of One India was not diluted by subnational loyalties to any great extent. The aspiration was there, the endeavour was there, big kingdoms and empires arose, but the goal was not reached.

What stood in the way was the sheer size of the country, a point generally overlooked but specially noticed by U.N. Ghoshal.[29] Holding together big kingdoms was by no means easy, and their life was much shorter than that of smaller ones. This was a major problem down to modern times. Both Aurangzib and Bahadur Shah contemplated division of the empire; this was as much due to the difficulty in administering the vast empire as the need to settle family feuds.[30] The problem was very much there under the British too. Down to 1833, the three Presidencies were virtually independent, and opinion was strongly divided on the issue of centralization.[31] Further, one-third of the country was under Princely rule. It was not the sanctity attached to treaties that came in the way of total annexation of Princely India. There was a strong body of opinion against extending the bounds of the directly-administered territories. British success in unifying India and establishing a strong centralized administration was as much due to the sea changes in the means of communication as to other factors.

In the medieval period, there were two new factors affecting the progress towards unification. There was first the rapid growth of regional languages and emergence of subnational sentiments centering round them. This did not prove to be much of a hurdle. On the contrary, the regional languages came to be the principal purveyors of the common religious heritage and the all-India classical culture to the masses, and did yeoman service to the cause of unification. This help too came at a time when the Hindus were in wilderness, and it helped to minimise the damage done to their religion and culture. Also, the confrontation with the Muslims overshadowed and held in check the possible rivalries and conflicts that might have arisen within the Hindu ranks by the growth of subnational sentiments.

The real setback was caused by Islam and the establishment of Muslim rule. The Hindu vision of One India was shattered; it was a divided India that was there for the time being.

This major fact apart, within the Hindu world, the ruling classes lost their homogeneity and got greatly vivisected. Cultural development was much more at the regional level than the national. But the homogeneity, the consciousness of oneness attained earlier, was not obliterated. The little flames of the old spirit and outlook were to be seen wherever Hindu authority survived; the embers did not die out at the grass-roots level anywhere. The Bhakti saints lived and propagated in their respective regions; they spoke in the language of the people; their following was mostly local. Yet, their vision was all-India, and the Bhakti movement as a whole had an all-India sweep. In the realm of scholarship, literary, theological and other studies in Sanskrit and other all-India classical languages came to have a strong regional flavour, but the inter-regional links were not wholly lost. On the whole, the all-Indianness of the Hindu cultural development during the period was subdued and on a lower key.

In the political field too, whenever the Muslim chips were down, there were assertions of Hindu power and revival of the old ideal e.g., the resistance offered by Vijayanagara, the rise and fall of Hemu in the second battle of Panipat, 'a forgotten Hindu Hero' as R.C. Majumdar has said, and the rise of the Marathas with their *Hindu-pad-padshahi* cry. Less known, there was the Rajput plan to overthrow the Mughuls in the time of Bahadur Shah. Of this incident, Satishchandra writes, "If the Rajput tradition be accepted, the Rajput Rajahs planned not only to recover their countries, but to expel the Mughul influence from Rajaputana completely, and even dreamt of bringing the entire Hindustan under their sway." Nothing came out of the move, because there was no agreement on who was to wear the imperial mantle — Jai Singh of Amber or Ajit Singh of Jodhpur.[32] Despite these manifestations of the Hindu spirit, belief in the invincibility of Muslims and the Mughul charisma had a strong hold; the aspiration for freedom and forging of one Hindu India remained only in the realm of vain hope.

The coming of the British heralded a change. From one angle, the Hindus had only exchanged masters, and their religion and culture had to encounter vigorous Christian proselytization instead of the Islamic one that had lost much of its punch. This apart, what mattered most was the Renaissance spirit ushered in. For the Hindu, it was not so much the rediscoveries made by the European savants that mattered as much as the value and respect they attached to the old Hindu heritage. The Hindu shed his inferiority complex or the proud aloofness to which Al-Biruni referred. Now he held his head high, was ready to face criticism, and willing to absorb new ideas. The Hindu Renaissance heralded by Ram Mohan Roy brought in its wake Hindu Nationalism. Swami Vivekananda, Bal Gangadhar Tilak and Aurobindo were the best representatives of this twin development. In all their thinking, Hindus were one, India was one. This was not a subject for debate. This rapid resurgence of the vision of One India in the Hindu mind and the phenomenal growth of nationalism in the nineteenth century became possible, because it was only a revival of the old-time ideal and outlook.

THE MUSLIM HERITAGE

The vision of One India came naturally to the Hindu, who was native to the soil, with all his interests, socio-economic as much as religio-cultural, rooted in it. Indian Muslims comprised mostly local converts, and they too were native to the soil. But this was not true of the small immigrant class, the Ashraf, the members of which maintained their distinctness and kept aloof from the main body of Muslims till the middle of the eighteenth century. The social and economic standing of the local converts was, however, such that they did not count for much in public life. Only the sentiments and attitudes of the Ashraf mattered most, and as the elite of the community their influence was great. Shedding alienness and getting indigenized constituted a slow process and was a matter of time. This process could not gather its natural momentum because of the close contact the Ashraf continued to have with the land they had left, and also the bond of common religion and culture and the strong sense of *Quam* or community feeling which held the world of Islam in one piece. Besides major military incursions and waves of immigration due to unsettled conditions in Central Asia and elsewhere, there was a continuous trickle of migrants down to the middle of the eighteenth century. These included scholars and divines who were invited with open arms as hailing from home, and also soldiers of fortune from the Middle East and Central Asia, who were rated high and employed in large numbers by all Indian rulers, including the Hindu. The traffic was always one way; those who came, whether as conquerors or as peaceful settlers, never went back. "No outstanding Indian Muslim migrated to Persia or anywhere else except to the Hijaz."[33] The steady stream of migrants of all classes from home helped in sustaining old-world sentiments and attitudes undiluted. Throughout the medieval period, the Ashraf had two homes to which they were equally attached — the one they had left, their spiritual home; the other, India, wherein they had settled down and were flourishing.

The old-world ties tended to get weak with the passage of time and changing circumstances. There was first the religio-political bond stemming from the supremacy of the Khalif as the spiritual and temporal head of the Islamic community the world over; every Muslim ruler derived his authority to govern from the Khalif only. This classical conception could be sustained only for a short time. Later, there were frequent scrambles for the high office, and rival claimants demanded the obedience of the faithful. Also, soon enough, many Muslim rulers exercised the authority of the Khalif within their own domains without seeking or obtaining specific sanction. In India, while the early Sultans were circumspect, the Mughuls felt strong enough to ignore the Khalif's claim to obedience, and dispensed with the formality of obtaining his sanction at the time of ascending the throne. They even claimed the dignity of the Khalif for themselves, though not in too prominent a way as it would have shocked the orthodox and evoked opposition. Akbar and Shahjahan avoided confrontation by conceding the Ottoman's primacy; only it was not made clear whether the respect shown was one due to a great potentate or to the supreme head of the Islamic community, the Khalif. Early during his reign, Akbar addressed Sulaiman the Magnificent as "the Khalif on earth, the refuge of the princes of the time, and the adjuster of the lords of the age."[34] Much of what Akbar did in later years however showed no great concern for the feelings of the orthodox. Later, when Tipu Sultan failed to obtain the recognition of the Mughul as a ruler, he sought and obtained it as from a higher authority, the Khalif.[35] The old-world bond arising out of obedience to the Khillafat had clearly lost its potency, but it had not wholly vanished. How the nearly-dead embers could shoot up to flame was seen in the Khilafat movement of 1918-20. The dissident Shias owed no obedience to the Khalif, but they evinced a similar attachment, though less strong and defined, towards the Shah of Iran, the land wherein most Shias lived.

There was also the politics of the Islamic world of which the Muslim rulers of India were members. There were invasions whenever there was power vacuum at Delhi. At the height of the power of the Mughuls, special attention had to be paid towards the security of the north-west frontier; in the years of decline, the invasions of Nadir Shah and Ahmed Shah Abdali seemed to herald the birth of a new dynasty. In turn, strong rulers at Delhi cast covetous eyes across the frontier. Fight with Iran over Kandahar was a constant feature, and the ambition of reconquering the Central Asian homeland has been described as the *folie de grandeur* or the great hereditary folly of the Mughuls. The mountain barriers however kept them away from over involvement.

Of greater importance was the religio-cultural factor. The Indian Ashraf sought to model themselves on and be every bit like the elite of the Islamic world outside. The Quranic and religious tradition of the Arabs and the literary and cultural tradition and life style of the Persians constituted their primary heritage. They stood by these and reacted to every trend and development of significance outside. The India of the Ashraf was a part of the Islamic universe, and with them attachment to the land of domicile had a secondary place, though as time passed this tended to be more and more important.

There was at the same time a growing consciousness of pan-Indian Islamic unity; it was a unity within a unity that gathered momentum with the passage of time and the compelling needs of common living in an alien land. The solidarity of the immigrant Muslims as a class emanated from the political predominance they had gained and the prime necessity for unity to preserve it in the face of Hindu hostility.

The Muslim rulers also inherited from the Hindus the concept of *chakravartikshetra* or the vision of One India. What distinguished them from their predecessors was the steadfastness with which they pursued this goal. While Malik Kafur's invasion of the South was mostly a plundering raid, soon after, under Muhammad-bin-Tughluq, in 1323, Madurai, deep down in the south, became the headquarters of a Muslim province. Though the hold of the Delhi Sultans over the distant region proved to be transitory, the achievement was comparable to that of Asoka and Aurangzib. The expansionist spirit was at work continuously. Akbar said in his Happy Sayings, "A monarch should be ever intent on conquest, otherwise his enemies rise in arms against him."[36] According to Jadunath Sarkar, to the Mughuls, unification of India was a primary and great objective, and they never resiled from it. As Y.A. Raikar observes, "Aurangzib actually, in one sense, died for the unification of India. Restless to realise that object, he risked his real best."[37]

A significant aspect of the progress of Muslim arms was the establishment of a strong centralized government, eliminating all possible rivals. This was a marked departure from the old Hindu tradition of being content with mere acceptance of suzerainty and payment of tribute. It was, however, in keeping with the invaders' own tradition, which allowed no quarter to the enemy who was subdued. Further, the Hindus, who were strong in numbers and in land and money power, could not have been held under subjection without such a government.

There is another interesting aspect. Tarachand has pointed out that in pre-Muslim India, there was a lack of centrality, territorially viewed; no states crystallised around specific centres as it happened in Europe in the case of London, Paris and Rome.[38] The view overlooks the fact that there were many centres providing centrality for long periods, specially at subnational levels, e.g., Pataliputra, Ujjain, Kanchi and Madurai. There is, however, no doubt that this aspect gained greatly in importance with the coming of Muslims. This was largely due to the fact that the invaders came invariably through the north-western passes of the Himalayas, and whoever held Delhi gained the upper hand. Delhi provided centrality to Indian polity throughout the medieval period.

The situation changed with the coming of the British. Their strength lay in their power over the seas, and it is Madras, Bombay and Calcutta that provided centrality to political life during British rule. Of them, Calcutta attained primacy, and enjoyed the status for a century and a half, though Delhi retained some of the charisma of the old days. The shifting of the capital to Delhi in 1911 was primarily due to pride and sentiment — it was the crowning symbol of the British supplanting the Mughul. The centrality attained in the medieval period was much more than territorial. The power struggle, whatever form it took, was in essence between two blocks, Hindu and Muslim, and this had all-India dimensions. Similarly, during British rule, it is the anti-imperial struggle that provided centrality to politics. The impact in both cases was to bring together the elite and dominant classes all over the land for appropriate political action. This was an important aspect of the process of unification.

In brief, the Muslim vision and heritage of One India centered round four facets — pan-Indian Islamic unity; the maintenance of Muslim political predominance; bringing the whole land under Muslim rule; forging of a steel frame, a centralized government, to retain power. Also, the Hindu-Muslim confrontation itself deepened all-India consciousness on both sides. Subject to the several reservations made earlier, we may endorse K.M. Panikkar's observation, "The conception of political unity (of India as whole) was broadly speaking an Islamic conception."[39] The British only took the country a step further in the same direction.

The great vision, the hopes and aspirations entertained by the Muslim ruling classes, were shattered by the decline of the Mughuls and the loss of political predominance. Further, since land, trade and commerce were in Hindu hands, they had no economic viability and little to fall back upon. There was a sea change in the life of the Indian Muslims — the Ashraf who had held aloof came closer to the Muslim commoners; pan-Indian Islamic consciousness, which had been confined to the upper classes, percolated to the grass roots. Indian Muslims emerged out of the travails of the eighteenth century and the following decades as an integrated community, with the claim to be a nation.[40] In the changed situation, there were two courses open — to merge with the

Hindu syncretically in all matters of common interest on an equal footing, or continue with the fight for predominance and special status. Opinion was sharply divided over what was best. Muslims the world over had known no subjection, and were unaccustomed to sharing power with others. It was a novel situation they faced in India. While those democratically inclined favoured moderation and compromise, the diehards had greater sway. In later days, the core of the communal problem under the British centered round the Muslim claims based upon 'political importance' grounded in history. It was this assertion in its extreme form that led to Partition and the creation of Pakistan. The Muslim vision of One India based on their political predominance had been shattered. The desire now was to preserve that predominance at least in the areas where they were numerically strong. The Partition left a larger proportion of Muslims in Hindu India. These were to continue the struggle for their rightful claims as national minority and also for their old-time special privileges — a challenging legacy indeed.

The Role of Subnationalism

THE GENERAL TRENDS

The vision of One India was a reality from the earliest times, but the gulf separating One India from the villages and the little worlds was very wide. It was not at all easy to maintain links with the poor means of communication available, besides other factors. The several moves aimed at fusion at lower levels and the emergence of subnational political and cultural entities were not only natural but also necessary. At the dawn of historical times, we have a picture of countless little worlds with different dialects and cultural life all over the land. The spread of the Aryan culture had made great headway, and subnational unities too were becoming visible. As G.S. Ghurye observes, the latter trend, "the cracks in the homo-geneous-looking frontage of culture," was only making concrete in the cultural province what was happening in the political and military fields.[41] The history of Tamil as a developed language goes back to the Sangam classics, which date back at least to the beginnings of the Christian era. Kannada and Telugu emerged a little later.[42] The birth of the modern vernaculars of the northern belt, phonetically linked with Sanskrit, was much later, between the tenth and the thirteenth centuries. This coincided with the invasion of Muslims and the establishment of Muslim rule. By the beginning of the medieval period, the linguistic subnational map of India was clearly etched. It is important to note the sea change that had occurred.For the most part of the ancient period, Sanskrit and the associated all-India classical culture (inclusive of the Buddhist and Jain classical heritage) stood out like the towering Himalayas amidst countless little hillocks of local dialects and cultures. At the close of the period, however, with the process of fusion and unification that had gone on and the emergence of the regional languages and cultures of the present day, Sanskrit and the all-India culture came to constitute only the highest range amidst other high ranges that had erupted.

The rise of the regional languages was a historic necessity. The number of local dialects was too many. Once the knowledge of writing became universal and literary media emerged, the rise of the major regional languages, bringing together and fusing several dialects, was only a matter of time. When Sanskrit ceased to be a spoken language, Pali and Prakrit took its place. When they too in turn ceased to be spoken and became classical, the modern vernaculars emerged. It is sometimes said that the two trends, one favouring all-India homogeneity and the other favouring local developments, were opposed to each other, working at cross purposes continually, and the unity of India of the Asokan days was lost with the diversification of scripts and the rise of the regional languages. These views have only a limited validity. The two trends were to a great extent well-co-ordinated; they were only two facets of the same process. The regional languages were the principal instruments for the spread of the Aryan religious heritage and culture throughout the land, and also for taking the higher culture down to the masses. In this process, as explained earlier, the Aryan culture itself became a composite culture absorbing much from the local contacts. Throughout the medieval period, Sanskrit and the higher Aryan culture acted as co-ordinators and inculcated homogeneity at the all-India level; the development of the regional languages and cultures was within the framework set by them. Indeed, it was only with the dawn of the modern age and growing secularism that the regional languages came of age and began to have an independent development. In brief, from the point of cultural unification, the rise of the regional languages was seminal and highly significant in three ways — they laid the foundation for the growth of subnationalism, political and cultural, bringing closer countless little worlds; they helped in forging cultural unification of the whole land as they were primarily engaged in conveying the treasures of the all-India culture to the people at the regional level; they enriched the common culture of the land with their own contributions making it as much regional as all-India in orientation, and helping it in gaining general acceptance. The role of linguistic subnationalism in the pre-modern age was positive and constructive, and far from disruptive.

As regards manifestation of subnationalism in its political aspect, from early times, there were small and stable states within the bounds of the later-day linguistic-culture zones, which coincided with the historical geographic zones into which India could be divided, as made out by Y.A. Raikar — the Indus basin: Punjab and Sind, Rajaputana, Gujarat, Malwa linking north and south, and Bundelkhand; the Gangetic basin: Delhi (Western Hindi), Kanauj (Eastern Hindi), Bihar (Maithili) and Bengali Orissa; Deccan; South India between Tungabhadra and Kaveri; and Extreme South: South Tamilnad and Kerala.[43] Since regional languages emerged initially in the South, it was there that kingdoms with noticeable subnational characteristics first appeared —the Chera-Chola-Pandya in the Tamil zone, the Gangas and Hoysalas in Karnataka, the Western Chalukyas, Rashtrakutas and Yadavas in Maharashtra, and the Eastern Chalukyas and Kakatiyas in the Telugu region.

There is another aspect to the issue — nationalism associated with big empires *vis a vis* subnationalism associated with small states. It is a common misconception that nationalism and big empires contributed towards peace, stability and progress more than subnationalism and small states. In India, it was the small states that flourished most of the time. Y.A. Raikar is on strong ground when he says, "Though so much of emphasis is laid upon Indian unity in reconstructing Indian history, it is to be noted that large empires are only a short-lived and feeble feature of Indian polity throughout history," and there would be great peril "if the history of India is mistaken to be the history of the empires."[44] The smaller states, it should be remembered, were not tiny principalities, but large, viable kingdoms. When large empires like those of the Mauryas or the Guptas, and later of the Mughuls, disintegrated, there was no anarchy or chaos. Economic progress and cultural development did not come to a stop. Most of the significant achievements were when small kingdoms flourished. While the focus of nationalism was the whole land, that of subnationalism was the region; one laid stress on horizontal unity and the other on vertical unity. The rise of small kingdoms and big empires in turn provided the necessary balance for the operation of the two forces and ensured that both types of unity did not suffer. Laying stress on the constructive aspect of subnationalism, Y.A. Raikar writes, "The evolution of a region is an interesting phenomenon. A basically geographical unit gradually attains some degree of cultural homogeneity and in the course of history it is transformed into a political state. This gives a new significance to its culture expressed through the local language. Under the patronage of the ruling dynasty, not only a vertical development of that culture is achieved, but also there is a horizontal spread of certain cultural traits with the expansion of the state. This leads to cultural synthesis. With the decay of power, it contracts and remains localised in its original home. This process is eternally operating throughout Indian history."[45] Endorsing this view, B. Subba Rao says, "India is a large cell not with one nucleus but several", and S.C. Malik cautions, "It is apparent that all universal schemes that do not take into account the specific regional factors in India will prove to be misfits in a traditional structure of civilization like that of India."[46]

As stated earlier, the growth of the modern regional languages and of subnationalism centering round them was more or less a medieval phenomenon, and the establishment and prevalence of Muslim rule at the time had its profound impact. A few Muslim rulers like Nasrat Shah of Bengal and

Muhammad Adil Shah of Bijapur were great patrons of Hindu saints and vernacular learning. Based on this fact, some have grossly exaggerated the role of Muslims. But for their coming, one scholar observes, the Hindus would not have had the courage to displace Sanskrit. I.H. Qureshi writes, "The greatest contribution of the Muslim rulers was the encouragement of the contemporary vernacular languages which broke the artificial barriers created by the insistence on Sanskrit as the medium of expression, and opened the floodgates of literary and religious activity."[47] The decadance of Sanskrit literature often referred to by scholars was qualitative, not at all quantitative. This trend had set in well before the tenth century, as noted by the eminent Sanskritist M.A. Mehendale and others.[48] The flowering of the regional languages had begun in earnest in most parts well before Muslim rule took root. If Muslim rule was beneficial, it was because of its negative role. Under the new dispensation, there was no great movement of Hindu shcolars from court to court or from one center of learning to another; Hindu learning became insular and regional. The drying up of court patronage made for increased dependence on the middle and the lower classes. And this increased the tempo of the trend already there — that of carrying the higher learning and culture associated with Sanskrit, Pali and Prakrit to the people at large through the vernaculars, and the general development of the regional languages.

As regards the political aspect of subnationalism during Muslim rule, it was the imperial and centralizing trend that was dominant. Only when the power of Delhi was weak, regional Muslim kingdoms flourished, specially in the outskirts — Gujarat, Bengal and the South. The rise of these provincial kingdoms was conditioned by the geographical and historical factors referred to earlier. Also, the imperial rulers took note of the prevailing subnational sentiments and traditions in fashioning policies. Jahangir wrote in his memoirs, "It is agreed that the boundary of a country is the place upto which people speak the language of that country." Aurangzib's 21 administrative divisions corresponded closely "to the natural and linguistic divisions of India." Also, to some extent, local people were associated with the administration, and some of the governors patronised local cultures.[49]

The main political issue of the time was how the Hindus reacted to Muslim rule. Muslim military prowess had acquired an aura of invincibility not only in India but in the rest of the world too.[50] Organized all-India revolt was not within the realm of possibility for reasons stated earlier. However, Hindus offered resistance whenever there was a chance. The progress of Muslim arms had been halted at the local or little world level, and the authority of the rulers made less effective. There were volcanic eruptions at higher levels only when the power of the government was pronouncedly weak and the administration highly unpopular. The reign of Aurangzib and the Mughul decadence thereafter provided such an occasion. Subnationalism came to its own in the political field in a big way with the rise of the Marathas, Rajputs and Sikhs. In the case of all the three, the need to safeguard hearth and home provided the material motivation, the call of religion gave the emotional drive, and the bond of racio-linguistic unity and common faith gave them solidarity, confidence and strength.

MARATHA NATIONALISM

There was a vein of rebellious sentiment from Jnanesvar to Tukaram and Ramdas as reflected in Marathi literature. But there was no sign of any political upsurge from the Yadavas to Shivaji. As S.N. Sen observed, the Maratha Watandars or chiefs loved their feudal independence more than religion —"There was no sacrifice he could not make for it; even apostacy from his religion was not too high a price to pay for its retention."[51] It is the Mughul expansion into their heartland that roused their will to resist. Doggedness and grim determination on the part of the Watandars would have been of little avail if a leader of the calibre of Shivaji had not arisen. Also, the emotional drive would have been absent if the Bhakti saints had not prepared the ground from the time of Jnanesvar, and the Pandarpur movement was not at the height of its popularity at the time. Ramdas was the spiritual father of Maratha nationalism as much as Shivaji on the political side.

Scholars have differed over the question of the specific

objectives Shivaji had in view. Clearly his main object was
to save the Marathas from being conquered by the Mughuls
and also to recover the lost lands. He founded a Maratha
state united by race, language and religion. It was *Swarajya*
or one's own state. The term *Maharashtra Dharma* widely
used indicated the bond being as much linguistic and religio-
cultural as political. One of Shivaji's well-known sayings was
"This is not the kingdom of Shivaji; it belongs to Dharma",
and "It is for the protection of cows and Brahmanas." It was
a *Hindavi Swarajya* he had in view.[52] Characteristic of the
Hindu tradition, as stated earlier, this did not imply or involve
confrontation with Islam or any curtailment of the religious
freedom of Muslims.

Shivaji's vision does not appear to have extended beyond
unifying Marathas and freeing the Maratha land.
M.G. Ranade writes, "The idea of forging a confederacy of
Hindu powers all over India, and subverting Mussulman
dominion appears never to have seriously been entertained
by him."[53] Shivaji had an ideal, but he was no visionary. In
his time, few would have dreamt of supplanting the Mughuls.
Placed as he was, it would not be incorrect to surmise that
even Shivaji would have acquiesced and entered the Mughul
world, if only Aurangzib had been considerate and liberal.
Akbar had persuaded the Raja of Mewar to fall in line, but
Aurangzib was not Akbar. As things transpired, following the
treaty of Purandhar (1665), Jai Singh had prevailed upon
Shivaji to visit Delhi and pay homage. Aurangzib queered
the pitch by offering a Mansab of 5,000 only and imprisoning
Shivaji when he protested in open court. If it were not for
the highly imperialistic and anti-Hindu policy of the emperor,
there was yet room for conciliation. It is clear that not paying
homage to the Mughul was never an article of faith with
the Marathas. Shahu's acceptance of a Mansab was not
something forced upon him. According to S.N. Sen, "he was
sincere in his belief in the legitimacy of the Mughul claim"
to universal domain.[54] The later Peshwa approach too was
far from rigid in this respect.

The idea of ousting the Mughul and establishing a Hindu
rule over the whole land, the vision of a *Hindu-pad-padshahi*,
appeared to be something practicable only with the thumping
military successes of Baji Rao I. According to S.N. Sen, most

of his wars "could be invested with religious character".[55]
The idea might have caught Hindu imagination all over the
land and inspired Hindus to action if Maratha policy had
not become imperialistic and antagonised Hindus as much
as Muslims. Maratha chauvinism was no new phenomenon.
According to G.S. Sardesai, even under Shahji in Bijapur
service, in Karnataka and the Tamil countries, Marathas were
predominant in the army and the civil services, Marathi was
the court language, Maharashtran system of administration
and of maintaining accounts was in force, and miniature
Maharashtras had arisen.[56] Under the later Peshwas,
Marathas antagonised everyone so thoroughly that in North
India they had come to be known by the common name *ganim*
or enemy, a name of which they were once proud while facing
the Mughul might.[57] At the time of the battle of Panipat,
no Hindu ruler was on their side. Maratha imperialism blasted
the prospects of the *Hindu-pad-padshahi*.

Assessing the character of Maratha nationalism, Tarachand
observes, "In the political structure created by Shivaji and
inherited by his successors, the idea of an exclusive Maratha
people united by national and moral bonds and devoted to
the maintenance of their Maratha identity, welfare and
independence never became prominent."[59] The standard he
has set is perhaps too high. The national bond was no doubt
weak in many respects. But, it cannot be doubted that
Maratha nationalism was anterior to Shivaji, had its glorious
period, and has continued in a subdued form down to our
times — Maratha imperialism was itself a facet of Maratha
nationalism.

THE RAJPUTS AND RAJASTHANI NATIONALISM

The Rajputs were a Hindu caste just like others. While they
were to be found in different parts of North India, they were
mostly in Rajasthan, constituting about ten per cent of the
population of the region. Whatever be their origin, they were
the ruling class at the time of the Muslim invasion. Holding
on to their desert fortresses, they put up the best and most
prolonged resistance that the Hindus exhibited in the whole
land. As such, the term Rajput came to be a synonym for

valour and chivalry. Originally looked down upon as *vratyas* (barbarians) by the orthodox highbrows, they came to be accepted as Kshatriyas of blue blood not to be found elsewhere. The Rajputs stood for the whole local community — it was Rajasthani nationalism or Hindu nationalism, of which the Rajputs were the spearhead.

There was one weak spot of magnitude in the Rajput armour. Divided into 36 clans and with several ruling dynsties, they were unable to coalesce and form a compact kingdom. The utmost achieved was acceptance of the primacy of Jaipur and Jodhpur. The resistance that Rajput rulers put up was mostly individual. Unable to unite among themselves, they could hardly be expected to give a lead to any pan-Hindu struggle covering the whole land. The only instance perhaps of a plan to this effect being mooted was the one mentioned in *Vir Vinod* of Kaviraj Shyamal Das referred to earlier.

In sharp contrast to their dogged prolonged resistance, the Rajputs finally acquiesced and came to be close to the Mughuls. They had their share of power, getting most of the Mansabdaris given to Hindus, and some of them contracted matrimonial alliances. The Rajputs retained their distinctness and subnational identity under the Mughuls, and the regiments they raised for them were entirely Rajput in composition. They were a part of the Mughul nobility and were deeply involved in the Mughul court politics. A testing time came when they were confronted by the anti-Hindu policies of Aurangzib, and again in the years of Mughul decline when Hindu power was asserting itself everywhere. They were, time and again, torn between loyalty to the Mughul and the call of religion. They disapproved Aurangzib's policies; they were discontented and protested. They did not, however, raise a banner of revolt or join forces with the Marathas. By and large, they were no less loyal to the Mughul cause than the Muslim nobles. If the Mughul authority vanished, they preferred to revert to their earlier independent status than exchange masters.

Rajput nationalism was born of the stubborn and prolonged fight put up against Muslims. It survived many trials. Though they had been humbled and acquiesced, the Rajputs retained their national identity and flourished under the

Mughuls. After the Mughuls too, they retained their political importance, since they came to be a part of the Princely world under the British. This went a long way to ensure the survival of the old-time sentiments and loyalties down to modern times. All through, Rajput nationalism was broadbased — it drew sustenance as much from the racial factor as from language and religion. There was also the deep attachment of the people towards their rulers, and the traditional loyalty evoked. As such, Rajput nationalism was not that of a caste group; it was for the most part Rajasthani nationalism.

SIKH AND PUNJABI NATIONALISM

Sikh nationalism was an aspect of the emergence of the Sikhs as a religio-political community. The founder of the Sikh faith, Guru Nanak (1469-1538), was a radical reformer like Kabir, Dadu and others. It is significant that, outside the Punjab, only moderate reformers like Chaitanya and Basavesvara registered success and founded great sects. It was in the Punjab alone that the radicals could leave a deep permanent impress. The prime determining factor for their success here was the fact that the scene lay in the north-western region, which was most prone to attack by Muslim invaders and also bordered on the outside Muslim world. Hari Ram Gupta has stated that there were nearly seventy Muslim invasions during the five hundred years preceding Nanak.[59] Also, because of proximity, the extent of proselytization and the impact of outside Islamic culture were great. More than half the population of the frontier region were converted to Islam. In this highly strife-worn region, it was only natural that the Hindu social system and institutions should receive the severest drubbing, and these were fast crumbling when Guru Nanak and his successors entered on the scene. The anti-caste, anti-idol worship and anti-priest message of Nanak was like lighted tinder to dry wood.

Sikh religious history lays great stress on the persecutions suffered and the lives of those who died martyrs. However, it is important to remember that, under the Great Mughuls, treatment of non-Muslims in the Punjab could not have been less liberal than elsewhere. The progress of Sikhism was

closely linked with political happenings; religion and politics
could not be easily separated. The fifth pontiff Guru Arjun
(1581-1606) was the first great martyr. According to Jadunath
Sarkar, in a weak moment, he had blessed the banners of
Khusrau, the rival of Jahangir to the throne; when a heavy
fine was imposed for his disloyalty, he refused to pay and
died a martyr.[60] From the time of the succeeding Guru, Har
Govind, for a whole century, as Shafaat Ahmad Khan
observes, the Sikhs were making "a desperate attempt to
conquer the country of their birth, and to carve out a
principality in which the purest doctrines of the Khalsa could
be realised", and it is this which the Mughuls were trying
to put down with a heavy hand.[61] In every confrontation,
John Malcolm observes, there was "implacable sense of injury
on one part, and the insolence and violence of insulted power
on the other." Also, "To unite and to act in one body, and
on one principle, was, with the first Sikhs, a law of necessity;
it was, amid the dangers with which they were surrounded,
their only hope of success, and their sole means of
preservation."[62] In similar situations, the Hindus elsewhere
had not acted with fervour and determination. The early Sikh
Gurus too were pacific in their outlook. It was only after the
martyrdom of Guru Arjun in 1606 that Sikhs started
organizing themselves to form a militant community. Nearly
after a century, stirred by the anti-Hindu policy of Aurangzib,
Guru Govind Singh, the last Guru, accorded the development
the status of a dogma by giving Sikhs two swords to fight
with — the *faqiri* and the *amiri* (that of a saint and that
of a ruler). It was a highly militant version of the stand saint
Ramdas had taken earlier in Maharashtra.

The welding together of the Sikhs to form a militant
religio-political community, determined to stand up to their
rights, was very opportune. After Aurangzib's death, political
life was disturbed throughout the land; it was particularly
so in the Punjab, with frequent invasions by Afghans from
Kabul and their oppressive rule. *Seir Mutaqherin* noted that
Sikhs grew in numbers as they were considered to be a sure
and safe refuge from Afghan oppression.[63] In the great
struggle between the Marathas and the Afghans for
supremacy, the real victors were the Sikhs; they filled the
political vacuum created by the enfeeblement of both of them.

They consolidated their position under twelve Misals or miniature kingdoms; it is these that Ranjit Singh welded into a single Sikh state.

Sikh nationalism centred round a definitive faith — the teachings of the ten Gurus enshrined in the *Granth Sahib*, the book itself becoming the prime object of adoration and worship. The language and script of the sacred book came to be the linguistic bond holding the community together, and there was deep sentimental attachment towards them on religious grounds. The oldest book in the Punjabi language is a biography of Guru Nanak, *Janam Sakhi*, written by a disciple, and the growth of the language was closely linked with that of the sect. While emerging as a separate sect Sikhs established their own places of worship and evolved their own rituals. The five jewels that Guru Govind Singh wanted every Sikh to possess and cherish had the trappings of a regimental uniform — *kesh* (long hair), *kanga* (comb), *kirpan (sword)*, *kara* (steel bracelet), and *kaccha* (a pair of knickerbockers or loin cloth worn in a particular way). These made Sikhs distinctive and prominent in any gathering. Strict conformity to the prescribed external forms of the faith was enjoined on every member. The democratic organization that was set up to run the affairs of the community, the Khalsa, was all powerful, and every Sikh had a sense of belonging and of sharing power. The close-knit community, steeped in faith and conscious of its power, was very much on par with the Puritans and the Jesuits at the height of their influence and popularity. Every contemporary referred to the fervour and enthusiasm exhibited by the Sikhs. *Seir Mutaqherin* was all praise for the fortitude and courage of Banda and his followers at the time of execution.[64] Another contemporary observed that nobody would have taken any notice of the Jat Sardars if they had not embraced the new faith — "now they have put on the iron bracelet, fifty of them are enough to keep at bay a whole battalion of the King's forces, such as they are. This shows the force of prejudice and the value of military reputation."[65]

When power came their way with the rise of the Misals and the creation of the Sikh state by Ranjit Singh, the Sikhs acquired a strong mundane base and deep material interest closely linked with religion. It was but natural that political leadership should be in the hands of the Sikhs, and the army was predominantly Sikh. So long as the Sikhs were on the defensive and fighting for self-preservation, democratic functioning of the Khalsa was possible and had its advantages. It was different when it came to governance of a multi-caste multi-religious community of which the Sikhs were only a part. But the Khalsa claim to supremacy was there to contend with. The Sikhs had risen to power under its leadership —*Raj Karega Khalsa*, the Khalsa shall rule, had been the slogan. The Khalsa had always been associated with policy-making and political happenings. When the Sikhs rose to power, it was natural that it should resent being ignored. In 1761, on the capture of Lahore, the victorious Misal chief issued a coin in his own name. The Khalsa forced him to withdraw it, and issue a new one in the name of the Khalsa in the accepted form.[66] But the Khalsa could not run a government when a state emerged. The Misal chiefs had acted independently often enough. Ranjit Singh was not subject to the dictates of the body over-much. But its formal supremacy was there and had to be respected. It was a Khalsa state (*Sarkar-i-Khalsa*) that he headed. He considered himself a servant of the Khalsa and did not assume any regal honours. The principal coin issued was known as Nanak Shahi. The governing spirit of the state was "Khalsa nationalism", "a product of the idea of the Sikh commonwealth or an outcome of the *espirit de corps* among the Sikhs", as Fauja Singh Bajwa observes.[67] This is the view of Sikh nationalism that is generally accepted by scholars.

Striking a new line, in his interesting study *A History of the Sikhs*, Khushwant Singh has held that the Sikh movement was broadbased and secular, that it was Punjabi nationalism that had emerged. His thesis is that Nanak's followers came from all communities, and paid homage to the ideal he had set forth — "There is no Hindu, there is no Mussalman." And, "it was this ideal which gave birth to Punjabi consciousness and Punjabi nationalism."[68] Sikhism was a bridgebuilder, seeking to bring together the two great communities in the spiritual field. In the field of politics and public affairs, though the leadership was Sikh, the goal was to keep both the Afghans and the Marathas out — Punjab was to be for the Punjabis. Liberalism and tolerance succeeded in securing for the Sikh rule the massive support of the whole community.

This view has come in for sharp criticism,[69] and in the face of the strident Akali spirit that permeated throughout, Khushwant Singh seems to have no case at all. But a closer look reveals that his thesis rests upon a strong-enough ground, and this is for a reason on which he has laid very inadequate stress. Until we come to the closing decades of the last century, it would be wrong to consider the Sikhs to have been different from the Hindus. Nanak was only one of the many radical reformers among the Hindus, though the most important and successful. When Nanak said "There is no Hindu, there is no Mussalman", he was only exhibiting the eclecticism and universal outlook of Hindu religion and culture. His attempt to be a bridgebuilder between the two opposed faiths was in keeping with the Hindu tradition. When the Sikh Gurus attacked caste, spoke against idol worship, and inveighed against superstitious beliefs and practices, they were addressing the Hindus, and referring to their shortcomings. They borrowed freely from other Hindu reformers who were seeking to convey the same message. The Hindu myths and legends were part of their stock. It was mostly the Hindu that answered the call of the Gurus. When the Sikhs fought for their faith and their rights, they always felt they were fighting for the whole of the Hindu community. This may be seen in the events connected with the launching of the crusade by Guru Govind Singh in 1699, which proved to be momentous. By way of preparation, to seek the blessings of Goddess Durga, he performed a *homa* (sacrifice), which lasted for six months and was officiated by Pandit Kesho of Benares.[70] What he was fighting for, he stated clearly in his *Bichitra Natak*, with reference to the martyrdom of his father:

"To Protect their right to wear their
    caste-marks and sacred threads,
Did he, in the dark age, perform
    the supreme sacrifice,
To help the saintly he went to
    the utmost limit,
He gave his head, but never
    cried in pain."[71]

While such was the approach of the Sikhs, the non-radical
or orthodox Hindus reciprocated the sentiment of oneness and
unity. In their view, the Sikhs were neo-Kshatriyas fighting
for them; their role was the same as that of the Rajputs,
who were close to orthodoxy. The complete identification of
non-Sikh Hindus with the Sikhs gave Khalsa nationalism the
solidarity, popularity and strength which it may not have
otherwise attained.

There were other factors too that made Khalsa nationalism
less communal and more broad-based and secular. In driving
back the Afghans from Kabul and holding the Marathas at
bay, thus preserving the peace of the region, they earned the
gratitude of all. As Khushwant Singh says, they "built up
(perhaps unconsciously) the notion that the Punjab would be
better off if it were ruled by Punjabis rather than remain
a part of the kingdom of Kabul or the Mughul empire", or
fall into Maratha hands.[72] Again, there was the proletarian
aspect. Many have viewed the Sikh uprising as "a specific
form of a lower class movement", and held that the restricted
religious appeal came in the way of its gathering greater
momentum and heralding a general peasant uprising .[73]
Most important of all was the attitude towards the Muslims
who constituted the majority. Sikhism emerged as a syncretic
faith, holding Islam in great respect. There could be no quarrel
with the Muslims as such. The Sikh struggle was with the
Muslim ruling classes, Mughul and Afghan, and also with
the Hindu zamindars who were ranged with the rulers. There
was, however, a phase of bitter communal antagonism lasting
for several decades following the martyrdom of Guru Govind
Singh and the execution of Banda. There was also the
persisting Afghan menace, and the attempts to revive the
old *jihad* spirit. When peace returned and the Sikhs were
in power, the Muslims did not fare badly under their rule,
and that despite the troubled past and haunting memories.
Shafaat Ahmad Khan writes, "On the whole, it must be stated
that though the Muslims under Ranjit Singh were subject
to some serious disabilities, such as the prohibition of *Azam*
in parts of the Punjab, there is no evidence to show that
the community was denied the exercise of most of its religious
and civic rights. In his reign, career was open to talent, and
many able Muslims secured positions of supremeresponsibility

and trust in Ranjit Singh's service." Also, he says, "Muslims were not given inferior rights, nor were they treated as second-class citizens."[74]

Thus, despite the patent limitations, Sikh nationalism partook the character of Punjabi nationalism in good measure because of the general acceptance gained, and Khushwant Singh's thesis stands largely vindicated. However, an important reservation is to be made to what has been stated above. The character of Sikh nationalism underwent a radical change from the mid-nineteenth century onwards. The eclipse of Muslim power had removed the emotional factor that had helped the Sikhs to gain in numbers and importance; their own loss of power made them lose the prestige and support that power had brought. They were now reduced to a simple minority. On the religious front, the rise of the Arya Samaj brought in a powerful rival in regard to gaining converts from among the unweaned orthodox Hindu. With the general acceptance of the radical ideas propagated in good measure by the Hindu community at large, the need for formal change of faith was no longer felt, and there was even a trend towards reversion to the ancestral faith. These developments put the Sikhs on their guard, and the desire to maintain their distinctness and importance, both as a religious and a political community, became intense. In this, they were greately helped by the policy pursued by the Government of India in respect of army recruitment and development of the Canal Colonies in the Punjab. The Sikhs were now primarily interested in maintaining their special and sectional interests as a community. Sikh nationalism took a communal turn, and became a part of the communal problem of the country.

General Appraisal

To restate the strength and weaknesses of the territorial consciousness and national outlook of the pre-modern age, their manifestation and intensity depended upon the degree of homogeneity and solidarity attained. The greatest impediment came from the pre-modern conditions of life —poor transport facilities made closer relationship difficult, and ignorance of the knowledge of printing had a similar impact on the intellectual field. The vastness of the country too was a major decisive factor. Life was intense, but confined; insularity was inescapable owing to the conditions of the times. The progress made was despite these handicaps. Caste and sectarian differences made for heterogeneity and gave rise to tensions and conflicts. But Hindu eclecticism and spirit of tolerance ensured that these did not go out of control. In the long run, sectarian differences provided variety; the oscillation between rigidity and flexibility of caste made for steady orderly progress, and gave stability to the system of caste itself. Village self-sufficiency and absence of marked class differences ensured economic stability and made for homogeneity at the local level. Decentralised industrial development centering round villages and absence of regional rivalries made for economic well-being without rousing conflicts and tensions. The pace of progress was slow, comparable to that of a meandering river. Absence of uprooting revolutionary movements in any field was a characteristic feature. In pre-Muslim India, the homogeneity and solidarity attained and the territorial consciousness and national outlook evinced at the different levels, local regional and all-India, were consistent with what was possible.

With the coming of Muslims, Islamic fundamentalism and the aggressive expansionist outlook made for a divided society. Despite provocations and trying circumstances, the Hindu attitude favoured mutual accommodation and synthesis to the extent necessary for harmonious living. It was the Muslim approach that required radical change, specially on the part of the immigrant Ashraf class. That Islam's success was only partial, and most Muslims were local converts and heirs to the indigenous tradition, made such a change not only desirable but also inescapable. But the spirit of fundamentalism and exclusiveness ingrained in the alien Islamic heritage, and the keenness to maintain the dominant position attained unimpaired, made the process of acculturation and integration slow, halting and difficult. The progress made by the close of the Mughul age was, however, considerable. Those who had come to conquer and convert went to live in peace as good neighbours. The *jihad* was mostly gone; it was no more than an occasional feeling of alienness nearly vanished. Hindu-Muslim relations had assumed the familiar inter-caste pattern with both its strength and weakness. On the vocational side, the new comers had got fitted into society as the ruling class, and found employment largely in the army. The local converts pursued their hereditary callings without being disturbed. The emerging trading classes among Muslims such as the Bohras and Lohanas had no difficulty in finding entry into the business class that had become cosmopolitan to a great extent. In the field of public employment, though there were preferences, racial and religious prejudices had assumed a low key. The politics of the land was conditioned by mundane and secular factors and self-interest, not so much by racial and religious considerations. A strong middle class, cutting across race, religion and caste, was emerging. Most important, by and large, there was a general acceptance of the equilibrium reached, and the Hindus and the Muslims had come to form a single community in matters of common concern. The heterogeneity in social structure and way of life was one that was always there, though now more pronounced than earlier. It could be said that 'an Indian community' comprising both the great religious groups had emerged, though the path of integration yet to be traversed was long. This is clear from any casual perusal of memoirs, travelogues and other contemporary records.

There was, however, one ingredient of seminal value lacking in the process of integration — the emotional and sentimental base, the cement that alone could bind the two communities firmly together without fear of breaking off. Common external danger arising from British imperialism was helpful for the growth of national sentiment cutting across religious barrriers as seen from the history of the freedom struggle. This might have proved a clincher if it were not for this grave shortcoming. Both the Hindus and the Muslims took to Western education and absorbed with avidity the Western intellectual tradition, and at the same time enriched Western scholarship. But no such development had taken place in the encounter between the Hindu and the Muslim cultures. There had been no meeting of minds, no growth of syncretic scholarship, no emergence of an integrated intellectual elite.[75] The two did not develop genuine regard for each other's religion and culture. To this day, one cannot name a

distinguished Muslim Vedic scholar or a Hindu noted for
proficiency in Quranic studies. The attitude was the same
towards Christianity on the part of Muslims elsewhere too.
A distinguished scholar observes, "There isn't a single Muslim
scholar in all history ... who has written an authentic essay
on Christianity."[76] Persistence of this lacuna has been
largely in the way of integration and development of a
broadbased national outlook.

Many scholars have been hesitant to accept that pre-modern
India had developed territorial consciousness and national
outlook to any significant extent. In their view, patriotism
centering round villages and their little worlds was only
parochialism glorified; the One India of the Hindu was a vision
that came nowhere near realisation; that of the Muslims
marked the success of the racial and political ambition of
a small class only; subnationalism to the extent it surfaced
was saturated with racial and communal exclusiveness; on
the whole, there was no evidence in the political field of a
healthy all-India national outlook down to modern times. For
instance, with reference to Ancient India, P.V. Kane writes
that though the Hindus had several common bonds making
for homogeneity, "this did not make for a deep seated and
effective sentiment of nationhood or national unity."[77] With
reference to later times, S.N. Sen admits that Shivaji left
the Marathas "fairly united under a ruler of their own with
a national banner and common objective to strive for." But
he hesitates to term the spirit behind *Swarajya* and
Maharashtra Dharma national. He writes, "In that age the
idea of nationality was yet unborn, but race and religion still
stirred the deepest chord in the sentiments of the rude
soldiery."[78] Fauja Singh Bajwa writes that Khalsa
nationalism "was really no nationalism in the modern and
usual sense of the term."[79] A.L. Srivastava writes of the
times, "This was an age of political consciousness and
tribalism for the Punjab, and not that of nationalism in any
part of India."[80] The dissatisfaction in all these cases has
been with reference to the level of progress registered, or to
the source of inspiration or the sentiment of unity being
associated with a section of the community only. The
measuring rod used is nationalism envisaged as an ideal. To
be perfect, nationalism should be of the open type as defined

earlier: it must rest on deep attachment towards every section of the community in equal degree; to be strong it must be based on purposive unity to realise vital common ends. Such a nationalism need not necessarily come in the way of humanism or international cooperation. It has to be remembered that in the whole course of history, the ideal has never been reached by any community. Scholars refer without any hesitation to English nationalism from Tudor times. This was fanatically Episcopalian, attached to the Established Church of England. While the Puritans were able to hold their own, the emancipation of the Roman Catholics came only in 1831 with their admission to Parliament, and this too was only a beginning. The breaking off of Catholic Ireland and the persistent demand for autonomy by the Scots and the Welsh too made apparent the chinks in the British nationalist armour. The nationalism of the French, the Dutch, the Spanish and the Portuguese was equally tinged with religious fanaticism. It was only with the impact of the spirit of secularism generated by the French Revolution that nationalism got divorced from religion. But, then, it fell into the clutches of linguistic chauvinism much more than earlier and the nation-state ideal was bedevilled by the problem of National Minorities and the issue of divided loyalty. If we realise that True Nationalism was and remains in the realm of the ideal only, we would be in a position to assess the progress towards Indian nationhood prior to the modern age at its true value. Taking a broad view, it could be said that territorial consciousness and national outlook played a significant role all through Indian history consistent with the conditions of the times, and the problems of the present day in this respect are very much rooted in the past.

Notes

1. Satchidananda Murty, 66. Elphinstone observed, "These communities contain in miniature all the materials of a state within themselves, and are almost sufficient to protect their members if all other governments were withdrawn."—*Report on Territories Conquered from the Peshwa*, 20.
2. D.D. Kosambi has noted the survival of some aspects of communal ownership of land to the present day in a small part of Goa.—*Myth*

*and Reality,*Chap.V. After an in-depth study, Ramakrishna Mukherjee, p.150, observes, "In a broad sense at least; land was held in common by the village community, so that all transactions in land within a village could be undertaken by the villagers with the permission and direct supervision of the village assembly or council."

3.   Two representative opinions may be cited. Tarachand observes that the traditions of village panchayats as distinct and separate from caste panchayats were obscured, if not altogether extinguished, in the North during the Middle Ages.—Vol.I, 106. In the opinion of Nazrul Karim, taking all the evidence available, it would appear that the administration of the villages was oligarchic, not so much democratic, despite representation of all the communities on the Panchayats.—pp.22-3. Also, H.G. Franks, 3-4; Sri Rama Sharma and G.N. Sharma in *Medieval Indian State,* 24 & 106-11; and Percival Spear, 110.

4.   Nanavati and Vakil, 150.

5.   C. Rajagopalachari, 33.

6.   Nazrul Karim, 81-2. Also, S.C. Gupta in Tapan Raychaudhuri, Vol. I, 22-4,38.

7.   Percival Spear, 107.

8.   Y.A. Raikar, 46.

9.   M.N. Srinivas and A.M. Shah, The Myth of Self-Sufficiency of Indian Villages—*The Economic Weekly,* Vol.XII, No.37, pp.1375-8.

10.   Moncton Jones, 7, 159.

11.   C. Rajagopalachari, 33.

12.   Madras Record Office, Judicial Sundries, Police Committee, 1805, Vol.I B, No.45, pp.491-5 *et seqq.*

13.   Commenting on the strength and vitality of "the indigenous, non-official powers" and the weakness of the British administration at the beginning of the century, D.A. Washbrook writes that, with the machinery available to him, Curzon could not have gone the way of Peter the Great—"it (the Government of India) was more 'a mighty and magnificent machine for doing absolutely nothing'." —pp.40-8, 332 *et seqq.*

14.   B. Subba Rao, 34.

15.   Bal Krishna, Indian Theory of the Universal State, in S.R. Tikekar, 180.

16.   G.S. Ghurye in Nanavati and Vakil, 118.

17.   For instance, Romila Thapar, p.7, writes, "What we would recognize as a Hindu today would hardly have been recognizable in the ancient period. The recognizable Hindu begins to emerge in the post-Gupta period in the post-fifth century A.D. There is ample evidence from the sources of the ancient period to suggest that religious sects and groups in pre-Islamic India did not identify themselves as Hindus or as a unified religion. The followers of Buddhism provide a striking contrast in precisely their form of religious organization." The view has its strong points. In their successful confrontation with Mahayana Buddhism to the extent of wiping it out of existence, the castes and sects allied to the Brahminical tradition acquired a clearer identity and gained in importance. Most of the sects and theological schools of the present day no doubt emerged after the Gupta period. Even

so, amorphousness and looseness of structure have always been characteristic of Hindu religion and society. The semantics of the issue apart, unless we take a wider view and equate the Hindu with the Aryan from the beginning, much of the socio-political history of the ancient period would be incomprehensible. We have to accept the existence of a Hindu consciousness in the form of an expanding Aryan consciousness from the earliest times, and also of a sense of community arising therefrom. This was subdued and did not stand out in the absence of a serious external challenge until Islam and Muslims appeared on the scene. On this score, the intensity and vitality of the consciousness need not be doubted. See also pp. 11-5 above.

18. P.V. Kane, Vol.III, 137. Manu is clear that the community was only of Aryans; the Dasyus were excluded "whether they speak the language of the Mlekkhas (barbarians) or that of the Aryans."—G. Buhler, Chap. X-45.

19. R.C. Majumdar, *Imperial Kanauj*, xvi.

20. Santiparva of *Mahabharata*—P.V. Kane, Vol.III, 67.

21. G.S. Ghury observes that monasteries established by Sri Sankaracharya "left out India beyond the Ravi as beyond their purview", and the fundamental and overall unity felt all over India "almost practically comes to be confined to and concretized in respect of the political India of today."—In Nanavati and Vakil, 117-8. No evidence is cited in support of the view. Perhaps the region beyond the Ravi was mostly Buddhist, and as such the Brahminical monastery he founded at Srinagar in Kashmir was not, expected to function there.

22. Buchanan, *Mysore, Canara and Malabar*, Vol.II, 304-6. Q. Crauford, 72-6. A. Sterling, 92-5.

23. P.V.Kane, Vol.III, 136-7. K.M. Panikkar, *Foundations of New India*, 66. S.N. Sen, *Maratha Military System*, 17-8.

24. B. Subba Rao, 24-5. K.V. Sundararajan, Determinant Factors in the Early History of Tamilnadu—*Journal of Indian History*, Vol.XLVI, Sl.136 (April 1968), 56.

25. Percival Spear, 3. Also, Y.A. Raikar, 30.

26. Banarasi Prasad, Presidential Address, *Proceedings of the Indian History Congress*, 1966, p.viii.

27. P.V. Kane, Vol.III, 69, 235.

28. G. Buhler, Chap.VII, 198-203.

29. U.N. Ghoshal, 517.

30. Satishchandra observes that belief in imminent disintegration of the empire was wide spread in the last year of Aurangzib's reign, and this found expression in some of his own letters —pp.40-3, 55.

31. S.V. Desika Char, *Centralised Legislation*, 41-6.

32. The Rajput plan referred to in *Vir Vinod* of Kaviraj Shymal Das. Satishchandra, 34-5.

33. Aziz Ahmed, *Islamic Culture*, 47.

34. *Ibid.*, 28, 37.

35. *Ibid.*, 53.

36. R.C. Majumdar, *The Mughul Empire*, 115.

37. Jadunath Sarkar, *Mughal Administration*, 228. Y.A. Raikar, 35.

38. Tarachand, Vol.I, 71.

39. K.M. Panikkar, *Foundations of New India*, 66.
40. K.M. Panikkar observes, "At the beginning of British rule, the Muslims were a nation, while the Hindus were an incohate mass of people slowly trying to achieve self-realisation based on their common religion and culture."— *Ibid.*, 67.
41. G.S. Ghurye in Nanavati and Vakil, 119.
42. It may be noted that the relative antiquity and chronological sequence of the different Dravidian languages is a matter of dispute among scholars.
43. Y.A. Raikar, 6-8. Also, Subba Rao, 18-23.
44. Y.A. Raikar, 44.
45. *Ibid.*, 45.
46. B. Subba Rao, 35. S.C. Malik, 173.
47. I.H. Qureshi in R.C. Majumdar, *The Delhi Sultanate*, 452.
48. M.A. Mehendale in R.C. Majumdar, *The Struggle for Empire*, 297-8.
49. Satishchandra, xx-xxi. Tarachand, Vol.I, 83.
50. A.J. Toynbee, *A Study of History*, Vol.VIII, 222 *et seqq.*
51. S.N. Sen, *The Maratha Military System*, 3.
52. N.K. Behere, 164-5.
53. M.G. Ranade, *Rise of the Maratha Power* (1961), 39-40, 48.
54. S.N. Sen, *The Maratha Administrative System*, 185.
55. S.N. Sen, *The Maratha Military System*, 59.
56. G.S. Sardesai, Vol.I, 79.
57. S.N. Sen, *The Maratha Military System* 146.
58. Tarachand, Vol.I, 106.
59. Hari Ram Gupta in R.C. Majumdar, *The Mughul Empire*, 305.
60. *Ibid.*, 309. Beni Prasad held the same view — p. 138.
61. Shafaat Ahmad Khan in *Maharaja Ranjit Singh Centenary Volume*, 6.
62. Malcolm, 33-4, 90.
63. *Seir Mutaqherin,* Vol.III, 341.
64. *Ibid.*, Vol.I, 89-91.
65. "An Account of the King, of his Dominions and of Nujhaf Khan" —*Bengal, Past and Present*, Vol.VIII, Sl. No.16, (April-June 1914), 158.
66. S.S. Bal in *The Medieval Indian State*, 128.
67. Fauja Singh Bajwa in Bisheshwar Prasad, 204. Also, Review by Bajwa, *Enquiry*, Vol.II, No.1, (Spring 1965), 135.
68. Khushwant Singh, Vol.I, 48.
69. Note 67 above. Also, Asirvadi Lal Srivastava in *Journal of Indian History,*, Vol.42, Sl. No.125, pp.581-2.
70. Hari Ram Gupta in R.C. Majumdar, *The Mughul Empire*, 317-8.
71. Khushwant Singh, Vol.I, 74-5.
72. *Ibid.*, 183.
73. Satishchandra, 51. Khushwant Singh, Vol.I, 101-87 (Agrarian Uprising).
74. Shafaat Ahmad Khan in *Maharaja Ranjit Singh Centenary Volume*, 39-40.
75. Humayun Kabir in *Report of Seminar on National Integration* (1958),10.
76. Charles Malik, cited by W.C. Smith, 104-5.
77. P.V. Kane, Vol.III, 136-7.
78. S.N. Sen, *The Maratha Military System*, 17-8.
79. Fauja Singh Bajwa in Bisheshwar Prasad, 204.
80. A.L. Srivastava in *Journal of Indian History*, Vol.42, Sl. No.125, pp.581-2.

Bibliography

BOOKS CITED IN THE TEXT AND NOTES

Acharya Hrdayam of Azahiya Manavala Perumal Nayanar, with Commentary by Manavala Mahamunihal, Varavara Muninthra Granthamala, published by P.B. Annangaracharya, 1966.

Ahmed, Muhammad Aziz, *An Intellectual History of Islam*, Edinburgh, 1969.

— *Studies in Islamic Culture in the Indian Environment*, Oxford, 1964.

— *Political History and Institutions of the Early Turkish Empire of Delhi* (1206-1290), Lahore, 1959.

Ali, M. Athar, *The Apparatus of Empire: Award of Ranks, Offices and Titles to the Mughal Nobility, 1574-1658, O.U.P.,* 1985.

Ali, Mrs. Meer Hassan, *Observations on the Mussulmanns of India*, edited by W. Crooke, 2nd edition, O.U.P., 1917.

Ambedkar, B.R., *Castes in India—Their Mechanism, Genesis and Development*, 1917.

Ananda Rangam Pillai—*The Private Diary of Ananda Rangam Pillai from 1736 to 1761*, Vols.I to XII, Edited by J.F. Price and K. Rangachari, Madras, 1904.

Ansari, Ghaus, *Muslim Castes in Uttar Pradesh*, Lucknow, 1960.

Araish-i-Muhfil or The Ornament of Assembly of Sher Ali Afsos, Translated from Urdu by Major Henry Court, Calcutta, 1881.

Bajwa, Fauja Singh, *Military System of the Sikhs during 1799-1849*, Delhi, 1964.

Bawa, V.K., *The Nizam between Mughals and British— Hyderabad under Salar Jang I*, New Delhi, 1986.

Behere, N.K., *The Background of Maratha Renaissance in the Seventeenth Century*, Bangalore, 1946.

Bharatiya Samskriti Kosh (Marathi), edited by Mahadeva Shastri Joshi, Vols.II & VII.

Binyon, Lawrence, *Akbar*, 1963

Buchanan, Francis, *A Journey from Madras through the Countries of Mysore, Canara and Malabar*, Vols.I & II, London, 1807.

— *An Account of the District of Purnea in 1809-10*, Patna, 1928.

— *Journey through the Northern Parts of Kanara*, Karwar, 1956.

— *An Account of the District or Zila of Dinajpur*,

— *An Account of the Districts of Patna and Gaya in 1811-12*, Vols. I & II, Patna.

Buhler, G, *The Laws of Manu*, Oxford, 1886.

Chaitanya, Krishna, *The Betrayal of Krishna*, New Delhi, 1991.

Chakravarthy, G.N., *The Concept of Cosmic Harmony in the Rg-Veda*, University of Mysore, 1966.

Chaudhuri, S.B., *Civil Disturbances during the British Rule in India, 1765-1857*, Calcutta, 1955.

Chunder, Bholanath, *The Travels of a Hindoo to Various Parts of Bengal and Upper India*, with an Introduction by J. Talboys Wheeler, Vols.I & II, London, 1869.

Cockburn, Rev. William, *A Dissertation on the Best Means of Civilizing the Subjects of the British Empire in India and Diffusing the Light of the Christian Religion throughout the Eastern World*, Cambridge, 1805.

Coomaraswamy, Anand K. and Horner, I.B., *The Living Thoughts of Gotama the Buddha*, London, 1948.

Coser, Louis A., *The Functions of Social Conflict, London 1965.*

Coulson, Noel J., *Conflicts and Tensions in Islamic Jurisprudence*, Chicago, 1969.

Crauford, Q., *Sketches chiefly relating to the History, Religion, Learning and Manners of the Hindoos*, London, 1790.

Das Gupta, T.C., *Aspects of Bengali Society from Old Bengali Literature*, University of Calcutta, 1935.

De Bary & Others, *Sources of Indian Tradition.* Columbia, 1958.

Desika Char, S.V., *Centralised Legislation,—A History of the Legislative System of British India from 1834 to 1861*, New Delhi, 1963.

Desika Char, S.V., *Readings in the Constitutional History of India, 1757-1947*, New Delhi, 1983.

Dharam Pal, *The Beautiful Tree*—Indigenous *Education in the Eighteenth Century*, New Delhi. 1983.

Dow, Alexander, *The History of Hindostan*, (Translated from Persian), Vols. I-III, London, 1803.

Edwardes, Michael, *British India, 1772-1947—A Survey of the Nature and Effects of Alien Rule*, London, 1967.

Elphinstone, Mountstuart, *Report on the Territories Acquired from the Peshwas* Calcutta, 1821.

— *The History of India* London, 1916.

Fitz-Clarence, Lt. Col., *Journal of a Route across India, through Egypt, in the Latter End of the Year 1817 and the Beginning of 1818*, London, 1819.

Forrest, George, *Lord Cornwallis*, Vol. I & II, Oxford, 1926.

Franks, H.G., *Panchayats under the Peshwas*.

Futuhat-i-Alamgiri of Isardas Nagar, Translation by Jadunath Sarkar. Typescript in the National Library, Calcutta.

Gadgil, D.R., *Origins of the Modern Business Class—An Interim Report*, New York, 1959.

Gellner, Ernest, *Thought and Change*, London, 1964.

Ghoshal, U.N., *Studies in Indian History and Culture*, 1957.

Ghurye, G.S., *Caste and Class in India*, Bombay, 1950.

— *Anthropo-Sociological Papers*, Bombay, 1963.

— *Vedic India*, Bombay, 1970.

Gladwin, Francis, *A Narrative of the Transactions in Bengal during the Soobadaris of Azzam Shah, Jaffar Khan, Sirfraz Khan and Alyvirdy Khan*, Translated from Persian, Calcutta, 1788.

Goetz, Herman, *The Crisis of Indian Civilisation in the Eighteenth and Early Nineteenth Centuries—The Genesis of Indo-Muslim Civilisation*, Calcutta, 1938.

Gopal, B.R., *The Chalukyas of Kalyani and the Kalachuris*, Dharwad, 1981.

— *Ramanuja in Karnataka*—An Epigraphical Study, Delhi, 1983.

Gopal, M.H., *Tipu Sultan's Mysore—An Economic Study*, Bombay, 1971.

Gospel of Sri Ramkrishna by M., Translated from Bengali, Swami Nikhilananda, Madras, 1981.

Grose, John Henry, *A Voyage to the East Indies, begun in 1750 with Observations continued till 1764*, London, 1766.

Guha, Nikhilesh—*Pre-British State System in South India—Mysore, 1761-1799*, Calcutta, 1985.

Hamilton, Alexander, *A New Account of the East Indies*, London, 1930.

Hamilton, Edith, *The Greek Way to Western Civilisation*, Penguin, 1952.

Hasan, Ibn, *Central Structure of the Mughal Empire*, New Delhi, 1970.

Hasan, Mohibbul, *History of Tipu Sultan*, Calcutta, 1971.

Hastings, Warren, late Governor General of Bengal, *Memoir relative to the State of India*, London, 1787.

History of Hindostan—Extracts from Ferishta and other Contemporary Sources, Vol.II, The Present State of Hindostan (1764).

Hoey, William, Memoirs of Delhi and Faizabad, being Translation of Tarikh Farabaksh of Muhammad Faiz Baksh, Vols.I & II, Allahabad, 1889.

Hutchins, Francis G., *The Illusion of Permanence—British Imperialism in India*, Princeton, 1967.

Irvine, William, *The Army of the Indian Mughals*, New Delhi, 1962.

Jordanus, Friar, *The Wonders of the East* (circa 1330), Ed. by Col. Henry Yule, London, 1863.

Joshi, Lalmani, *Studies in the Buddhistic Culture of India during the Seventh and the Eighth Centuries A.D.*, Varanasi, 1967.

Joshi, Pranabanand (Ed.), *Religion and Society in Ancient India*, Calcutta, 1984.

Kabir, Humayun, *Mirza Abu Talib Khan*, Patna, 1961.

Kane, Pandurang Vaman, *History of Dharmasastra*, Vols. I-V, Poona, 1930-77.

Karandikar, M.A., *Islam in India's Transition to Modernity*, Orient Longman, 1968.

Kareem, C.K., *What Happened in Indian History*, Cochin, 1971.

Karim, A.K. Nazrul, *Changing Society in India and Pakistan—A Study in Social Change and Social Stratification*, O.U.P., 1956.

Katre S.M. & Gode, P.K. (Eds.), *A Volume of Studies in Indology Presented to Prof. P.V. Kane*, Poona, 1941.

Keene, H.G., *The Fall of the Mughal Empire*, Delhi, 1971.

Khan, Yusuf Husain, *Nizamul-Mulk Asaf Jha I*, Mangalore, 1936.

Khantipalo, Phra, *Tolerance—A Study from Buddhist Sources*, London, 1964.

Kirby, Major Charles F., *The Adventures of an Arcot Rupee*, Vol.I, London, 1867.

Kirmani, Mir Husain Ali Khan, *A History of the Reign of Tipu Sultan*, Translated and Edited by Col. W. Miles, London, 1864.

Kohli, Sitaram, *Catalogue of the Khalsa Darbar Records*, Vol.I (1919) and Vol.II (1923).

Kopf, David, *British Orientalism and the Bengal Renaissance—The Dynamics of Indian Modernisation, 1773-1835*, California, 1969.

Koshambi, D.D., *Myth and Reality—Studies in the Formation of Indian Culture*, Bombay, 1962.

Lala Chhaganlal, *Bhakti in the Religions of the World*, Delhi, 1986.

Law, Bimla Churn, *Concepts of Buddhism*, New Delhi, 1991.

Law, Narendranath, *Promotion of Learning in India during Muhammadan Rule by Muhammadans*, London, 1916.

Macnicol, Nicol, *The Living Religions of the Indian People*, New Delhi, 1964.

Maharaja Ranjit Singh Centenary Volume, Cawnpore, 1940.

Majumdar, R.C. (Ed.), *The History and Culture of the Indian People*, Bharatiya Vidya Bhavan, Bombay.—Vol.I: The Vedic Age; Vol.II: The Age of Imperial Unity; Vol.III: The Classical Age; Vol.IV: The Age of Imperial Kanauj; Vol.V: The Struggle for Empire; Vol.VI: The Delhi Sultanate; Vol.VII: The Mughul Empire; Vol.VIII: The Maratha Supremacy; Vol.IX: British Paramountcy and Indian Renaissance, Parts I & II.

Malcolm, Lt. Col., *Sketch of the Sikhs*, London, 1812.

Malik, S.C., *Indian Civilization: The Formative Period*, Simla, 1968.

Marathe, K.B. (Ed.), *Sawai Madhav Rao Peshwa*, Vol.II, Poona, 1909.

Medieval Indian State, Proceedings of Seminar, Punjab University, March, 1966.

Mill, James, *The History of India*, Vol.II, London, 1820.

Mishra, Vikas, *Hinduism and Economic Growth*, Bombay, 1962.

Misra, Satish C., *Muslim Communities in Gujarat—*

Preliminary Studies in their History and Social Organization, Baroda, 1964.

Mitra, R.C., *Decline of Buddhism in India*, Viswabharati, 1954.

Moncton-Jones, M.E., *Warren Hastings in Bengal (1772-1779)*, Oxford, 1918.

Mujeeb, M., *The Indian Muslims*, London, 1967.

Mukherjee, Radha Kamal, *Economic History of India, (1600-1800)*.

Mukherjee, Ramakrishna, *The Rise and Fall of the East India Company— A Sociological Appraisal*, Berlin, 1958.

Mundy, Godfrey Charles, *A Various Universe—A Study of Journals and Memoirs of British Men and Women in the Indian Sub-Continent, 1761-1856*, Oxford, 1980.

Murty, K. Satchidananda, (Ed.), *Readings in Indian History, Politics and Philosophy*, London, 1967.

Nanavati, M.B. & Vakil, C.N., (Eds.), *Group Prejudice in India—A Symposium*, Bombay, 1951.

Narain, A.K. (Ed.), *Studies in the History of Buddhism*, Delhi, 1980.

Narain, Dhirendra, *Hindu Character—A Few Glimpses*, Bombay, 1957.

National Integration—Report of Seminar on, 16-17 April 1958.

National Integration—*All-India Colloquium on Ethical and Spiritual Values as the Basis of National Integration, 30 December 1966 to 2 January 1967*, Bombay, 1967.

Nigam, S.B.P., *Nobility under the Sultans of Delhi (1206-1398)*, Delhi, 1968.

Oddie, G.A., *Social Protest in India—British Protestant Missionaries and Social Reforms, 1850-1900*, New Delhi 1979.

— *Religion in South Asia*, New Delhi, 1991.

O'Malley, L.S.S. (Ed.), *Modern India and the West*, London, 1941.

Oriental Annual or Scenes in India, London, 1834.

Panikkar, K.M., *A Survey of Indian History*, Bombay 1962.

— *The Foundations of New India*, London, 1963.

— *The Determining Periods of Indian History*, Bombay 1962.

Paranjpye, A.C., *Caste, Prejudice and the Individual*, Bombay, 1970.

Peshwa Daftar—*Selections from the Peshwa Daftar*, Vols.1-37.

Prasad, Beni, *History of Jahangir,* Allahabad, 1962.

Prasad, Bisheshwar (Ed.), *Ideas in History*, Delhi, 1968.

Qanuni-i-Islam of Jafar Sharif, Edited by G.A. Harklots, O.U.P., 1921.

Raghuvamshi, V.P.S., *Indian Society in the Eighteenth Century*, New Delhi, 1969.

Raikar, Y.A., *Indian History—A Study in Dynamics*, Baroda, 1960.

Rajagopalachari, C., *Our Culture*, Bombay, 1963.

Ramesh, K.V., *Indian Epigraphy*, Vol.I, Delhi, 1984.

Ras Mala or Hindoo Annals of the Province of Goozerat in Western India, by Alexander Forbes. Edited by H.G. Rawlinson O.U.P., 1924.

Rawlinson, H.G. (Ed.), *An Account of the Last Battle of Panipat and the Events leading to it* by Casi Raja Pandit, O.U.P., 1926.

Raychaudhuri, Tapan (Ed.), *Contributions to Indian Economic History*, Vols.I & II, Calcutta, 1960 & 1963.

Reneck, Anthony de, & Knight, Julie (Eds.), *Conflict in Society*, London, 1966.

Rhenius, Rev. C.T.E., *Memoir of Rev. C.T.E. Rhenius comprising Extracts from his Journal and Correspondence with Details of Missionary Proceedings, by his Son, London, 1841.*

G. Roerich (Ed.), *Biography of Dharmaswamin—A Tibetan Monk Pilgrim*, Patna, 1959.

Roy Choudhury, M.L., *The State and Religion in Mughal India*, Calcutta, 1951.

Sankara Digvijaya—The Traditional Life of Sri Sankaracharya of Madhava Vidyaranya, Translated by Swami Tapasyananda, Madras, 1980.

Sardesai, G.S., *New History of the Marathas*, Vol.I, Bombay, 1957.

Sarkar, Jadunath, *History of Aurangzib*, Vols.I-IV, Calcutta, 1912-19.

— *Mughal Administration*, Patna, 1925.

Satishchandra, *Parties and Politics at the Mughal Court*, 1707-1740, Aligharh, 1959.

Scott, Jonathan, *Ferishta's History of the Deccan from the First Muhammadan Conquest*, 1794.

Scrafton, Luke, *Reflections on the Government of Indostan*, London, 1770.

Seir Mutaqherin—A Translation of the Seir Mutaqherin or A view of the Modern Times, by H. Raymond, Vols.I-IV, Calcutta, 1903.

Sen, Surendra Nath, *Studies in Indian History*, Calcutta, 1930.

— *The Administrative System of the Marathas*, Calcutta, 1925.

— *The Military System of the Marathas*, Orient Longman, 1958.

— *Early Career of Kanoji Angria and Other Papers*, Calcutta, 1941.

Sen, S.N. & Subbarayappa, B.V., *A Concise History of Science in India*, New Delhi, 1971.

Sharma, G.S., *Secularism: Its Implications for Law and Life in India*, Bombay, 1966.

Sharma, S.R., *The Religious Policy of the Mughal Emperors*, Calcutta, 1972.

Silverberg, James (Ed.), *Social Mobility in the Caste System in India—An Inter-disciplinary Symposium*, The Hague, 1968.

Singh, Khushwant, *The History of the Sikhs*, Vols.I & II, 1963.

Sinha, N.K., *Ranjit Singh*, Calcutta, 1951.

Sinha, R.M. & Avasthi, A., (Eds.), *Elphinstoné Correspondence, 1804-08* Nagpur, 1961.

Smith, Wilfred Contwell, *Islam in Modern History*, Princeton, 1957.

Spear, Percival, *Twilight of the Mughals—Studies in Late Mughal Delhi*, Cambridge, 1951.

Spear, T.G.P., "The Grounds of Political Obedience in the State" in *The Journal of the Punjab History Society*, April, 1935.

Spirit of India—Volumes Presented to Srimathi Indira Gandhi, Vol.II, Asia, 1975.

Srinivas, M.N., *Social Change in Modern India*, Bombay, 1968.

Sterling, A., *An Account of Orissa Proper or Cuttock*,

Stewert, Charles, *Travels of Mirza Abu Taleb Khan in Asia, Africa and Europe during the Years 1799-1803*. Translated from Persian and published in 1814. Reprint, 1972.

Subbarayappa, B.V.(Ed.), *Indo-Soviet Seminar on Scientific and Technological Exchanges between India and Soviet Central Asia, (Medieval Period)*, New Delhi, 1981.

Subba Rao, Bendapudi, *The Personality of India—Pre- and Proto-Historic Foundations of India and Pakistan*, Baroda, 1958.

Tarachand, *History of the Freedom Movement in India*, Vols. I-IV, Delhi. Vol.I—1961; Vol II—1974; Vol.III & IV—1972.

Tarikh-i-Ahmadshahi, Translated by Jadunath Sarkar, Sitamau, 1937.

Tennant, Rev. William, *Indian Recreations, Consisting chiefly of Strictures on the Domestic and Rural Economy of the Mahomedans and Hindoos* Vols.I & II, London, 1804.

Thapar, Romila, Harbans Mukhia and Bipin Chandra, *Communalism and the Writing of History*, New Delhi, 1969.

Tikekar, Sripad R. (Ed.), *Sardesai Commemmoration Volume*, Bombay, 1938.

Tirumalai, with Periya Vacchan Pillai's Commentary, Published by Krishnaswamy Iyengar of Puttur

Titus, M.T., *Islam in India and Pakistan*, Calcutta, 1945.

Tuhfat-Al-Mujahidin, of Shaykh Zaynud-Din. Translated from Arabic by S.M.H. Nainar. Madras, 1942.

Washbrooke, D.A., *The Emergence of Provincial Politics—The Madras Presidency*, 1870-1920, New Delhi, 1976.

Yasin, Muhammad, A Social History of Islamic India, 1605-1748, Lucknow, 1958.

Index